953.1
K965

Ex Libris copy 1

Presented by

DAWN OVER SAMARKAND

DAWN OVER SAMARKAND
THE REBIRTH OF CENTRAL ASIA

BY JOSHUA KUNITZ

NEW YORK
COVICI · FRIEDE · PUBLISHERS

COPYRIGHT, 1935, BY JOSHUA KUNITZ

All rights reserved. No part of this book may be reproduced in any form without permission in writing from the publisher, except by a reviewer who may quote brief passages in a review to be printed in a magazine or newspaper.

Manufactured in the United States of America
THE VAN REES PRESS, NEW YORK

To
ANGELO HERNDON

ACKNOWLEDGEMENTS

In preparing this book I had recourse to scores of studies, monographs, memoirs in the Russian language. I cannot acknowledge all of them. The authors to whom I am particularly indebted are: Faizulla Khodzhaiev, Rakhim Khodzhibaiev, Boris Lapin, Zakhar Khatzrevin, A. Briskin, P. Alekseenko, F. Boshko, Orest Rovinsky, T. Dzhurobaiev. For my information about the early career of Enver Pasha, I am indebted to Louis Fischer's *The Soviets in World Affairs*. The quotations on pages 127, 128, 162, and 163 are taken from *Soviet Rule in Russia* by Walter Russell Batsell (The Macmillan Company, 1929).

I wish to express my warmest gratitude to my colleague, Herman Michelson, as well as to Mr. Nathan Ausubel, and Mrs. Lydia Gibson Minor, for their reading of the manuscript and their many valuable editorial suggestions. Needless to say, the responsibility for the inadequacies of this book rest solely with me. I wish also to express deep appreciation to my friend Edward Dahlberg whose enthusiastic response to the material hastened the publication of this book.

CONTENTS

INTRODUCTION   11

I
OLD AND NEW—IMPRESSIONS

I. THE EMIR
- FLIGHT OF EMIR   19
- SPIRITUAL RULER   21
- TEMPORAL RULER   22

II. MILLIONS OF DAYS
- NOBLE BOKHARA   25
- PEOPLES AND CONQUERORS   28
- THE WHITE CZAR   31

III. CONTRASTS
- WATER AND BLOOD   37
- IN THE SHADOW OF THE ARK   40
- UNREASONABLE HUMAN HERD   42

II
STRUGGLE FOR POWER

IV. GATHERING OF THE STORM
- BOLD SPIRITS   55
- EMIR'S FUTILE INCANTATIONS   57
- UNITED IN REVOLUTION   59

V. FIRST THUNDERBOLT
    EMIR PONDERS   65
    PARTING OF WAYS   71
    IN THE SHADOW OF EMPIRES   76

VI. A COLOSSUS PROSTRATE
    NOT ALL LENINS   81
    SPECULATING ON DIFFICULTIES   86
    BARKING JACKALS   93
    THE BASMACHI   97
    PERFIDIOUS ALBION   102
    VULTURE'S FEAST   106

VII. ANOTHER VICTORIOUS PAGE
    BRITAIN'S OUTRAGED DIGNITY   112
    THE EMIR IS DISCONSOLATE   116
    UNDER THE WALLS OF BOKHARA   122
    EPILOGUE AND PROLOGUE   126

VIII. RECEDING VERSUS EMERGENT
    REVOLUTION IN A QUANDARY   129
    THE THIEF AND THE UNIQUE ROSE   135
    MOSLEMS OF THE WORLD UNITE!   138
    HERE A MOSLEM SAINT IS BURIED   145
    A TICKET TO HEAVEN   148
    CONSOLIDATING FORCES   151
    BOLSHEVIK TECHNIQUE   154
    SHOWING WAY TO MILLIONS   158
    A WRONG MADE RIGHT   160

III
COMPLETING THE BOURGEOIS REVOLUTION

IX. WHERE COTTON IS KING
    WHITE GOLD   169
    WHITE PLAGUE   172
    FOR COTTON—FOR SOCIALISM!   175

X. LAND AND WATER 179
    ART AND PROPAGANDA 183
    POOR BEYS 186
    POOR MULLAHS 188
    THE INTELLIGENTSIA TOO! 192
    LIKE A DREAM COME TRUE 193

XI. TOWARD SOCIALISM
    FEAR OF THE UNKNOWN 197
    DIZZINESS FROM SUCCESS 200
    FASCINATION OF TRACTORS 204
    MTS AND COÖPERATIVES 208
    PLANNING MADE POSSIBLE 212

IV
BUILDING SOCIALISM IN TADJIKISTAN

XII. A BOLSHEVIK IN STALINABAD
    STRUCTURES AND SUPERSTRUCTURES 217
    NATIONAL IN FORM, SOCIALIST IN CONTENT 222
    IN HAPPY EXILE 227
    IBRAHIM BEK AGAIN! 229
    A BOLSHEVIK LEGEND 233

XIII. DUSHAMBE VERSUS STALINABAD
    DONKEYS—CAMELS—MULLAHS—MERCHANTS 237
    NO MOSQUES, NO CHURCHES, NO SYNAGOGUES 240
    STALINABAD PRESS—SELF-CRITICISM 243
    FOR SANITATION! FOR EDUCATION! 247

XIV. A SHEAF OF TRAVEL NOTES 251

XV. NEW WOMEN IN OLD ASIA
    GRAY OR DARK-BLUE COFFINS 274
    GREEN FROGS AND FREE WOMEN 278
    TACT AND REVOLUTION 287
    HUSBANDS AND SCHOOLS 291
    A TRANSITION GENERATION 297

XVI. THE END OF THE BASMACHI
    A TOUCH OF THE EXOTIC   302
    TWO DOCUMENTS   307
    A MEMORABLE NIGHT   311

V

SOVIET ASIA—1934

XVII. A FANTASY BASED ON FACT
    POIGNANT THOUGHTS . . . BITTER THOUGHTS   319
    A SOVIET RHAPSODY   322
    WE HAVE BEEN VICTORIOUS   327

XVIII. SOVIET ASIA SINGS
    SONGS OF SORROW AND REVOLT   331
    SONGS OF FREEDOM   336
    SONGS ABOUT LENIN   339
    NEW CONTENT—NEW FORMS   343

DAWN OVER SAMARKAND

"One of two things: either we shall set in motion the deep rear of imperialism—the eastern colonial and semi-colonial countries, shall revolutionize them and thus hasten the fall of imperialism; or we shall botch things here and thereby strengthen imperialism and weaken our movement. This is how matters stand.

"The point is that the entire Orient regards our Union as an experimental field. Either we correctly decide and practically apply the national question within the framework of this Union; either we establish really fraternal relations, real collaboration between the peoples within the framework of this Union—and then the entire Orient will see that in our federation it possesses a banner of liberation, a vanguard in whose footsteps it should walk, and this will be the beginning of the collapse of world imperialism. Or we, the entire federation, commit a mistake here, undermine the confidence of the formerly oppressed peoples in the proletariat of Russia, shear the Union of its power to attract the Orient which it now enjoys, in which event imperialism will gain and we shall lose.

"This constitutes the international significance of the national question."

—JOSEPH STALIN, *Report on the National Question*, delivered at the XII Congress of the Russian Communist Party, 1923.

INTRODUCTION

*No clouds! In a clear sky I see
The sun. No night to dim bright day!
No Czar! Our soil's forever free!
Well done, O Bolshevik!*

*You crushed the Khans, you did not spare
The age-long foe of tribes oppressed.
The victory the poor will share.
Well done, O Bolshevik!*

*Of all I've heard and seen I sing,
For now my blind eyes see anew....
I see, I feel the joy you bring—
Well done, O Bolshevik!*
　　　　　　　—Kar-Molli
(A blind seventy-year-old Turkoman bard)

BOKHARA, Samarkand, Dushambe, what romantic associations are evoked by the mere mention of these names! Down a yellow shimmering road a long line of conquerors—Alexander the Great, Genghis Khan, Tamerlane—and countless peoples and tribes move in endless caravans through the centuries, lured by the "pleasure domes" and "gardens bright" of Samarkand the Ancient and Noble Bokhara.... Incense-bearing trees, vineyards, pomegranates, pistachios, cotton fields, bazaars, camels, rugs, silks, harems... against a background of deep blue, gleaming towers of particolored mosques, turbaned mullahs reciting the sacred verses of the Koran, veiled maidens swaying gently to the weird monotone of an old chant....

Alluring echoes, these, of a romanticized, idealized past —an Occidental's literary reveries.

I recall our trip to Varsobstroy, the new hydroelectric station that was being built in the remote land of the Tadjiks, at the foot of the Pamir. We were a literary brigade: Egon Erwin Kisch, the Austrian journalist; Paul

Vaillant-Couturier, the French revolutionary writer; Luyn, a Norwegian writer; Bruno Jasiensky, the Polish novelist and poet; Anna Abramovna Berzina, the Russian writer, and Louis Lozowick, American artist. Our cars rattled up the narrow, rocky road that wound along the precipice overhanging the wild Dushambe. The mountains on both sides of the river were bare rocks, torn by deep gorges, red with the heat of the sun. Far in the distance loomed the snowy peak of Lenin-tau.

There was not a living being in sight, except for a rare native in bright cloak and silk embroidered skull-cap, prodding his long stick into the ribs of his obstreperous *ishak* (native ass), or an occasional eagle wheeling in the sky.

The country was primitive. Only here and there one saw traces of civilization: now a green patch of cultivated land rising on a steep incline—a triumph of human persistence and ingenuity; now an ethereally woven bridge arching perilously over the roaring Dushambe.

But those things had been there for centuries. Alexander the Great, during his famous passage to India, must have contemplated them as rude signs of a primitive life.

The ebullient Frenchman at my side, undaunted by the scorching heat and clouds of dust, grew eloquent over the rough grandeur of the scene: "Chaos... primordial chaos... *magnifique!*..."

"Never mind chaos..." grumbled Khodzhaiev, a young Tadjik, a member of the State Planning Commission of Tadjikistan. "We are beginning to harness this chaos. There has been chaos here long enough."

It was always so! Invariably those Central Asian Bolsheviks would put a damper on our innocent enthusiasms. Small wonder. They had dwelt there for centuries, in ignorance, in darkness, isolated from the rest of the world, oppressed by the Czars, exploited by the native rulers, the Emirs, the Khans, the Beys, and the all-powerful and fanatical Mohammedan clergy. One could scarcely blame them for being impatient with the magnificence of chaos and for finding romance "in this telegraph line we have put up here at the cost of infinite pain, in this road which we are building and which is to serve as an artery beating with the pulse of a modern Stalinabad joined to a modernized Samarkand and Tashkent."

"This is our romance," insisted Khodzhaiev. "Bolshevik tempo, comrade, Bolshevik tempo!" And after a pause: "If you ever write about Tadjikistan, please don't fall into the error of most of the Europeans who visit us, don't descend to exoticism, don't become worked up over the magnificence of chaos." Khodzhaiev pronounced "magnificence of chaos" with irony. "Please don't expatiate on the beauty of our apparel, the quaintness of our villages, the mystery hidden beneath our women's *paranjas,* the charm of sitting on rugs under shady plane trees and listening to the sweet monotone of our bards, of drinking green tea from a *piala*—and eating *pilaf* wth our hands. Really, there is little that is charming about all that. Take any cultured Central Asian, cultured in a modern sense, that is, and to him most of the local customs mean simply backwardness, ignorance of the most elementary rules of sanitation and prophylactics."

We felt that Khodzhaiev was annihilating a half—the best half, we thought—of our prospective books on Central Asia. We hastened to defend ourselves, attempting to assuage him by diplomacy, reminding him jocularly that if we ever wrote anything about Central Asia, it would be not for Uzbeks and Tadjiks, but for Europeans and Americans, and that a touch of the exotic might make our books more palatable to the West.

"But that would be pandering," Khodzahiev argued indignantly. "You would not be describing Soviet Central Asia. If your reader is interested in exoticism let him read books about us written ten or twenty or fifty or a hundred years ago—it would all be the same. But you are in Soviet Asia, and it is your duty to give what is most characteristic, what distinguishes our Soviet Republics. You must deal with the living, not the dead."

Khodzahiev was, of course, right. He was speaking of a

modern romance, a contemporary epic—the rebirth of Central Asia. And that romance, he felt, demanded not rhetoric but arithmetic, not exclamation marks but figures.

Central Asia is in a paroxysm of change. The immemorial droning of the somnolent East is drowned out by the strains of the *Internationale* mingled with the sirens of new factories and the hum of American and Soviet motors. Among the traditional *paranjas* of the veiled women there are appearing in ever-increasing numbers the bobbed hair and the khaki uniforms of the revolutionary youth. Mullahs and beys have been supplanted by Soviet commissars and Red factory managers. Mosques and *mederesse* (religious academies) are being crowded out by Communist Universities, workers' clubs, people's theaters, libraries, movies. An anciently entrenched oriental feudalism is being shattered by the vast sweep of modernity, by industrialization, electricity, collectivization, science.

For years now Central Asia has been a medley of clashing values. The revolution has unleashed a whirlwind of passion. The old fights back, desperately, brutally. But the new is triumphantly advancing. Even those who cling to the old cannot resist the magnificent upsurge of the new. History has executed a sudden *volte face:* the West is carrying its civilization back to its place of origin. Western revolutionary scientific ideas have been hurled against eastern tradition with unparalleled daring, and the emotional overtones of this collision of two world systems are surely the most dramatic aspects of the epoch-making advance of Bolshevism in the Orient.

Yes, a storm is raging over Asia. The heart of the old continent is on fire. From Moscow the revolutionary flames have raced across the burning steppes of Turkmenia and enveloped the Asiatic extremities of the old empire. And the end is not yet. Beyond Khiva, Bokhara and Samarkand, beyond Turkmanistan, Uzbekistan, Tadjikistan, these rising outposts of Bolshevik influence in the East, there are the teeming colonial and semi-colonial peoples of Asia—Persia, Afghanistan, Mongolia, India, China....

INTRODUCTION 15

Central Asia has become a source of infinite wonderment to the peoples of the Orient, including the Central Asians themselves. It is significant that within the last few years the Karategin, Darvaz, and Pamir mountain Tadjiks have evolved the so-called "songs of wonderment," a new genre of folk poetry. Each of these new songs expresses the bard's thrill of amazement at first beholding the achievements of the new Socialist Soviet Republics.

Thus, to take only one example, the Tadjik bard Munavvar-Sho, for instance, is ineffably impressed by what he saw in the capital. His song begins with an enumeration of all kinds of possible and impossible wonders that he had once seen or heard or remembered—"soot and ashes in the caverns of the moon," "a kingdom bathed eternally in the lunar quiet of the night," a "multitudinous bazaar where the silence is never broken," the men of Darvaz who when they caress their lovely damsels find "eternity too short and a second much too long...." However, Munavvar-Sho has visited the new city of Stalinabad, the capital of Tadjikistan, and has grown much wiser. He now speaks contemptuously of all those wonders he once believed. He dismisses them as trifling, mere "fables." The one thing he now *really knows,* the one *really* great wonder is the city of Stalinabad where he saw "a great, big square with clubs and cars and cinemas and factories and lights."

News spreads fast in Central Asia. Mountains, deserts, rivers and national boundaries present no serious obstacle. Everything spectacular happening in Soviet Asia is immediately known in all the surrounding colonial and semi-colonial lands. In remote Khokanyor, for instance, the whole village—men, women and children—had gone out to meet the first tractor shipped from the center. When they saw that the tractor could not be brought down the very steep hill, they decided to carry the machine down in their arms. For weeks the tractor driver was the most respected man in the village. On the other side of the border Afghans sat day and night and watched the tractor working.

And at Sarai Komar, the center for the development of Egyptian cotton in Tadjikistan, I saw a delegation of

Afghans who came from across the Pianj to ask the local Soviet authorities to help them organize a collective farm.

"But you are not Soviet citizens," protested the Tadjik official. "Your country is Afghanistan. We can't come there and organize collective farms."

"Why not?" asked the naïve Afghans. "You have a strong army."

The thing appeared quite simple to the applicants—come with your army and organize collective farms.

"It's a long and very complicated story—why not," dodged the official. "But why not get together your belongings and come to us? We'll organize you in a kolkhoz all right. We'll settle you on good land, and give you credits. Remember we can use here another million and a half willing workers. Just go back and think it over."

Disappointed, the Afghans left. I do not know whether those particular Afghans ever came back. But I do know of a few collective farms in Tadjikistan organized by Afghan immigrants. I have also met a number of Afghans in one of the brick factories in Stalinabad, the new Tadjik capital.

Great Britain is filled with foreboding. Japan is rattling the sword. Hyashi says Japan will not brook Soviet influence in Sinkiang or the rest of China. The United States is wavering, loath to see Japan gobble up China and loath to see Soviet influence spreading in the Orient. Of late it has begun to lean more to the side of Japan. Asia is in a great ferment. One little spark may set off an explosion powerful enough to shatter to bits the whole elaborate world structure of modern imperialist-capitalist civilization. And it is as likely as not that that spark may be generated around Uzbekistan or Tadjikistan, the two young Soviet Republics which have risen out of the ashes of ancient Bokhara in the very heart of Asia.

# PART ONE

OLD AND NEW—IMPRESSIONS

"Since the time of the formation of the Soviet Republics, the states of the world have divided into two camps: the camp of capitalism and the camp of socialism.

"There—in the camp of capitalism—national enmity and inequality, colonial slavery and chauvinism, national oppression and pogroms, imperialist brutalities and wars.

"Here—in the camp of socialism—mutual confidence and peace, national freedom and equality, dwelling together in peace and the brotherly collaboration of peoples.

"The attempts of the capitalist world for a number of decades to settle the question of nationality by the combination of the free development of peoples with the system of the exploitation of man by man have proved fruitless. On the contrary, the skein of national contradictions is becoming more and more tangled, threatening the very existence of capitalism. The bourgeoisie has been incapable of organizing the collaboration of peoples.

"Only in the camp of the Soviets, only under the conditions of the dictatorship of the proletariat, mustering round itself the majority of the population, has it proved itself possible to destroy national oppression at the roots, to establish an atmosphere of mutual confidence and lay the foundation of the brotherly collaboration of peoples.

"Only thanks to these circumstances have the Soviet Republics been able to beat off the attacks of the imperialists of the whole world, internal and external, only thanks to these circumstances have they been able successfully to liquidate the Civil War, and to secure their own existence and commence economic reconstruction."

—*Declaration from the Constitution of the Union of Socialist Soviet Republics.*

I
THE EMIR

> *Humanity is plagued by four evils—fleas, bedbugs, mullahs, and the Emir's officials.*
> —Tadjik proverb.

Flight of Emir

THE Bokhara Emirate was overthrown in September, 1920. The Emir, abandoning his hundred wives, but taking along his letter of credit on the English bank (fifty-four million gold rubles), fled from his capital, followed by a host of officials, mullahs, merchants, and several of his comeliest *bachi* (young boys). The news spread like wildfire: The *Djadids* (bourgeois progressives) have seized power in Bokhara; they are being helped by the Bolsheviks.

A strange silence fell upon the land. From early dawn, great clouds of dust rose above the road leading from Bokhara through Denau to Dushambe. Thousands of the Emir's horsemen moved stealthily in the direction of Eastern Bokhara. Like a thief in the night, Emir Said-Alim entered Denau. No sumptuously dressed cortège now, no music, no harem—only a pitiful horde of frightened followers.

Four nights the Emir spent in Denau. Nigmatulla, the Bek, was so anxious to please his majesty that he became hoarse issuing orders to his servants. But knowing the Emir's lechery, Nigmatulla was somewhat worried about his sisters whom he had kept unmarried because he could not find in wild Denau men of sufficient wealth and social standing to satisfy him. Now, that the Emir was his guest, Nigmatulla was in a quandary. At a conference of the local officials, therefore, he urged that something quite extraordinary be presented to the Emir for his delectation and amusement. According to the stories of the local peasants, seven youngsters, daughters of the poorest peasants, were selected. They were flat-breasted little creatures, with not a single hair on their bodies. Among them was little Khozid, a slip of a girl, pale, thin, transparent. The old mother begged for mercy. Nigmatulla was adamant: "You ought to be proud, you foolish woman, that the Emir is so kindly disposed to your ragged little brat."

The first day, peasants by the thousands milled around the house where the Emir was lodged, anxious to get at least one glimpse at the divine being they so often blessed in their Friday prayers. By the end of the second day, however, there was not a peasant left in Denau. They had all sought refuge in the villages, hiding their young wives and daughters, smearing dung over the faces of the prettier youngsters.

To deflect popular resentment, the Emir incited the peasants to rob the Jews, who, he charged, had brought the Bolsheviks into the land. And, it is reported, to replenish his own depleted fortunes (the English bank was alas too far!) he seized the wealthiest Jewish merchants in the region, decapitated them, and confiscated about three-quarters of a million dollars' worth of silver. The prettier Jewish women he ordered seized and distributed among his followers. But his henchmen excelled even him in greed and lawlessness, forcibly taking the grain, the horses, the handsome boys and girls from the peasants. An outcry of anger and indignation shook the town. On the morning of the fifth day, when the tidings came that the Bolsheviks were in pursuit, the Emir and his ignominious train resumed their hasty retreat to Dushambe.

In Dushambe the Emir attempted to organize a force to resist the onslaught of the approaching Red Army and the revolutionary Bokharan detachments. He drew to himself the blackest forces who sensed in the advance of the Reds their inevitable end. English imperialism, too, was not slow in offering aid to the Emir. But the peasants, for the most part, refused to send their sons to fight for their oppressor. They knew what a restoration of the Emir would mean. Deserted by his people, the Emir could not withstand the pressure of the Red troops that were advancing inexorably through Baisun, Denau, Dushambe, Faizabad, Kuliab, and on March 5, 1920, Emir Said-Alim-Bakhadur-Khan, the last of the Mongit dynasty, fled to Afghanistan.

Spiritual Ruler

Noble Bokhara—"high, holy, divinely descended Bokhara"—capital of the ancient Bokhara Khanate; home of a long line of mighty temporal and spiritual rulers, the Emirs, who next to the Turkish chalifs wielded the greatest authority among the Moslem peoples.... Bokhara—glorious citadel of Arabian-Persian culture; for centuries the "heart of Islam" in Middle Asia; birthplace of great orthodox scholars and expounders of the Koran; center of two hundred and fifty mosques and one hundred and fifty *mederesse*.... From the Volga, the Crimea, the Caucasus, the Siberian deserts, the Pamir mountains, Chinese Turkestan pilgrims and students of the Koran and of Sunnite lore came here to kneel in reverence before the grandeur, the sanctity of the great city and its divine ruler.

Bokhara was a powerful theocracy in its day. Headed by the Emir, the Bokharan clergy was omnipotent. Education, justice, domestic relations, everything was in its hands. Through the centuries, the Emirs and their hosts of mullahs (who were three per cent of the entire population; practically the only people who were literate were mullahs) had perfected a splendid apparatus for regimenting the emotions and aspirations, the very lives of the Bokharan peoples. Wealthy and disciplined, the Moslem clergy under the Emirs formed a powerful army for crushing any signs of spiritual independence or intellectual heterodoxy anywhere in their domain.

Fearful that secular modern education, that science would undermine the established feudal order, the Emir and his mullahs fiercely opposed every tendency in that direction. Education was religious education. Culture was traditional culture. The sole function of the few elementary schools, conducted by mullahs or students from the religious academies, was to give the squatting pupil a smattering of religious dogma, a fair knowledge of Mohammedan ritual and practice, and a familiarity with a few Moslem prayers. The entire elementary "education" reduced itself to a few years of reciting by rote some verses from the Koran. In the elementary schools, few learned to read, fewer to write. In the higher institution of learning, in the *mederesse*, the course of studies differed in quantity rather than in quality from that pursued in the elementary school. Modern languages, natural sciences, higher mathematics, all these were strictly taboo. The citadel of ancient Arabian-Persian culture had to be preserved. The Emir's theocratic rule had to be kept intact.

In the isolated Bokharan towns and villages, the mullahs were everything—teachers, judges, spiritual guides. People went to them for advice, seeking their authority whenever any matter came up for a decision. This custom was hoary with age, and no one could question it with impunity. For the poor, overtaxed subjects of the Emir, the only consolation, the only hope lay in death, in the glorious beyond; but even the keys to the beyond were in the hands of the mullahs. If any bold subject of the Emir ever dared to rebel or even grumble, he would be torn to pieces by the mullah-incited mobs. The Emir's spiritual authority was not to be questioned.

Temporal Ruler

The Emir's temporal authority was also absolute. The heads of the various government departments, the ministers, were appointed by him and were responsible solely to him. The country was divided into administrative units—provinces, counties, villages. The corresponding administrative offices were those of *Bek, Amliakadar,* and *Aksakal.*

The custodians of religion and education in each bekdom were the *Raizes* and their subordinates. The financial department was administered by the *Ziakets*—the central and local tax collectors. Finally each bekdom had its own judicial apparatus consisting of the chief *casi,* generally a mullah, and his subordinate *casii,* also mullahs, throughout the amliakadardoms. All offices were under the direct control of the Emir's ministers.

The Emir paid no salaries. The Beks, the Amliakadars, the Aksakals, the Ziakets, all worked on a commission basis, receiving a stipulated percentage of the moneys they collected. The more they collected, the greater the commissions. The system lent itself to endless abuses.

Nepotism was rife. Officials filled their departments with friends and relatives. Offices were opportunities to mulct the population by taxes, bribes, extortions, expropriations. To get into office one had to make generous gifts to the high officials surrounding the Emir. Office-holding was a business and bribes to one's superiors were a good business investment.

To support the Emir and his rapacious officials and mullahs, the population was taxed mercilessly. There was a tax on the crops (one-sixth of the yearly yield); a tax on the cattle and produce bought and sold on the market; a head tax on each member of the family; tolls to be paid for crossing bridges and using the roads—taxes without end, and a large share of all this revenue would find its way into the Emir's coffers. More, the Mohammedan religion provided for a fund—*vakuf*—to be devoted to satisfying the spiritual needs of the faithful. Ten per cent of every Moslem income had to go into the treasury of the mosque. This money, according to the Holy Books, had to be used for the maintenance of religious schools, the development of "science," aiding the poor, and supporting benevolent institutions. But even the *vakuf* had for a long time been appropriated by the Emirs and the upper clergy for their personal use.

While the population was being impoverished, the Emir was accumulating more and more wealth. Not satisfied with his income as head of the state and head of the mosque, the Emir also went in for money-making as merchant and industrialist, taking advantage of his position of absolute monarch to exploit the people. Besides the huge sums spent on maintaining the luxurious court and harems, on bribing the Russian officials, and on sumptuous presents to the Russian Czar and his family, the Emir invested more than 100,000,000 rubles in commerce, in railroad companies, and in Russian and foreign industrial concerns. As in the early period of European feudalism, so in Bokhara no distinction was made between what belonged to the state and what belonged to the ruler. The vast riches of the country were regarded as the Emir's personal property; the state treasury was the Emir's treasury; the whole of Bokhara, the Emir's estate.

More than a hundred million! And that was not all. Add to that the sums the Emir received for the great stocks of cotton and caracul he had shipped to England in 1919-1920, then add the moneys he deposited in the French and English banks, and you get an idea of the immense personal fortune of Noble Bokhara's divine ruler. No wonder that when the Soviet Government of Bokhara was organized it found the country in an incredible state of devastation and wretchedness. The Emir had done nothing to develop industry, stimulate commerce, improve agriculture; he had not adopted a single measure to provide for the health of the people, for their education and culture. There was not a single theater in Bokhara, and only one small privately owned moving picture place. Of the annual eighteen million rubles that the Emir received in revenues, an infinitesimal portion was spent on the people's most elementary needs. Three tiny hospitals and an abominably laid pavement in the main streets of the capital—these were all that the Bokharans ever received from their government. Not one kopeck from the Emir's huge income was spent on irrigation, on roads, bridges, schools, or sanitation. The masses had to shift for themselves as best they might. Everything was in a state of ruin and neglect.

II

MILLIONS OF DAYS

    Along the road,
    Old and long,
    Passed to and fro
    Alexander who conquered the world,
    The great Caesar,
    And the murdered Genghis.
    And Tamerlane left his traces,
    And the Mongols took vengeance,
    And China attacked.
    They murdered men
    And they robbed the gardens.
    Blood, blood.
    It was bad for the living where Jugi went.
    Along these roads
    Very ancient,
    Across these steppes
    And mountains and valleys,
    Went slaves and widows,
    Their necks in iron chains,
    Five, ten, hundreds of millions of men,
    Condemned, weakened,
    Hunted out by sorrow—
    And they came again to sorrow.
    And ruin flew from Peking to Rome,
    Ruin went from Moscow to Bombay,
    And the unconquerable army moved.
    And all the roads were spread with human bones.
        Translated from the Uzbek of Gafur Gulam
        by Langston Hughes and Nina Zorokovina.

Noble Bokhara

NOW the Emir is gone. He is selling caracul in Cabul. The jeweled crown has been removed from Bokhara. Bokhara's age-long rival, Samarkand, has become the capital of the new State, the Uzbek Socialist Soviet Republic, while Tashkent, another rival, has become the flourishing center of contemporary Uzbek industry and culture. After a long and turbulent life, old Bokhara seems to be at rest, waiting.

I rise early and take a stroll in the company of Shokhor, the local correspondent for a Moscow paper, through the outskirts of the old city. There are gray streets, gray fences, gray walls, low, flat-roofed gray houses, all merged into one monotonous mass of corrugated gray, the same as they have been for centuries, hardened, immutable. As one gropes one's way through the endless labyrinth of Bokhara's narrow alleys, a queer sensation of timelessness creeps over one—millions of days, thousands of months, hundreds of years—as silent, as soft, individually as indistinguishable as the vague silhouettes of the few veiled women who glide mutely along the walls. A sleepy Uzbek with rolled-up trouser legs, his Mongolian face and sturdy limbs the color of chocolate, sprinkles the street from a water skin. In the distance, in the pale blue haze, gleam the minarets, tiled in turquoise and peacock colors. A stork rises from the gigantic cupola of a mosque and glides above the city. It is soon joined by others and still others. The sacred birds hail the rising sun as they have hailed it countless mornings in the past. A *muezzin* calls the faithful to the morning prayer in the same tones, in the same words, as a thousand years before. Outwardly, at least, it seems that life here still remains as changeless as the surrounding desert. For centuries men as identical as peas in a pod were being born here and grew and aged and died, while the same sun poured the same scorching rays on the same gray walls in the summer, and the same cold rains turned the gray dust into the same thick clay in the autumn. And behind the windowless walls husbands and wives and children lived in the same ancient Mohammedan traditions, with masculine and parental prerogatives inviolate, with polygamy, forced marriages, and bride-purchasing at the very foundation of the family structure.

Somewhere on the remotest outskirts of the city beyond the high embattled walls we find the notorious dungeon built by Nasrullah Khan, the Emir who seized the throne in 1826 after beheading, as a simple matter of precaution, his three brothers and twenty-eight other close relatives. The bleak structure is well enough preserved to give one an idea of the way in which Eastern tyrants treated political prisoners. The upper section is about forty feet square and far below the level of the ground. The entrance is a trap door. The lower section, a deep cellar underneath the first, is twenty feet square and pitch dark. The prisoners had to be lowered into it by means of ropes. Bokhara annals relate that Nasrullah considered incarceration in such a dungeon insufficient punishment for rebels. He therefore filled it with rats, snakes, and other vermin. When the dungeon was unoccupied the pests were kept in condition by being fed on raw meat! I peer into the black pit and think of the hundreds of fighters for a truly noble Bokhara who had suffered within its walls and I realize that this dungeon built by Nasrullah Khan is actually more symbolical of old Bokhara than all the exotic sights I am likely to see here during my journey.

In the distance looms the Tower of Death, the highest building in Bokhara. They threw criminals from the top of that tower, and at times also political rebels and religious heretics. In that tower, they impaled people, violated girls, killed unfortunates by the score. There is one spot in that tower where they punished thieves by chopping off their fingers or arms before taking them through the streets as object lessons for the populace. Yet in spite of all these cruel punishments, Bokhara was proverbially a land of lawlessness. No law-making body, except the Emir; no law, except the *shariat* (interpretation of the Koran) and the *adat* (common law); no personal or property rights, except those granted at the despot's will. Any one could at any time be seized, flogged, clapped in jail, deprived of his property, beheaded at the behest of the Emir. There were no elective offices of any kind. As in all arbitrarily ruled countries, graft, bribery, corruption, venality and violence were rife in Bokhara.

A characteristic feature: the judge (generally a mullah)

in pronouncing sentence also determined the amount of the fine, a part of which was to go into his own pocket. The fine was presumably in proportion to the punishment, and it was quite natural therefore for the judges not to be chary of handing out severe sentences and collecting heavy fines. Justice was candidly class justice. A transgression which in the case of a rich defendant incurred the mildest reprimand—the mere fact of his being haled before the court not infrequently having been regarded as sufficient punishment—involved in the case of the poor man severe flogging and imprisonment. Fine, imprisonment, flogging, drafting into the army for life-long service, execution—these were the most usual and frequent punishments. The venality and the cruelty of the courts were such that the population, particularly the poorer classes, feared them more than the plague. In the villages the peasants would most often settle their disputes by arbitration, thus avoiding the paying of extortionate fines to the Emir's mullah-judges.

Peoples and Conquerors

On my way back to the center of the city the memory of Nasrullah Khan and his weird dungeon haunts me. "Elsewhere light descends upon the earth, but from Bokhara it ascends," says a native proverb. And another declares that "Whoever says Bokhara's walls are not straight, he is cast out of God." I think of the past: numerous peoples and nationalities hemmed in by hungry steppes and impenetrable mountain ranges; living in poverty, darkness, bigotry; exploited by a host of feudal landlords, merchants, mullahs and tax-collectors; kept enslaved by continuous artificially stimulated racial and religious dissension; decimated by malaria, dysentery, typhoid and a hundred other plagues; tortured by fleas, lice, scorpions, jackals, wild boars, vermin and beasts of every other kind and description.

In the accepted literature—exotic tales of peoples and

conquerors; underneath—millennia of destruction, poverty, slavery; mountains of corpses; oceans of blood. And my first morning impressions of Bokhara's "eternal sameness" were also more than a little nonsensical—an idealization of a quiescence that has simply not existed. Surely even here man's spirit has manifested itself periodically with cataclysmic violence and incandescent brilliance. More than once had the blue cupola of silent years over the land been shattered by the thunder and lightning of momentous mass eruptions.

As far back as the fourth and fifth centuries, the Iranian peoples here—the Tadjiks—had formed a number of powerful states—Baktriana, Transoxiana, Sogdiana—the fame of which resounded throughout the then known world. Roads renowned in history, joining India with China, had wound their way through these regions—arteries of trade and commerce, sources of wealth and power for the states through which they ran. A great blessing these roads were, but also a great curse: the countless peoples migrating interminably from the depths of Asia swirled along them, sweeping everything before them in their path, destroying cities and states, and forming new ones in their stead, which in turn were overwhelmed by the next wave of still fresh and vigorous migrants, and so on through the ages. Medeans, Persians, Tokhars, Greeks, Parthians, Huns, Turkomans, Chinese, Arabs, Mongols, Russians—all of these and more had at one time or another moved in hordes along these roads; some vanishing without a trace, others settling and amalgamating with the older dwellers.

Alexander the Great—Alexander the Two-Horned in native legend—founded here a number of cities in which fourteen thousand Greeks had settled and finally merged with the Baktrians, but not without leaving some impression on the culture of the country. In the seventh and eighth centuries the Arabs came and formed the flourishing state of Maverannger. In the frenzy of religious proselytism, they extirpated Parsism, Buddhism, Mazdaism, Nestorian Christianity and proclaimed the everlasting glory of Allah and his Prophet. But the Arabs, too, like the Greeks and the others, were absorbed, assimilated. Only a few of them have remained, kinsmen of the Prophet, still cherishing a semblance of their ancient Arabian tongue. Then the Karliuks swooped down upon the land. In the tenth century it was they who were in the zenith of power. But like water in the surrounding deserts, they too were swallowed by the older population and only seven thousand of them have survived in what was formerly eastern Bokhara, now Tadjikistan. Then toward the beginning of the thirteenth century came the vast Mongolian hordes led by the great conqueror Ghengis Khan. And after him, in the last quarter of the fourteenth century, Timur, or Tamerlane.

The historians grow ecstatic when they speak of Tamerlane. He was "the most amazing conqueror the world has ever seen," writes one, "for he sacked Moscow one summer and was at the gates of Delhi (India) the next; he dethroned no less than twenty-seven kings and even harnessed kings to his chariot." And another writes of the "glorious pages Tamerlane had written into the history of Central Asia." One of Tamerlane's chief sports was to bury alive hundreds of captives or to pile up huge pyramids of living people and pour clay mixed with debris over them. True, he created an ephemeral empire which extended from Mongolia to Syria and included India and Russia, but at what price for the people who fought his battles! True, in Samarkand and elsewhere he built great and beautiful monuments for himself and his kin, but he built them on the dead bodies of millions of anonymous and forgotten subjects. And now only a few magnificent ruins remain to tell the Soviet children of Uzbekistan the sanguinary story of Tamerlane's exploits.

Then came Sheiharri-Khan in the seventeenth century, leading the nomad Uzbek tribes. This was no temporary invasion, but a permanent occupation. The Uzbek tribes settled in Central Asia and made Bokhara their capital. The ancient Maverannger vanished: it was replaced by the Bokhara Khanate of the Uzbeks. The Uzbeks formed other khanates, those of Khiva, of Kokand, etc. The Tadjiks who had successfully absorbed all the other invaders had to yield to the superior numbers of the Tiurko-Mongols. Great and fundamental changes in the life and culture of the country were brought about by the new invaders. The Uzbeks had marked their arrival by the razing of cities, the destruction of the elaborate system of irrigation. Retreating before the horrors of the Tiurko-Mongolian conquests, the Tadjiks fled into the ravines and caves of the Hindukush and Alexander mountain ranges. The whole composition of the population in Bokhara changed: the Tadjiks had permanently retired into the mountains, and the Uzbeks now filled the plains. Yet, strangely enough, it was the culture, the habits, the religion of the Tadjiks that ultimately survived in Bokhara, and the official language in the Bokhara Khanate and of the upper and more cultured classes of the Uzbeks was not Uzbek but Tadjik. Thus came into existence in the seventeenth century the theocratic, patriarchal Uzbek Khanates in Central Asia. Nasrullah-Khan was only one in a long line of despots. The khans of Kokand and Khiva were fully his match in tyrannizing over enslaved peoples.

The White Czar

It was in the reign of Nasrullah-Khan that the last major invasion of Central Asia came to a head. Russia's cynical seizure of the three Central Asian Moslem khanates—Kokand, Bokhara, and Khiva—and heedless expropriation of the semi-nomad Kirghiz, Turkoman, and Uzbek tribes are among the blackest pages in the gruesome history of Czarist imperialism. As far back as 1717, Peter the First attempted to worm his way into Central Asia by siding with one khan against another and mixing up in their feuds. But only disaster came of that. His successors found it advisable to go on with their "civilizing mission" a little more cautiously, creeping up slowly but inexorably from Siberia and the Urals in the North and the Caspian in the West, and steadily crushing the age-long "anarchy" created by "those semi-nomadic, marauding" Asiatics.

First the Kirghiz were smashed. A few years later the Czar had his troops on Syr-Daria. After that began the conquest of the khanates. In the sixties Kokand was battered, and two of its most important towns—Turkestan and Tashkent—were wrenched away. Learning from England's imperialist policy, Russia avoided noisy public annexations, and allowed situations created by victories "to ripen." Beaten and robbed, the Khan of Kokand became an abject slave of Russia. But in 1873-1874 he was forced into a struggle with his subjects who were exasperated by Russian imperialist aggression. In 1875 another, a more general, revolt took place. The Khan, abandoned even by his two sons, who joined the insurgents, quitted his capital with his harem and his treasures and took refuge under the wing of the Russian Czar. The insurrection was crushed by the invading troops, and Kokand was formally annexed to the Romanov Empire.

Bokhara was gobbled up in 1868. The Emir's frantic efforts to raise a defensive holy war against the Russian "infidels" were vain. In the end he was forced to cede to the Czar the larger part of his khanate, including Samarkand, to open the markets of the remaining part to Russian merchants, and pay an indemnity of two million rubles. The Emir of Bokhara became a vassal of the Czar.

Finally, in 1873, came Khiva's turn. The Khan of Khiva, too, had to accept the suzerainty of the Czar.

In the meantime, Alexander II had created in Tashkent the government of Turkestan, headed by a sort of vice-emperor, whose pomp and magnificence were calculated to give to the natives an exalted idea of their real sovereign, the "Great White Czar"! After one hundred and fifty years, Central Asia finally lay prostrate at the feet of the Romanovs.

Here the Czar's government, instead of its usual policy of Russification, adopted a policy similar to that of the French in Algeria. Legally and geographically, the native peoples were kept segregated from the Russian invaders and allowed to retain their old Moslem forms of life. Russia's "civilizing mission" reduced itself to economic exploitation of the natives through their rulers. On the very rare occasions (1898 and 1916) when the frantic natives broke out in revolt, the Czar's government resorted to savage repression, annihilating whole villages and killing native peasants by the hundreds.

With the growth of Russian capitalism, Turkestan and, in a lesser degree, Bokhara and Khiva were converted into a source of raw materials, especially cotton, for Russian industry. The development of native manufactories was artificially blocked; the manufacture of textiles in these territories was prohibited altogether. While many Russian manufacturers and a few native merchants made large fortunes, the Central Asian masses remained wretchedly poor. The peasantry was progressively pauperized, ground down by an army of native money-lenders, who acted as middlemen between the peasants and the Russian cotton industrialists.

The natural economy of the Bokharan villages was being rapidly modified; industrial crops, especially cotton, and an exchange economy began to play an increasingly important rôle. The Russian capitalists were opening banks, trading posts, offices in Bokhara, buying up the raw cotton from the peasants and selling them in return manufactured products. The economic and social structure of Bokhara was beginning to change. Something parallel to what had happened previously in Turkestan was now taking place in Bokhara: growth of commercial capital, disintegration of the feudal and patriarchal relations, pauperization of the peasant masses, and the sharp differentiation of the village population into the extremely poor, the landless, the tenant farmers, at the one pole, and the rapidly prospering landlords and kulak class, at the opposite.

Cotton-growing requires a good deal of preliminary labor and capital investment. Since the Bokharan peasants were poor, they naturally had to rely on advance credit. Even relatively well-to-do peasant households had to do borrowing. In certain regions seventy-five per cent of the peasants' total investment in cotton-raising was on borrowed money.

Bokhara, like the rest of Central Asia, had evolved special forms of credit for the cotton grower: loans from private cotton firms and loans from individual usurers. In describing the latter form, the Russian investigator, N. Koryton, wrote in 1904:

> These "benefactors" help the native peasant in the moment of his greatest need by lending him a small sum at an enormous interest, not less than four per cent a month. The transaction takes place before a common judge, and in the debtor's note the interest is always added to the sum borrowed. That is, if the sum of a hundred rubles is borrowed for one year, the note is made out for 148 rubles. Furthermore, if the usurer doubts the debtor's paying capacity, he takes as security a mortgage on the debtor's real property, at the same rate of interest as above and at a valuation of half the property's actual worth. Foreclosures of such mortgages are the usual thing here. Russian usurers have acquired vast tracts of land at the expense of the ruined native peasants.

The introduction of cotton-growing in Central Asia as a whole proved disastrous to the well-being of the lower economic strata. In the cotton districts of Turkestan, for instance, thirty per cent of the entire population were landless, forty per cent had only one head of cattle per family or no cattle at all, thirty per cent were altogether propertyless and homeless. A vast army of landless peasants and agricultural workers wandered from one region to another in search of jobs. The indebtedness of the poorest section of the peasantry mounted by almost 100 per cent from 1909 to 1911. The same was true of Bokhara and Khiva. Peasants lost their land. Farm tenancy was on the increase. Only the richer peasants, the kulaks, the beys, those who could afford to cultivate cotton without having to resort to loans, found cotton-growing profitable.

OLD AND NEW—IMPRESSIONS

Also, the usurers and the Russian firms waxed rich on cotton. For the majority of the native peasantry the transition of Bokhara from a primitive natural economy to commercial farming was the cause of infinite suffering and widespread ruin. The poor were becoming poorer, the rich richer; while wealth was being concentrated in the hands of the Russian bankers, the native money-lenders, and the beys.

The fact that Bokhara, like Turkestan, was a colonial country made the situation even worse. In America, in Europe, in Japan, to a lesser degree in Russia, the peasant's loss of land was in a measure compensated by the simultaneous growth of industry which absorbed a great deal of the surplus village population. In Bokhara this was not the case. The Czar's government brooked no industrial development in its colonies; and the fate of Bokhara's peasants was no concern of the Romanovs.

Is it any wonder that, ruined, hopeless, and desperate, the Bokharan peasants, like their brothers in Fergana, began to join in lawless bands of brigands, scouring the hills, attacking travelers, raiding settlements, robbing the well-to-do? Many terrible stories have been told about the notorious bandits, the *Basmachi,* of Central Asia. But the origin of this great social evil in Bokhara is scarcely ever disclosed.

The nomad Kazak, Kirghiz, and Turkoman tribes in the rest of Central Asia were even worse off than the agricultural peoples. Their pastures were being taken away from them and settled by Russians from the over-populated central and southern districts of Russia. The government's purpose was to reduce the agrarian unrest in Russia proper by colonizing new lands. Deprived of their pastures, their sole source of livelihood, the nomads retired farther and farther into the barren steppes where they were rapidly dying out.

So it was for decades under the Czars and the Emirs. Then came the February Revolution of 1917, and the feudal monarchy collapsed. Then came the October (Bolshevik) Revolution, and the laboring masses of Central Asia immediately, in 1917, organized a Soviet Government in Tashkent; in 1919, in Khiva; in 1920, in Bokhara. For the first time in their long history, the Central Asian peoples took their destinies firmly in their own hands.

III

CONTRASTS

*Along these ancient roads which have seen so
        many things,
From China to Iran, from India to Turkestan,
Across the whole world the myriads of the proletariat
Will pass quick and fast as a steel caravan
In union and solidarity.
These ancient roads are our immortality.
And along these roads
Will pass a gale of liberty
And not the smell of blood.*

—Gafur Gulam

Water and Blood

THE sun has risen higher, and old Bokhara is stirring to life. An *arba* appears—a queer wagon on two huge wheels as tall as a man, hitched to a camel on which a drowsy Uzbek, gray little skull cap on shaved head and tattered cotton-padded cloak wrapped about him, rocks rhythmically. Soon people on asses, on horses, and on foot, begin to fill the streets. The bearded patriarchs in their long multi-colored robes and huge turbans wound fantastically around their heads look like veritable Abrahams or Jacobs out of the Old Testament. Through a rickety gate a bare-foot youngster in white blouse with a red kerchief round his neck darts out and vanishes around the corner—a little Communist, a pioneer!

And here is a *chai-khanah* (tea house), an open platform set high at the edge of the street, spread with carpets and blankets, decorated with many blue china teapots. The proprietor crouching over a huge samovar spits on its surface and rubs it vigorously with a soiled towel. Another samovar is already going full blast. The customers, their legs folded under them, blow into their *pialas* (large china cups without handles) and enjoy their national drink, green tea. Others are crouching around the *chilim*, the huge tobacco bowl with rubber pipe attached to it, waiting for their turns to take one long voluptuous suck after their tea. The pipe passes from one mouth to another, and no one seems to have any hygienic qualms. Already two old fellows are matching their wits at the ancient game of chess, while near them reclines a wandering bard with his *dutar*, chanting lazily:

> *Glory, glory without end to Him*
> *Who blew a breath of life into a handful of dust.*

This, of course, is not one of the Red *chai-khanahs*, owned by the State Coöperative and patronized by the younger element. There one sees colorful posters plastered all over the back wall, ridiculing the beys and the mullahs, exposing the machinations of the English imperialists, urging preparedness for further revolutionary battle, preaching collectivization, and, above all, hygiene. There one sees stands with Uzbek and Tadjik books and papers and pamphlets printed for the most part in the Latin alphabet. There things are much cleaner, more sanitary, "cultured." This obviously is a private establishment, run as it has been run here for ages.

Everywhere we come across *hauzehs* or remnants of *hauzehs*—unclean, stagnant pools of greenish water where water boys used to fill their sheepskins to carry them to the neighboring households. We come to the famous *Liabi-Hauz*—Holy Pool. It is an enormous reservoir which was once the royal water basin. For hundreds of years the city has drunk its waters flowing from the distant river through uncovered ditches on the sides of the street. Liabi-Hauz stands in the square, the very center of the city. The water boys clamber down its worn stone steps, and with a skillful movement of their bodies dip their goat skins and fill them. Then they carry them to all parts of the city loudly proclaiming their wares. When the water boy finds a customer, he bends his sweating bag, and out of the opening, once the throat of a goat or a sheep, water pours into the earthenware pitcher. Seeing those disease-bearing pools of filth and being nauseated by their stench, I understand the pride of the local residents in the huge water tower, erected in 1929, opposite the Emir's palace, on the city's main square. Such an ugly water tower in such a prominent place would be inconceivable in any other city in the world. But in Bokhara water is precious. Bokhara stands in an arid desert. Water is its wealth, its strength. The canals are its arteries; water, its blood. And to the Bokharans, even to Russians living in Bokhara, nothing less than the main square would be an appropriate place for such a tower.

A wreath of stories and legends has been woven around Liabi-Hauz. In popular imagination the fate of almost every historical personage in Central Asia is in one way or another bound up with this source of Bokhara's life. This is how a contemporary Bokharan novelist writes about Liabi-Hauz:

> The Liabi-Hauz was dug by the Christians who fled here from the fires and the lions of pagan Rome. Exhausted by thirst, frenzied by the thousands of miles they had traversed, they dug here a ditch with bare hands, bare fingers. But they reached no water. And they filled the ditch with the tears of anger and the most transparent of tears—the tears of impotence. The old men maintain that even now the water of Liabi-Hauz is different from that of any other pool. It is transparent and bitterish like tears.
> The pagans who came here in the footsteps of the Two-Horned Alexander to make war, themselves drank and watered their horses from this pool.
> Genghis Khan, displeased by the resistance of the inhabitants, made an oath that he would not rest until the blood of his enemies reached his horse's knees. Corpses were piled up higher than the houses, but the blood, instead of flowing along the land, was soaked into it. There were no more heads to be chopped. The conqueror's oath seemed unrealizable. And then

Genghis rode into Liabi-Hauz and halted—the water almost reached the horse's knees. Forty boys, forty youths, forty adults and forty old men were beheaded over the water of Liabi-Hauz. Their blood coloring the water reached his horse's knees.

And the crippled Timur made an ablution in Liabi-Hauz before he went out to conquer the world. He had been told that only he would subjugate the earth who passed through the black tears of anger and through the most transparent of tears—the tears of impotence.

In the years of the Civil War when the grenades set the Ark on fire, Liabi-Hauz was filled with fire-brands, weapons and treasures.

Liabi-Hauz was the last pool into which the last Emir, Said-Alim Khan, spat when he abandoned his capital forever.

Now the water carriers are quarreling and resting here. What have they to do with legends, with the past; with the tears, the blood, and the spit left here! Do we ever stop to think while quenching our thirst about the hands that had dug this pool?

Those hands are gone. Only the gray stones that frame Liabi-Hauz lie here as of yore.

In the Shadow of the Ark

By midday, the bazaar, through which we are now making our way, is swarming with people—the majority are Uzbeks, but there are some Kirghiz, Bokharan Jews, Tadjiks and Russians. Most of these gaily attired natives are distinctly Mongolian; there are, however, quite a few of Iranian origin—round heads, oval-shaped faces, strong, prominent, straight noses, broad foreheads, and big eyes set in large orbits. The latter are for the most part dark, though occasionally one encounters a reddish-haired and blue-eyed native. These are mountain Tadjiks, the purest type of the Iranian aborigines in Central Asia. A fine, graceful lot. You will scarcely find a fat or flabby specimen amongst them. Their long, well-developed arms and legs come from mountain climbing, hunting and swimming. Some Tadjiks, though, the valley Tadjiks, are more of a Mongolian cast: high cheek-bones, flat noses, narrow eyes—centuries of mixing with the Uzbeks and Kirghiz. When in doubt, one can distinguish the valley Tadjik from the Uzbek by the Tadjik's heavier growth of beard.

Around us there is arduous selling, buying, haggling, shouting. Occasionally the violent honking of an automobile creates something in the nature of a peristaltic movement down the street. Like a huge morsel in a narrow gullet, the car makes its way slowly through the dense crowd which gives way in front of the car and immediately draws together behind it—it seems another Soviet official will once more be late to still another conference.

A beautiful girl, escorted by a rather proud-looking fellow in Young Communist uniform, arrests my attention. She and her companion are Bokharan Jews whom my companion Shokhor seems to know, for, in the manner of the natives, he places his hand on his breast and bows very courteously. Not so many years ago, Jews in Bokhara (not Russian Jews, but natives) were forced to live in a ghetto, were not allowed to enter the Moslem section of the city after sunset, or ride on horseback, or to appear without a rope around their waists as a sign of humiliation, or, at one time, without wearing a headgear of prescribed form, color, and material. Now all this has been swept away by the Revolution. No more humiliation, no more persecution—equality.

In front of the Workers' Coöperative, of the Uzbek State Trading Company, stands an Uzbek in high canvas boots, dark trousers, and white blouse of the militiaman. Here and there one sees the khaki uniform of a native Red Army man. As elsewhere in the Soviet Union and perhaps even a little more, the Red Army man here is treated with love and pride. The proximity to the border, I suppose. All along is the bizarre commingling of the receding and the emergent, the old and the new. Shokhor is indefatigable in pointing out every Soviet institution, every school, Red *chai-khanah,* every newspaper kiosk, the union headquarters, the Uzbek library and of course every unveiled woman we meet.

Nearby, crowning a high hill, are the black ruins of the Emir's castle, the "Ark," including the harem, the state prison, and the Emir's treasury, and encircled by a crumbling loess wall about seventy feet high. The ruins lie there just as they were left in 1920, when the palace was half destroyed by a people in revolt. Inside, the rooms have been renovated. The Regional Executive Committee of the Soviets has its offices there, above the dungeon. The ancient walls are decorated with graphs and revolutionary posters. Young Bolsheviks are scurrying through the halls. Delegations of workers, of peasants, of unveiled women come and go in an endless procession. The atmosphere here is that of any Soviet institution anywhere in the Great Union. As we go out we see urchins digging in the debris, hunting for souvenirs. One of them unearths a fragment of a pitcher decorated with the Emir's arms, another, the inlaid handle of a knife. Through the fine loess dust gleam the Tower of Death and the beautiful Meshit-i-Kalan mosque next to it. We sit down to chat and rest in the shadow of the ruins. From the square below come the incessant clanging of the coppersmiths, the loud blare of a Red Army band, and the sweet odor of *shashlik*, and far above shines a silver plane, winging its way to Samarkand, to Tashkent, to Chelkar, to Samara, to Moscow.

Unreasonable Human Herd

Everything seems peaceful in Bokhara. Yet I know that only yesterday some beys (rich individual peasants) and some traitorous officials were executed by the Soviets. Everything seems tranquil here, yet every item in the local papers is proof of the progressively mounting impact of the revolution in the deserts, mountains, and valleys surrounding Bokhara. Everything seems quiet here, yet I know that in adjacent Tadjikistan, formerly Eastern Bokhara, the peasants and the Red Army are scouring the

OLD AND NEW—IMPRESSIONS

hills in pursuit of Ibrahim Bek, a notorious brigand, and his armed detachment who had recently come from Afghanistan to disturb the collectivization campaign and to start a counter-revolution.

I ask Shokhor about Ibrahim Bek: Who are his backers? To which strata of Central Asian society does he appeal? Are his slogans economic or religious or nationalist?

But Shokhor is not eager to talk about Ibrahim. He suggests that I wait till I get to Tadjikistan to find adequate answers to my questions. "Meanwhile," he advises, "better prepare a background. To understand Ibrahim Bek, you must understand the specific nature of the Bokharan Revolution. Ibrahim is not merely an echo of the past. His adventure is bloody proof that civil war and imperialist intervention are still gruesome realities here. To understand what's happening now in the mountains of Tadjikistan, you must first penetrate to the very soul of ancient, fanatical, obfuscated Central Asia. For a foreigner, this is an almost impossible task. I am an outsider myself, a Russian, and personally, I have found contemporary native art—folk songs, folk poems, ordinary letters written by one native to another—much more revealing of the Central Asian revolution than anything one can read in the official press or observe with his own eyes."

Here Shokhor shows me the booklets which he carries under his arm—a number of anthologies of local poetry and prose—songs of mountaineers, songs of water-carriers, mule-drivers, peasants, collective farmers, unveiled women, short stories, sketches, fragments from novels.

"If you wish to get the real feeling of the clash between the old and the new in Bokhara," he exclaims, while impatiently flipping the pages of Lapin's *Story of the Pamir*, "this is the stuff to read. Some of it is unforgettably, poignantly beautiful. And as a reflection of the revolution, I know nothing to equal it."

Shokhor's eyes sparkle, when he finally finds the piece he is looking for.

"Here, for example, you have the spirit of the old, the counter-revolution, at its best, its sincerest. It's a magnificent piece of Oriental writing. Not until I read it, did I realize how appealing, how persuasive and how dangerous therefore our enemy can be. Read it, you must read it," he shoves the book into my hands. "And don't be afraid to yield to its insidious charm. I'll give you an antidote as soon as you are through."

What Shokhor hands me is a reprint of a letter written in 1924 by the Tadjik Bakhrom Amri-Khudoiev of Cold Springs, on the Pamir, to his Tadjik kinsman Sobyr Djon, a student at the Central Asian Communist University at Tashkent. On the eve of the October Revolution, Sobyr Djon had left his native Tadjik village and went to Bokhara to prepare for the career of a Moslem divine. In Bokhara he fell under the influence of the underground liberal movement among the Moslems, known as the *Djadid* movement. As the Revolution unfolded, Sobyr Djon, together with many of his colleagues, gradually advanced toward an enthusiastic acceptance of the principles of Bolshevism. He took an active part in the overthrow of the Emir, as well as in the Civil War that raged in Bokhara several years after the establishment of the Bokhara People's Soviet Republic. By 1924 Sobyr Djon was a student at the Communist University. In 1927 he died of typhoid fever. Khudoiev's letter was found among Sobyr Djon's papers and turned over to the archives of the City of Tashkent. It was first published in 1930 by the Russian traveler Boris Lapin in his *Story of the Pamir*. It reads:

In the Name of the Merciful God, His Name be Blessed! From Bakhrom, the Bek of Cold Springs, to his beloved and wise teacher, Sobyr-Djon, son of Shod Makhmad, of Cold Springs, blessings and greetings.

I hasten to communicate to you the news that the old Visir Bobo has gathered the autumn yield from nineteen mulberry trees, and has filled his bins so as to last until next spring. Also in exchange for two donkey-loads of salt, he has sold the dried oatmeal to some travelers from the land of Vakhi.

These Vakhi people told us of Russians stationed in

OLD AND NEW—IMPRESSIONS

their country, who were taking count of the number of smoking chimneys, hoofs and human souls.

There is also a rumor that the Russians will tax our hills. This rumor comes from the Ishan-Khodja of the Upper Vakhi.

In view of all these tales we have decided to address you this epistle, hoping God is Merciful, and the Russians will deliver it as far as Podnojie Druzhby.

O Mullah, Mullah! Will you ever come back to this House of Sorrow? Where waters tumultuously rush by, and your brothers are dying? Where sheep are grazing, and wolves are feasting?

You were our beacon when the world was a gloomy cavern, and you have failed us as deeply as we had believed in you.

O Mullah! Will you, drunk with the odor of musk, still remember the faint aroma of the syndjid tree whose fruit you had loved so well as a boy?

Then you, as all of us, did not allow your imagination to soar beyond the Tzygan glacier or the mountain pass of Lysia Smert.

Do you remember the day when your knapsack was filled, and old Mo-Beebee gave you the bast-shoes which she had herself woven with her infirm hands?

You were then a mere little crow, the first to leave the old rookery.

You were the first spring waft to leave the home of the four winds, the first copper penny out of the pauper's bone-framed purse.

That was a joyous occasion, because you were the first of our ravine before whom were to open the glamorous gates of the Veritable Book.

For seven long years you were away from your native hamlet. Those were seven years of daily waiting.

The dying fought death. The women in agonizing labor pains aided nature to heighten the great happiness of your homecoming.

But you never came back to teach us the intricacies, nor to illumine the darkness of our faith.

Then I, your old friend, followed in your footsteps, and twelve days later I reached Garm. The town was then in the hands of the Bek Ubaidullah.

You were not there. You had gone forth still farther, to Kokand.

I remained at Garm to study in the midst of ten-year-olds.

Later we heard that you had come back to Karategin, in the year when Said-Emir was banished, and that you were then helping the Russians to conquer Moslem lands. (A great unforgivable sin!)

Then your letter came to tell us of your sojourn in the thrice damned Red House of Science in Tashkent. Amen. May Allah be praised!

Truly these are the very forty thousand years of ill grace, as the exalted Mukhammad Boo Khanifi used to say. (May his soul rest in peace.)

The women are filled with white rot—the men are decaying stalks.

The cruel war has destroyed piety, and sowed thorns on the Moslem flax fields.

We lived in dependence and happy poverty.

The mighty were strong like oaks, and we, the poor and weak, clung to them like young shoots of ivy.

Before my eyes were hundreds of milestones erected by the teachers of the world. Now, like a madman on ruins, I know not where the sun rises and where it sets.

I am terrified by the valleys. Menacing boars of faithlessness trample our meager fields. Bewilderment assails us, and you are not here, O Mullah, to teach knowledge and faith.

You have betrayed us!

You were a rock, but turned into a bog. We do not know who tempted you, and wherein did you find allurement.

In your letter I felt the spirit of swine eaters, heretics and false commentators of the Law.

Cursed be he who taught you the word of negation. May

he be damned and his father burned. Let in his ears ring forever and ever the voice of doom, as loud as the chariots of Hell.... Same to you—my heart, my soul, O Mullah!

You are trying to feed us the venom of Russian teaching. Does it occur to you what our destiny might be if we follow you?

So be it!

We will share all that belongs to the mighty. We will take the cow of the wealthy and divide it into seven parts of poverty—will yet the cow give milk?

We will share the fields that have been hoed by our forefathers and give it to lie-a-beds and idlers—will the earth be more bountiful and give more bread to our land?

We will shut our eyes to the grandeur of Allah, and believe our souls will sprout grass in their graves—will we achieve immortality and omnipotence, like God?

No, my Mullah! No! No!

The demon, dull and indolent, has taken possession of the women. He is peeping out of their eyes, and kindles a covetous gleam. He makes their breath quick, their tongue sharp and unruly.

With sidewise glances, like bitches, our mountain vixens are seeking out the thin-shouldered youths, and their brain is stuffy and impatient....

Suppose we follow your teaching, O my soul, and the hills will not get richer, the ravines more fruitful, and highways less impassable. What then?

How will you ever look into the eyes of your old mentors, when led on your Day of Judgment over the bridge as thin and sharp as a razor?

Mullah, we live in humility. The poor are subdued by their poverty, and the rich enjoy the vanity of their wealth. Beware! Like a granite rock stands our mighty faith.

Mullah, do not come back. Do you hear the far cry of our hills? They say: "For thousands of years have we lived here guided by the laws of Allah and His prophet, and there can be no change, there can not! See, our summits quake, our mighty glaciers crumble away, ready to crush

you. We do not want to know you! We shall defend our unreasonable human herd from your teaching.
From the sinful, sinful slave
                                    MULLAH BAKHROM.

Month of Khut, year 1344.

"Now this letter," bubbles Shokhor as soon as he sees me lift my eyes, "is to me the most convincing embodiment of the spirit of counter-revolutionary Bokhara—obtuse, inert, slavish, bigoted, self-righteous, fanatical, risen in holy wrath against the heretical teachings of the new swine-eating prophets of Marx and Lenin. It is beautiful in its passionate imagery. The style breathes the spirit of the Old Testament. Have you noticed the author's primitive horror of a census? An interesting detail which accounts for the paucity of statistical information about pre-revolutionary Central Asia. And have you noticed that it was a clergyman, an Ishan, who spread the rumor about the *Russians* making ready to tax the hills? This is also characteristic. The *Ishans* and the *Mullahs* were always playing on the native's indiscriminate resentment against the Russians as representatives of foreign aggression and exploitation. The counter-revolutionary Moslem clergy was always ready to identify the Bolsheviks with the Russians just as the counter-revolutionary Russian clergy was always insisting that Bolshevism was a Jewish invention. You can understand, then, why to the author Sobyr Djon's siding with the Bolsheviks was equivalent to his helping the Russians 'to conquer Moslem lands.' Also, why to him the Red House of Science, the Bolshevik university, was thrice damned.

"What is more interesting, however, is the fact that by 1924 the essential tenets of our Party, however distorted and misconstrued, had penetrated as far as the Pamir. Khudoiev's metaphor about the 'cow of plenty' being divided into 'seven parts of poverty' is simply his poetic way of saying that he is opposed to socialization; his suggestion that the earth will not yield more bread if the land is given to the 'lie-abeds and idlers' is an argument against collectivization, and his irony about souls sprouting 'grass in their graves' is an attack on our materialistic Communist philosophy. Another feature is Khudoiev's reference to the women. That by 1924 our propaganda in Central Asia was beginning to bear fruit in the remotest regions, is evidenced by his assertion that 'the demon... has taken possession of the women.... He makes their breath quick, their tongues sharp and unruly!' And observe, despite his boast that 'like a granite rock stands our mighty faith,' the author confesses that he is 'terrified by the valleys,' and by the 'menacing boars of faithlessness' who 'trample our meager fields.'

"The concluding paragraph of the letter is the quintessence of the old Central Asia's *Moslem* credo: 'For thousands of years have we lived here guided by the laws of Allah and His prophet, and there can be no change....' "

Satisfied that his explanations have been thoroughly successful in dissipating any favorable impression the letter may have made on me, Shokhor now opens another booklet, an anthology of verse.

"And here is your quietly victorious answer, composed only a few years later by one of the Tadjik peasants, Munavvar-Sho:

To the Prophet

In the year of the great war I strolled along the road
(It was a scorching day)
Among the ruined Hissar towers
(The earth was in a mist).

My legs could scarcely carry me
(I was hiding from the horsemen)
Through the waters of the foul-smelling rice fields
(Everywhere lay corpses).

From a ruined cell emerged my old teacher, the guide of my childhood years, a Mullah and a lord of learning. And he cried to me: "Hearken to my prophecies. Years will pass. You will recall my words."

Years have passed. I remember your words, O teacher.

You said: "Crowns will not fall."
    They fell.
You said: "Thrones will not collapse."
    They collapsed.
You said: "The words of the Koran are eternal—
Our women will never unveil."
    They unveiled.
You said: "The mosques will never be empty,
Islam shall reign eternal."
    Hardly.
You said: "The blood of the ruler is sacred."
Look, behold,
Here it is on the steel of my sword.
You said: "From our land they will never flee, the merchants, the Mullahs, the Khans and the judges."
    They fled.

Mullah, teacher,
Where are your prophecies?
Mullah, teacher,
The thought of you makes me tired...."

Night comes suddenly in Bokhara. As I am finishing the poem, the sun is sinking fast on the horizon. On our way back to the hotel, Shokhor recites from memory a poem about Lenin by an Uzbek peasant bard:

The poplar can lift its top above the mountain peaks
Only if its roots drink water enough;
No hills of sand can fill the hollow of the sea
Unless they are as big as the Pamir Mountains;
A man can make the whole world say his name
Only if he commits some awful crime
Or brings something good to the whole wide world.

Many crimes have made the earth shudder
But few men have done good deeds.
The greatest of good deeds was done by Lenin,
The urn of virtues, he who freed the earth.

*The peaks of the Pamir may be leveled
And the oceans cover up the earth
And in their place new mountains rise
Ten times as high as the Pamir—
Ages may walk with iron tread across the earth—
Men may forget where their fathers lived—
Men may forget their fathers' tongue—
But they will not forget the name of Lenin.*

*The name of the greatest of men will never be forgotten:
Would not seas of tears have been shed without him?
Would not the earth have bled dry without him?
Did he not stop the great Russian war?
Did he not dry our tears?
Has he not warmed us with the rays of his soul?
Has he not crushed the beys, the lice of the earth?*

*We don't know where he found so much strength;
Our weak eyes can't see into the soul of this great man.
But this alone we know:
Lenin's equal in mind and heart
Earth has not yet begotten.*

*Now we live, now we try,
However little, to be like him—
The hero who brought us freedom.*

PART TWO
STRUGGLE FOR POWER

"It is no exaggeration to say that at the present time the establishment of correct relations between our Russian Socialist Federated Soviet Republic and the peoples of Turkestan is of colossal universal-historical significance.

"For the whole of Asia and for all the colonial peoples of the world, for thousands of millions of human beings the attitude of our Workers' and Peasants' Soviet Republic toward the weak and heretofore oppressed peoples is of practical import.

"I earnestly request you to give this question your utmost attention—to make every effort to establish—by example, by deed—comradely relations with the peoples of Turkestan—to prove to them by your acts the sincerity of your desire to eradicate all traces of Great Russian imperialism, to struggle tenaciously against world imperialism, with British imperialism at the head of it."

—LENIN, *to the Communist Comrades in Turkestan, November,* 1919.

"We want a voluntary union of nations—a union that would not tolerate any oppression of one nation by another, a union based on the completest mutual confidence, on a clear consciousness of our brotherly unity, on a perfectly voluntary mutual agreement."

—LENIN, *Letter to the Workers and Peasants of the Ukraine, concerning the victories over Denikin, December,* 1919.

IV

GATHERING OF THE STORM

> *O land of mine, here only dreams are bloodless....*
>
> *O God! Shatter the roofs of the palaces*
> *Over the crowns of the vile khans...*
> *O God! Lead us out of this horrible dungeon,*
> *And make the trembling princes kneel before their slaves....*
> —Sadreddin Aini, Tadjik poet.

Bold Spirits

THE first time Emir Alim Khan had felt vague tremors of a revolutionary movement in his realm was in the years of the Russo-Japanese War and the revolution of 1905. The great social disturbances in the center of the Empire had spread to the backward minority peoples on the peripheries and reached even Bokhara. It was the more advanced Tartars and Tiurks from the Volga, the Crimea and the Caucasus who were serving as connecting links between the progressive Moslem movements in Russia and Central Asia. The very name "Djadid"—the New—of the few nationalist societies in Central Asia was borrowed from the Tartars whose nationalist papers, periodicals, and satirical journals were avidly read by the small group of intellectuals in Turkestan and Bokhara. However, in the course of time Djadidism in Bokhara, from a purely cultural, legal movement agitating for secular education and a few minor administrative reforms, developed into a genuine underground organization with a considerable membership, several branches, and numerous sympathizers from among the most progressive nationalist elements in the Khanate. This change came primarily in response to the stimulus of the Turkish and Persian revolutions in 1908.

Now the Bokhara Djadids, in addition to combating religious fanaticism and advocating modern secular schools, began to agitate for a more liberal political and religious censorship and to demand a general lowering of taxes as well as the establishment of a well-regulated system of tax collections. Though it was never fully formulated, the Djadids also hoped for a number of legal guarantees that would in some way enable native capital to be developed unhampered. The sweetest dream of the Djadids, vaguely envisaged by a few of the bolder spirits, was a bourgeois-democratic constitution similar to that of the Young Turks.

The Emir of course persecuted the Djadids. Even the cultural aspects of their work met with the savage opposition of the government and obstinate resistance of the ignorant masses who were completely under the sway of the mosque. Still a few Djadid schools did manage to survive. The rallying ground for everything that was alive and forward-looking in Bokhara, these schools played an important rôle in forging the leadership of the impending revolution.

The February 1917 events in Russia, the overthrow of the Czar and the rise of the Provisional Government, brought the Bokhara Djadids into the open.

Hopes ran high in Bokhara. There were rumors that the Emir was preparing to issue a manifesto granting all kinds of liberties to his subjects. Indeed, in response to a congratulatory telegram from the Djadids, the Provisional Government of Russia sent a dispatch to Miller, the representative of the Russian Government in Bokhara, and to the Emir, urging immediate reform. Assured of the support of the Russian Government, the local revolutionary organizations began to raise their heads, growing ever more militant and aggressive in their demands. However, the Provisional Government in Petrograd, too busy with its own immediate problems of continuing the imperialist war and of counteracting the second wave of revolutionary activity, paid no further heed to the problems of remote Bokhara. So preoccupied was it with the difficult task of stopping the advance of Bolshevism that it never took the trouble to appoint its own representative to Bokhara. It simply retained in this highly responsible post the Czar's representative, the arch-reactionary Miller. Naturally, Miller, instead of assisting the revolutionaries, coöperated with the Emir.

Emir's Futile Incantations

Still the clamor for reforms was so great that Miller felt compelled to persuade the Emir to issue a liberal Manifesto:

> As ever concerned with the welfare and happiness of Our subjects, We are now resolved to institute wide-spread reforms in the various branches of Our administration, eradicating all abuses and improprieties, on the basis of elections to offices as demanded by Our people.
> Reminding all Our subjects that the only possible basis for useful reform and all improvement is the holy Shariat, We call upon every one to aid Us in carrying out Our firm decision to illumine Bokhara with the light of progress and knowledge that will be useful to the people of Bokhara.
> Above all, We shall lay an unshakable foundation for the just administration of Our laws and the collection of revenues and taxes. Furthermore, We shall pay especial attention to the development in Our Khanate of industry and commerce, particularly with mighty Russia. All officials and government employes shall be subject to strict control, and shall receive specified salaries, and shall be forbidden to receive any other compensation for performing their official duties. Also, We shall adopt every possible measure to encourage throughout Our domain the growth and development of useful knowledge in full accord with the dictates of the Shariat.

In Our solicitude over the welfare of Our subjects who reside in Our capital, We have resolved to allow them to elect a council from among those whom the population deems most worthy and honorable and who would assume the responsibilities of bettering the sanitary and living conditions in the first city in Our Khanate.

We also deem it necessary henceforth to establish a state treasury, to adopt a state budget, and to keep strict account of all the revenues and expenses of the Government.

Believing that all Our subjects should be regularly informed as to the exact nature of Our efforts and decrees pertaining to their well-being and happiness, We hereby order the establishment in Our capital of a printing plant whose primary task should be the publishing, as need arises, of special news that may be of general use and that may help Our subjects to obtain useful information.

To provide for the welfare of Our people, We have made every effort to insure in Our Bokhara Khanate the development of self-government whenever and however circumstances may demand it.

To celebrate this solemn occasion, We, working hand in hand with Our mighty protectress, Russia, and with the consent and approval of Our people, hereby order the release of all those who are at present confined in Our prisons.

Friday, 28 Djemadiussani, year 1335 of Khojra, in the capital of Bokhara the Noble.

The manifesto satisfied no one. The left wing of the revolutionary organization regarded it as ludicrously inadequate; the reactionaries, backed by the still deluded masses, viewed it as a national calamity, a blow at the very foundation of the established order. In the demonstrations which followed, the reactionaries made the better showing. Seeing this, the Emir decided to avenge himself on his foes. His magnanimous gesture of granting them freedom was forgotten. Reaction went on a rampage. Thirty of the outstanding leaders of the revolution were arrested and mercilessly flogged. One of the leaders, Mirza-

Nasrulla, received 150 lashes. The Russian workers in Kogan—the European settlement near Bokhara—organized a protest. The Emir, frightened by the unexpected alliance between the Russian and Bokharan revolutionists, hastened to release his victims. Mirza Nasrulla died on the following day. On the eve of his death he composed his political testament. He wrote that he loved his people, and that his last deathbed hope was that his people would free itself from the yoke of slavery. He also wrote that death at the hand of the executioner did not terrify him, that, on the contrary, it made him happy, for he was certain that by his death he was hastening the hour of his people's liberation. Mirza was right. His death sent a shock of horror through the heart of every decent patriot. Despite the Emir's threats and prohibition, Mirza's funeral attracted a vast crowd. From an occasion for mourning, the funeral procession developed into an impressive revolutionary demonstration. Yet the timid right wing elements of the Djadids decided to retreat and henceforth to pursue a more conciliatory policy. A new and more moderate Central Committee was organized which undertook to carry on negotiations with Miller and the Emir in an effort to obtain from the latter, in return for a promise not to engage in subversive activities, an amnesty for the political prisoners and a status of legality for the organization.

United In Revolution

In his memoirs, Faizulla Khodzaiev, one of the leading personalities in the Djadid movement, and until recently the president of the Uzbek Republic, has an interesting description of these negotiations. He writes:

"Through such moderate decisions many had hoped to open the way for some legal Party work. To begin with, it was suggested that Mansurov, Burchanov and I discuss the matter with Miller.

"We went. Miller received us. Mansurov led the discussion. Miller said that although he did not promise success he would try to help and that of course the only way to proceed was to confer with the Emir, since there were no other means of exerting influence.

"And so, on the following day, in accordance with Miller's suggestion, we went to the Emir. We were joined by Miller, Vvedenski and several members of the Soviet of Workers' and Soldiers' Deputies.... On Friday morning we boarded a passenger train bound for Bokhara where we were met by several of the officials in the Emir's carriages. We were all seated in pairs, each pair accompanied by two of the officials. I found myself alongside Mansurov. We were driving through the market place just at the hour when the worshipers were leaving the numerous mosques, and in the very center of the *Registan* we were awaited by a crowd of about 5,000 people.

"All along the road the crowds jeered and threw stones at us. That boded little good for our delegation.

"We finally arrived.... Within a couple of hours we were all invited into the Emir's throne room. Escorted by the Russian authorities we proceeded thereto in pairs, not even inquiring as to why we were being taken there.

"In the throne room we met the entire administration of Bokhara: dignitaries of all ranks and chief mullahs arrayed in all their splendor. When we entered, we were greeted with shouts and cries and abusive language. The introductory words were delivered by Mansurov.

"He began something to this effect: 'We, the citizens of Bokhara, love and respect our fatherland and the existing order and although we criticized His Highness' manifesto as not having altogether fallen in with our aims, we now extend our hand to you, great people of the State. May the will of the Emir be done.'

"No sooner did Mansurov begin to speak, than they all jumped up, waved their sticks, called us traitors, heretics, infidels. Some of us were beaten up.

"The Emir finally rose and addressed himself to Mansurov and the officials thus: 'You, and you my subjects, there is some misunderstanding amongst you. All this will pass, calm yourselves. As it was, so it shall be.' With these words he quickly left the room. We heard the raging and raving of a huge mob near the very wall of the castle, demanding the surrender of our delegation. Only then did we realize the real purpose of the two friends, the Emir and Miller. However, we were not handed over to the mob, instead we were kept in the corridor and then amidst the shouts of the retreating crowd, were led back to our former places.

"There we spent the whole day listening to the shouts of the excited mob still clamoring for our surrender.

"And now the treacherous rôle of the representatives of the Russian Provisional Government fully revealed itself. Miller and Vvedenski made every effort to create the impression that they were the messengers rather than the collaborators of the Emir. They were busy running back and forth, now coming to us, now going to the Emir, now appearing before the people, supposedly to calm them, but in reality as desirous of our end as the mob outside was.

"But in contrast to them, there was another element at work, an element which had already cast off the yoke of czarism, and which later proved to be the emancipator of Bokhara—the national-revolutionary masses of the East working hand in hand with the Russian workers and peasants.

"Were it not for the interference of this group, the bourgeois babblers and traitors—Miller and his colleagues who under the mask of liberalism concealed their reactionary nature—would, no doubt, have handed us over to the brutality of the mob.

"It was they, the revolutionary Russian Army and the workers of New Bokhara, the Russian settlement, who frustrated the hellish plans of the Emir and his Russian henchmen. The first to come to our aid were the workers of New Bokhara with whom our young Bokharan party maintained the closest ties, then the revolutionary Army which was stationed in New Bokhara and on the railroad stations of Old Bokhara.

"But of all this our delegation knew nothing. During

our entire stay at the palace we were awaiting death either at the hands of the hangman or the infuriated mob.

"Then the unexpected happened—we were visited by Nasrulla Kushbegi and Urgandji. They both with one voice announced that the Emir regretted the entire affair, that he was indignant at the fanaticism of the mob, whose number by that time had swelled to 10,000, which for the last twelve hours was demanding the execution of the delegation or its surrender. However, neither thing happened since the Emir was anxious that everything end amicably. Then Urgandji added that by morning we would probably be released.

"Evidently the visit of the workers and the revolutionary soldiers had its effect on His Highness the Emir and his officials.

"Urgandji further stated that the members of the Soviet of New Bokhara were very tired and were therefore obliged to leave. We protested very energetically against the departure of the only trustworthy protectors we had and of course they agreed to remain with us.

"When Miller noticed how readily the Soviets offered to help us, he became alarmed and immediately began to make arrangements for our release.

"By twelve o'clock we were freed and on our way back to New Bokhara where we were met by cheering crowds of railroad and cotton-ginning factory workers."

This trip to the Emir brought about the end of both the Central Committee and the chairmanship of Mansurov. About two weeks later, a new Central Committee was formed at a general membership meeting of the Organization. This Committee made a final break with many of the evils of Djadidism, such as its confinement to the province of culture and its political wavering. The formation of a new Young-Bokhara party, to replace the Djadid, was begun and its program drawn up. At the same time there was a strengthening of the agitational and organizational activities in the villages and the provinces. In accordance with one of the first and most important decisions of the new Central Committee, work was begun among the

Emir's soldiers. Efforts were also made to revolutionize and unite those groups of craft workers and drivers in the cities who were in sympathy with the Young-Bokhara party, and who were potentially excellent material for carrying the struggle to the next stage, the overthrow of the Emir and the establishment, three years later, of the Soviet power in Ancient Bokhara.

V

FIRST THUNDERBOLT

TWO CAMPAIGNS: A Recitation

1st GROUP: *We are going into battle. We are going into battle against the Chadra and the Paranja.*
We are struggling for your freedom, O East, on our most distant borders.
We are fighting for the freedom of our sisters and the lives of our daughters.
And they—what do they want? Their truth let us see.

2nd GROUP: *They go to the edge of the world; proudly they wave the British flag.*
They slay our toiling brothers whose blood in rivers flows.
They pet our lords and crush their obedient slaves.
They stamp as foes the eyes that stare straight in their faces.

1st GROUP: *We go to fight to set you free, O China and O India!*

2nd GROUP: *But for them China and India are like a fat ram for pilaf.*

1st GROUP: *There is no place here any more for emirs or beys or mullahs.*
We need no god and no servants of his from this or other lands.

2nd GROUP: *There they have thrown the burdens of this earth on the broken backs of the poor.*
The cry of the babes, of the Hindu peasants is terrible to hear.

1st GROUP: *We want to open up for the peoples of the earth a new and shining world.*

2nd GROUP: *They want to keep the yoke on us, the rich man, the bey, the emir!*
They are preparing for us a glorious holiday of bullets and bombs and grenades.

IN UNISON: *There are open before you two roads. In front there rises the sun.*
Look where is good and look where is evil and fight!
That's our advice.

—PAIRAU SULYAIMONI

Emir Ponders

THE Bolshevik Revolution came down like a bolt from heaven upon the Emir. Self-determination of Peoples! Down with Imperialism! Down with the Landlords and the Bourgeoisie! We Demand Peace, Land and Freedom! Long Live the Workers' and Peasants' Soviets! Long Live the International Revolution! These, he had frequently heard from Miller during the preceding months, were some of the slogans emblazoned on the Bolsheviks' banners. He had also heard of that man Lenin—"a lunatic and a German spy"—but he took neither Lenin nor his slogans too seriously, for he relied on Miller's optimistic interpretation of events in Russia.

Now the sudden news: Kerensky has fled. The Bolsheviks have seized power! And a few days later, the New Government's fantastic Declaration of People's Rights, announcing the "final and irrevocable" liberation of all the people who had suffered under the "despotism" of the Czars; guaranteeing "the equality and sovereignty of all the peoples in Russia; the right of all the peoples in Russia to self-determination, including the right to separation and the formation of independent states; the abolition of all national and national-religious privileges and restrictions; the free development of national minorities and ethnographic groups inhabiting Russian territory...."

National freedom in Russia! To the Emir the whole thing seemed absurd, incredible. Here was a country extending over two continents, embracing five hundred and seventy-seven different peoples and tribes speaking one hundred and fifty different languages, a country whose entire history was one endless series of conquests and subjugations of neighboring peoples, a country which in the course of four hundred years had increased its territory at the rate of fifty square miles a day—from 800,000 square miles in 1505 to 8,500,000 square miles in 1900!—a country which for centuries had treated subject peoples with the utmost contempt, keeping them economically backward, and, with the exception of the Bokhara Khanate, ruthlessly suppressing their national languages, cultures, and institutions. And in this country the equality of peoples has been proclaimed the fundamental law in the land. . . . "A piece of strategy," reasoned the Emir, "a spectacular gesture intended to delude the non-Slavic peoples, through the flattery of their national aspirations, into supporting the government of a band of Russian anarchists and brigands." And he decided to watch his step most vigilantly.

A couple of days later came the "Proclamation to the Mohammedans of Russia and the Orient," signed by Lenin and a certain man Stalin. This was even more disconcerting. The Bolsheviks now addressed themselves specifically to the Moslem East, to the "Mohammedans of Russia, Tartars of the Volga and Crimea, Kirghiz and Sarts of Siberia and Turkestan, Tiurks and Tartars of Transcaucasia, Chechenzi and other mountaineers from the Caucasus," to all those "whose mosques and prayer houses were being destroyed, whose peaceful customs were trampled under foot by the czars and oppressors of Russia." Yes, the godless riff-raff at Petrograd were trying to make people believe that "henceforth" Moslem "beliefs and customs . . . national institutions and cultures" were "free and inviolable." "Build your national lives free and unhampered," wrote the Bolsheviks. "You have the right to them. Know that your rights, as well as the rights of all the peoples of Russia, are under the powerful protection of the Revolution and its organs—the Soviets of Workers', Soldiers', and Peasants' Deputies. . . ."

The Emir was perturbed, puzzled. Sitting in his cabinet under the glaring empty space where the Czar's and Czarina's portraits used to hang, he read and re-read and pondered the two Bolshevik documents. Even before he had fully realized it, his class instinct told him that they contained some profound and sinister significance. First, as to the right to separate and form an independent state. As things looked now that seemed exceedingly alluring.

Of course, time was when he wouldn't have thought of breaking away from Russia, even if it had been feasible. But that was months ago, under the Empire, when he, Emir Said-Mir-Alim-Khan, still held the high rank of general in the Russian army and of aide-de-camp to his friend and protector Czar Nicholas II. Then under the beneficence of Russia's power and prestige, he lorded it over his domain without fear of challenge. Occasionally, some annoying interference from the Sovereign's representative would occur, but that was made up a hundredfold by the great economic and military advantages which he and his closest friends derived from the association. After all, it was under the czars that he had become one of the wealthiest men in Asia. "Such riches as take one back to the days of the Arabian Nights," once remarked an admiring Englishman, "with a collection of jewels and precious stones worthy of the oldest Mohammedan state." In addition to the 100,000,000 rubles invested in Russian industrial and financial enterprises, he had thirty-five million pounds sterling in gold and silver coins and ingots. More precious than gold was his power: two and a half million good, pious, obedient subjects! True, there were a few malcontents. But Great Russia's friendly interest certainly helped keep them in the proper place. And there was never any trouble with respect to religious freedom and the preservation of Moslem tradition. In Bokhara, at least, there was no Russian meddling on that score. The Mohammedan faith and tradition, Allah be praised, existed here after the Russian conquest as they had existed here centuries before, without perceptible changes.

There was a time when the social structure of the Khanate seemed to the Emir as unshakable as those great pyramids that keep eternal watch over the African deserts. He himself was the supreme ruler, the very apex of the pyramid—the focus of all religious, executive, judicial and legislative authority in the realm—Chief Mullah, Chief Executive, Chief Casi, Chief Commander, Chief Merchant, Chief Everything. And immediately below him, supporting him and coöperating with him, were his highest ecclesiastical and state dignitaries and the financial aristocracy. A compact, scarcely differentiated social layer, rich and powerful, and inextricably bound up with his rule; impervious to new ideas, set against the slightest innovation, the iron stronghold of orthodoxy in his realm.

Below were other layers, broader and thicker, but less homogeneous, and less integrated—the so-called rural and urban middle classes. The most stable and loyal amongst them had always been the beys, the richest peasants. With the exception of his nearest collaborators, the beys were his most favored subjects. Their estates were for the most part not very large, but they comprised the best lands, not infrequently granted to them by himself. The Emir was proud of his strategy—the bestowal of such land upon the chiefs of tribes and clans secured for him the loyal coöperation and support of the most authoritative elements in the village. In essence, each bey was a petty feudal lord, his, Alim Khan's, vassal. The bey was not really a peasant, for he rarely worked on the land. He was most usually the local administrative officer of the Emirate, and his lands were worked by tenant-farmers who received one-fourth of the harvest. Altogether the beys constituted quite a distinct economic and social category. Their relative wealth and political power made their position in the village invulnerable and their influence irresistible. Living on their own lands which produced everything they needed, the beys like the aristocracy, were among the least susceptible to outside influences and the allurements of modernity. They were the backbone of conservatism in the Khanate.

In the city, the most numerous section of the middle class was the lower merchants. They were neither independent nor affluent—mostly middlemen and agents for Russian commercial and financial institutions. Always in debt to the Russian banks or the Bokharan upper class, always in the process of getting into or getting out of bankruptcy, this class was ignorant and subservient, but God-fearing, politically trustworthy and scarcely distinguishable from the rest of his subjects. Socially and psychologically the merchants were most closely related to the lower clergy and officialdom.

Associated with this perfectly trustworthy class was, however, the native professional intelligentsia, not a very numerous group but sufficiently "advanced" to chafe under what they were pleased to call the "glaring anachronisms" of Bokharan life. A perverse element, most of them liberals and revolutionists—Djadids. Yet on the whole, with the aid of the Czar, he had never found it very difficult to handle them. A little severity went a long way with them.

And right below was the thin layer of city workers—about ten thousand of them—truckmen, water-carriers, shoemakers, tailors, blacksmiths, leather workers, silversmiths, weavers, and craftsmen of various other kinds. There were no industrial workers, no industrial proletariat in his Khanate, for there were no industries. However, the several thousand workers in Bokhara were a pretty bad lot—a little too "civilized," a little too ready to pick arguments and kick up trouble, and a little too ready to listen to the Djadids and to hobnob with the Russian railroad workers and other Russian riff-raff in the New City, in Kogan. But there were so few of them and they were so poor and had so little influence on the general population that neither the Emir nor any of his aides ever took them seriously.

Then there was the large mass of the village population—the broad base of the social pyramid. A stolid, inert lot; poor and humble and touching in their profound devotion to tradition, the mosque, and their divine ruler. It was on their loyalty and obedience that the whole social structure rested. There had been sporadic peasant outbreaks, but those, Allah be praised, had been easily put down.

Such was life in the not very distant past under the Empire—a good, reverent, God-fearing folk welded together by the power of their ruler and the help of the Czar into one happy, harmonious family. Surely the thought of independence would have never entered the Emir's mind in the days of the Czar. Things, however, had changed. Ever since February Bokhara had been seething with agitation. The Young Bokharans had been making more and more a nuisance of themselves. The humiliating episode of the manifesto passed through the Emir's mind, and he felt a shudder running down his spine. That could not be dismissed too lightly. What was the use of the Bolsheviks' guarantees that beliefs and customs would be free and inviolable, when here one's own subjects, Moslems, Bokharans, were trying to tear everything down? And the most disturbing, the most ominous thing was the way the revolutionary Russian workers and soldiers and the members of the Soviet from the New City rose in defense of the Young Bokharans. So that's what the Bolsheviks meant by the rights of the peoples of Russia being under the protection of the Soviets of Workers', Soldiers', and Peasants' Deputies!

Now the Emir saw through the trick of the Bolsheviks. Just as Miller, the spokesman of Imperial Russia, had dealt with him as the representative of the Bokharan peoples, so now would the Bolsheviks, the spokesmen of the revolutionary Russian masses, deal with the Young Bokharans as the representatives of the Bokharan peoples. Feeling the whole world toppling on his head, realizing that his money, his lands, his investments, his throne, his very life were in peril, the Emir, in a frenzy of fear, issued a despairing call to all his ministers, mullahs, ishans, rich merchants, casii and other dignitaries of State and mosque to gather in secret council. His purpose was to check up the home forces that could be mustered against the Bolshevik menace as well as to discuss the possibilities of obtaining outside, especially British, aid.

Parting of Ways

The Djadids and the Young Bokharans, too, were deeply stirred by the tremendous overturn in Russia. The Bolshevik Declaration of Peoples' Rights and the Proclamation to the Mohammedans of Russia and the Orient gave expression, it seemed, to their fondest hopes. Those were days of profound exultation and passionate discussion. Before long, however, the fundamental differences inherent in the various attitudes ranging from the constitutional democratic of the bourgeois nationalists to the proletarian revolutionary of the Bolshevik internationalists began to come to the surface. Now that national self-determination was at last proclaimed, the bourgeois nationalist Djadids thought it best for Bokhara to overthrow the Emir, break away from Bolshevik Russia, form a constitutional democratic republic, and start on an ambitious career of capitalist development, with native capital guaranteed every legal advantage. Like the Emir, most of them on sober reflection came to doubt the ultimate sincerity of Bolshevik protestations concerning the right of each nation to form a separate independent state. An empty gesture, another Russian trick! Let them entrench themselves, and before long they will crush the slightest manifestation of "separatism" or "particularism" or "local independence." The Russian Bolsheviks were now advocating national rights, because they were trying, for their own safety, to demolish the old state structure. But as soon as the Old Empire was completely gone, they would hasten to build in its place "their own—Red, but Russian—empire." Once the old alignments were annihilated, the nationalism and particularism of the former colonial and semi-colonial peoples would no longer be useful to the new rulers! So reasoned the Bokharan bourgeoisie.

Other Djadids, the more revolutionary ones, vehemently defended the Bolsheviks, and expressed faith in their sincerity. They referred to history. They unearthed old documents. They insisted that self-determination of peoples was not a newly invented Bolshevik trick, but that it lay at the basis of Bolshevik ideology from the very inception of Bolshevism in 1903. They went farther back—to the early days of the Second International. The London Congress of the Second International, in 1896, had stated it clearly and unequivocally: "The Congress declares that it stands for the right of all peoples to self-determination." The same position had been taken by the Congress at Paris in 1900, at Amsterdam in 1904, at Stuttgart in 1907.

And Lenin had worked over this question for years. In a hundred different places, in articles, editorials, resolutions, Lenin always maintained that national self-determination meant precisely what it said—the freedom of every nationality to determine its political, economic, and cultural life. He fought tenaciously those among the Social Democrats who felt that "national self-determination" should be confined to the purely cultural or purely economic phases of a people's life and that Lenin's conception, if pressed to its logical conclusion, would tend to ignore the "international sentiments" of the working class and introduce narrowing "chauvinistic tendencies" into the international revolutionary movement. Lenin always insisted: "By self-determination we mean the right of a people to separate itself from alien national-collectives, the right to form an independent national state."

And in 1913 Stalin, in his *Marxism and the National Question,* wrote: "The Social Democracy of all countries is proclaiming the right of the peoples to self-determination. ... No one has the right forcibly to intervene in the life of the nation, to destroy its schools and other institutions, to break down its customs and usages, to suppress its language, to cut down its rights."

And in April, 1917—seven months before the Bolshevik victory—the All-Russian Bolshevik Conference at Petrograd (now Leningrad), in criticizing the Provisional Government, reiterated the fundamental Bolshevik principle that "all nations within Russia must be accorded the right freely to secede and to form independent states ... the denial of this right, and the failure to adopt measures guaranteeing its practical realization, amount to the support of a policy of conquests and annexations."

But the bourgeois nationalists who distrusted the Bolsheviks were not easily downed. If the Bolsheviks, they maintained, were honest, then they were hopelessly naïve. Surely, when confronted with the practical tests of government, all their ardor and theories would be dampened. Centralization of authority and unification would become the watchwords. Before long they would discover Bolshevik equivalents of the "white man's burden," "civilizing influence," "trusteeship," etc. The Stuttgart Congress, as well as the subsequent history of the Socialist parties in Europe, provided an excellent example of this. It was at Stuttgart that Socialists like MacDonald and Von Kole—one a citizen of Imperialist Britain, the other of Imperialist Holland—had refused "in principle to condemn any colonial policy which under a socialist régime may have a civilizing rôle to perform." As soon as the Socialists had found themselves with ministerial portfolios under their arms, the arch-revolutionary doctrines of 1896, 1900, 1904 began to evaporate. The same would happen with the Russian Bolsheviks. And then woe to those of the national minorities who had reposed their faith in them! They would be crushed—all in the name of helping "our backward brothers in the East"!

Furthermore, a thorough analysis of Bolshevik writing on this subject—maintained the bourgeois nationalists—revealed a curious fundamental contradiction: Always separation and unification in the same breath! The germ of this contradiction was contained in the Declaration of the London Congress in 1896. Immediately after announcing that all nations had the right to determine their own destinies, the Congress called upon the workers of all countries to unite in struggle for the overthrow of international capitalism and for the realization of the aims of International Socialism. Well, argued the bourgeois Djadids, suppose the several thousand workers in Bokhara suddenly turned Communist, while the rest of the two and a half million inhabitants preferred a bourgeois democracy—by joining hands with the Bolsheviks in Russia, by inviting Russia's help, several thousand Bokharan workers could, through sheer external force, establish the dictatorship of the proletariat in Bokhara too, and thus make Bokhara once again an appendage of Russia. What the bourgeois-nationalists, therefore, insisted on knowing was what it was that the Bolsheviks really stood for, separation or unification, national independence or international dependence?

The few young Bokharans who were most familiar with Marxist dialectics denied that there were any contradictions in the Bolshevik national program. It was all a matter of defining who was the exponent of the nation's will. And here they felt the Marxists had always been lucid and consistent. In the *Communist Manifesto,* in 1848, Marx and Engels wrote:

> *Formally,* though not *intrinsically,* the struggle of the proletariat against the bourgeoisie is in the first place a national one. The proletariat of each country must, naturally, begin by settling accounts with its own bourgeoisie. The proletariat must begin with the conquest of political power, must raise itself to the position of the national class, must constitute itself the nation; in this sense it is itself national, though not at all in the sense of the bourgeoisie.

Also Stalin, in 1913, made it quite clear that the whole purpose of the Bolsheviks' struggle for national self-determination in Russia was ultimately "to undermine the national struggle, to rob it of its sting, to reduce it to a minimum" and thus enable the laboring classes of the different peoples to unite against the common enemy—the bourgeoisie. "In this way the policy of the class-conscious proletariat is sharply distinguished from that of the bourgeoisie, which aims at intensifying the nationalist struggle and continuing and redoubling the nationalist agitation."

The Young Bokharans knew that *unification,* in Marxist theory, was always the fundamental motive of the apparently separatist slogan of national self-determination. It always meant "national" not "in the sense of the bourgeoisie," but in the Marxist sense of the proletariat seizing political power, and "constituting itself the nation" by winning over the vast majority of the working population. The same thought was expressed even more clearly by the April Conference of the All-Russian Bolshevik Party in Petrograd: "The question of the *right* of nations freely to secede is unjustifiably confused with the question of the *expediency* of the secession of one or another nation at one or another moment. *This latter question must in each separate instance be determined in entire independence by a party of the proletariat, from the point of view of the interests of general development and of the proletarian class struggle for socialism."* *

* The Communist understanding of self-determination is excellently revealed in *Resolutions of the Communist International on the Negro Question in the United States:* "... Complete right to self-determination includes also the right to governmental separation, but does not necessarily imply that the Negro population should *make use of this* right in all circumstances, that is, that it must actually separate or attempt to separate the Black Belt from the existing governmental federation with the United States. If it desires to separate, it must be free to do so; but if it prefers to remain federated with the United States it must also be free to do that. This is the correct meaning of the idea of self-determination, and it must be recognized quite independently of whether the United States is still a capitalist state or whether a proletarian dictatorship has already been established there.

"It is, however, another matter if it is not a case of the *right* of the oppressed nation concerned to separate or to maintain governmental contact, but if the question is treated on its merits: whether it is to work for state separation, whether it is to struggle *for this* or not. This is another question, on which the stand of the Communists must *vary* according to the concrete conditions. If the proletariat has come into power in the United States, the Communist Negroes will not come out for but against separation of the Negro Republic from federation with the United States. But the *right* of the Negroes to governmental separation will be *unconditionally realized* by the Communist Party; it will unconditionally give the Negro population of the Black Belt freedom of choice even on this question. Only when the proletariat has come into power in the United States the Communists will carry on propaganda among the working masses of the Negro population against separation, in order to convince them that it is much better and in the interest of the Negro nation for the Black Belt to be a free republic, where the Negro majority has complete right of self-determination but remains governmentally federated with the great proletarian republic of the United States. The bourgeois

When the bourgeois national Djadids finally grasped the full import of what the Bolsheviks meant by "national" self-determination they were horrified. They had yearned for a constitution, a parliament, an opportunity to develop native industry and trade, and to exploit their poorer compatriots without Russian competition or interference. They had dreamt of a prosperous and growing native bourgeoisie—liberal, cultured, modern—as the best social expression of a revolutionized Noble Bokhara. They had hated the Emir and his entire clerical-feudal set-up. However, now that they had discovered what Bolshevism actually stood for, they knew that they hated Bolshevism even more. For it was not the refined and cultured bourgeois intelligentsia, but the worker and peasant masses, led by the most class-conscious proletarian sections, who were to be the exponents of the national will! That would never do! If forced to make a choice, the liberal Djadids would regretfully choose the clerical-feudal forces of the Emir. One hope for a "democratic" government remained and that was Great Britain, although, in view of Britain's record in Asia, even that was highly questionable. Still if forced to the wall, the Djadid nationalists would choose even England in preference to the Bolsheviks.

In the Shadow of Empires

The Emir's and the bourgeois nationalists' hopes of British help were based on a sound evaluation of the fine web of geographical, historical, economic and political factors which entered into Russo-British relations in the East.

It must be remembered that Great Britain, besides being a world center of trade separated by a narrow channel from the European Continent, is a vast Asiatic Em-

counter-revolutionists, on the other hand, will then be interested in boosting the separation tendencies in the ranks of the various nationalities in order to utilize separatist nationalism as a barrier for the bourgeois counter-revolution against the consolidation of the proletarian dictatorship."

pire. In India, Persia, Afghanistan, Turkey, China, her interests in Asia are all-pervading. The Near East, the Far East, the Middle East—England is everywhere. Until the relatively recent rise of Japan, Great Britain's only serious rival on the Asiatic continent was Imperial Russia. Like an insatiable octopus, the monster from the north had for centuries been pushing its greedy tentacles further and further south, tightening their coils around the Crimea, the Caucasus, Central Asia, crawling out to the south and east to Constantinople, Persia, Afghanistan, India, Mongolia, China. It had a vast hunger for the cotton bolls and silk cocoons of the south, and a vast thirst for the warm Mediterranean and Indian waters. Everywhere it found Great Britain in its way. Not only that, but England herself had been fixing a covetous eye on the Caucasus with its oil and on Central Asia with its vast riches. For decades the two Giant Empires in the East were making ready to leap at each other in a life and death struggle. Occasionally, when the British lion was engaged elsewhere, the Russian octopus would snatch as great a piece of territory as it could. So it was during the Boer War. While Britain was busy in Africa, Russia grabbed at Tibet and Persia. However, in 1907, when Czarist Russia, enfeebled by war with Japan and internal revolution, became fearful of the ominous shadow of Imperial Germany spreading from the west, she temporarily abandoned her expansionist dreams, and entered into a military alliance with Britain against Germany. Yet the basic antagonism between the two rivals in the East remained.

Persia offers one instance. Ever since the Treaty of Torkmanchei (1828), Persia, deprived of her tariff autonomy, had been forced to yield greater and greater concessions to her northern neighbor. Czarism's most insidious method of directing Persia's economic policy was to grant loans at exorbitant interest to the degenerate Persian Shahs. When Russia launched a modern textile industry in the latter half of the last century, the Czars began to evince an increasingly keen interest in Persia's cotton-growing regions. Moreover, in order to assure the arid districts of Central Asia of adequate grain supplies, the Czars began to feel an overpowering urge to lay hands on the fertile provinces of Northern Persia. At the same time, England was pressing her imperialist weight against Persia from the South. Finally in 1907, this country of twenty million population, rich in oil, coal, iron, virtually lost her last shred of independence: Russia and Britain had divided her between themselves into "spheres of influence" —in the North, Russia; in the South, England, Afghanistan, too, after many years of friction between England and Russia, finally became an English dependency. With the World War, Russia's dormant appetite for southern lands and waters stirred once again. And in 1915, to stimulate the Czar to even greater sacrifices of the lives and the goods of his peoples, Great Britain and France were forced to sign a secret agreement guaranteeing to the Czar as one of the spoils of victory the Turkish capital, the resplendent city of Constantinople. Whatever the obstacles, the rapacious northern monster was pushing ruthlessly southward. The conflicting, fundamentally irreconcilable interests of the two temporarily allied imperialist rivals were challengingly reasserting themselves. What held them together was the dread of a victorious Germany.

In Bokhara it was clearly understood that the Bolsheviks' long-proclaimed threat of withdrawing Russia from the war and of confiscating all property belonging to landlords, banks and foreign concessions—and Britain had vast and profitable concessions in Russian gold, oil, and other fields—would break the truce between the two countries.

Also, it was correctly argued, the Bolshevik Declaration of Peoples' Rights and particularly the Proclamation addressed to the Moslem peoples of Russia and the Orient were bound to arouse the greatest apprehension and the bitterest resentment of the English imperialists in Asia. For it was precisely here in Asia—in India, in Persia, in Afghanistan, in Turkey, and even in China—that English imperialism was most relentless in exploiting the native masses. And the Bolsheviks' dramatic disavowal of Russia's czarist past, especially as regards her oppressed peoples of the Orient, naturally carried with it the implication of sharp censure of the predatory practices of the remaining imperialist countries, chiefly England.

There were in Asiatic Russia about thirty million Moslems, several million Mongols, Buriats, Jews, Armenians. All those nationalities, settled along the southeastern borders of the former empire, had national or religious or economic ties with millions of related peoples in the contiguous lands which were under English sway. And Great Britain would certainly be greatly alarmed over the possibility of the revolutionary enthusiasm of the released peoples sweeping across Russia's boundaries.

Even a greater revolutionary threat to England, it was felt in Bokhara, was contained in the Bolshevik announcement that, in addition to liberating all the peoples enslaved by the Czar, the new workers' government—voluntarily and without expecting any compensation—repudiated and canceled all czarist treatries, debts, capitulations and ambitions in the East. "Moslems of the East," read the declaration, "Persians and Turks, Arabs and Hindus, all of you whose lives and properties, whose liberties and customs have for hundreds of years been sold and bartered by the blood-thirsty European beasts of prey, all you whose lands are intended to be divided amongst the robbers who have started this war, we say to you that the secret treaties concerning the seizure of Constantinople signed by the now deposed Czar and confirmed by the now deposed Kerensky are abrogated and canceled. The Russian Republic and its government, the Soviet of People's Commissars, are opposed to the seizure of somebody else's lands. Constantinople should remain in the hands of the Moslems. We declare that the treaty about the partition of Persia is abrogated and canceled. As soon as military operations stop, the Russian armies will be withdrawn from Persia, and the Persians will be assured their right freely to determine their political destiny. We declare that the treaty pertaining to the partition of Turkey and the wresting of Armenia from her is abrogated and canceled."

The Emir and his councilors understood very well what the revolutionary domestic and foreign policy of the Bolsheviks meant to the peoples of the East—not only to those who had for long been chained to Russia's imperial juggernaut, but also to those who, like Persia, Afghanistan, or Turkey, were in constant dread of foreign aggression and occupation, as well as to those millions in India and China and Korea who had long been trampled under the imperial heels of England, France, Japan, and others. And they felt reasonably sure that in Central Asia it would be England who would lead the fight against the Bolsheviks.

VI

A COLOSSUS PROSTRATE

> The Shah said: "Two truths are struggling in heaven."
> The Shah said: "Why need you worry about bread?
> Poverty is needed in the world. Wealth is needed in the world.
> Let us wait for whatever lot befalls us.
> Glory to you, conquerors, who have drowned the world in blood.
> Glory to you, slaves, who have fed the world with bread."
>
> "Lying foolish old man," I answered the Shah.
> "Your words are contemptible," I answered the Shah.
> "Everything on earth comes from peasants' and workers' hands,
> Great and wonderful is their work," I answered the Shah.
>
> ...Your evil world, your shop of oppression,
> Your smithy of chains, your goat-skin of malice and fat
> Must fall before the songs of the Gatling guns
> In the firm hands of the poor peasants and workers of the world.
>
> The time has come. The arm of our class is strong.
> A new world, without classes, will arise from the ashes!
>
> —G. LAKHUTI, Tadjik poet.

Not All Lenins

FEARING for his throne, recognizing that compromise with the Bolsheviks was impossible, the Emir broke off relations with Red Petrograd and declared intercourse with Soviet Turkestan a capital offense. He began to negotiate definitely for help from the Russian Whites, the English imperialists, the Afghan government. He began feverishly to augment his army, increasing the already too heavy taxes and taking vigorous measures to stop the growth of revolutionary sentiment among his subjects and the increased activity among the Left Djadids.

The one great advantage he had over the Reds was that the class-conscious proletarian stratum in Bokhara—and not only in Bokhara, but in the whole of Central Asia, including the most industrialized Tashkent and Kokand regions—was exceedingly thin and narrow, a small group of Russian and native revolutionists in the vast mass of faithful Moslems. The readiness of the mob to lynch the very moderate Djadids during their visit to Alim Khan indicated what treatment real rebels could expect at the hands of the fanatics. Then the Djadids were saved by the revolutionary Russian soldiers and workers from Kogan. But obviously there were not enough Russian workers in the Khanate to effect an overturn against the will of millions of natives, even if such a course were desirable or feasible.

To overthrow the Emir, the Young Bokharans, still too weak to attempt anything by themselves, would have to invite outside help, especially from adjacent Turkestan, where the few Russian railroad workers and Bolsheviks who had happened to be in Central Asia during the October days formed a revolutionary soviet government at Tashkent. And that was precisely what the Young Bokharans did. They entered into a secret agreement with Kolesov, the chairman of the Soviet of People's Commissars in Turkestan, who promised to assist them with arms and men. They then began to make energetic preparations for an armed rebellion and the seizure of power. But because of unforeseen developments Kolesov proved unable to give the promised aid. The Tashkent Soviet was itself in a highly precarious situation and was busy fighting for its own life.

To understand why the Emirate maintained itself for three long years after the Bolsheviks had formed a government in Turkestan, it is essential to bear in mind that the course of the revolution in Bokhara depended in a thousand different ways on the vicissitudes of the struggles elsewhere in Central Asia, especially in the adjacent regions. Any Bolshevik mistakes or weaknesses or difficulties anywhere in Central Asia had their immediate repercussions in Bokhara. "The end of the Bolsheviks is at hand," the Emir would gloat. "The end of the Bolsheviks is near," the Young Bokharans would lament. And of course there were always, especially at the outset, plenty of reasons for the optimism of the one and the pessimism of the others.

The main reason was the overwhelmingly Russian composition of the revolutionary organizations in Central Asia. Even in the Bolshevik Party itself there was at first little harmony between the Russian and the few native workers and intellectuals. The general differences in race, language, tradition and culture were aggravated by the great and apparently irreconcilable psychological difference between the representatives, albeit proletarian and peasant representatives, of a victoriously imperialist people and of a subject colonial one.

The cardinal task of a proletarian revolutionary party in a colonial peasant country is to attract the peasant masses, to wean them away from reactionary, feudal, and clerical influences, is, in short, to revolutionize that most potent, though ordinarily inert, stratum of society. In contradistinction to the technique of the imperialists, who coöperate with the native rulers in exploiting the native masses, the technique of the Bolshevik posits unqualified coöperation with the native masses in eradicating both foreign and native capitalist exploiters. This is an exceedingly exacting technique, and calls for a highly experienced, homogeneous, and genuinely revolutionary organization and leadership.

The Bolshevik, particularly if he happens to be a member of a formerly dominant race or nationality, must win the confidence of the native masses, must convince them of his sincerity, must impress them with his tact, sympathy, familiarity with local conditions. He must be open, comradely. The least trace of prejudice or patronage in his attitude is bound to cause resentment and stir suspicion.

No one was more aware of all this than was Lenin. He once said to his Russian comrades:

> ... in the question of nationality it is not possible to proceed from the assumption that economic unity is necessary at any price. Necessary, of course, it is. But we must attain it through propaganda, through agitation, through a voluntary union. The Bashkirs, for instance, distrust the Russians because the Russians are at a higher level of civilization and have used their civilization to rob the Bashkirs. Consequently in these remote districts the name Russian means "oppressor." ... We must take that into account, we must combat it. But that takes a long time. It is not to be got rid of by decree. We must go to work on this very cautiously. Above all such a nation as the Russians, who have excited a hatred in all other nations, must be particularly cautious. We have only now learnt to manage better, and even that only some of us as yet. This tendency still exists in many of us, and we must wrestle with it.
>
> Consequently, we must say to the other peoples that we are internationalists through and through, and are striving for a voluntary union of the workers and peasants of all nations....

In Central Asia, especially, the Bolsheviks needed great diplomatic skill, for the influential native ruling groups were cleverly utilizing the prevailing fear and hatred of the Russians for their own purposes. As against the Bolsheviks' class slogans, they appealed to the nationalist, religious, and family loyalties and prejudices of the ignorant and fanatical natives. This was so everywhere—in Tashkent, in Khiva, in Kokand, and, of course, in Bokhara.

Unfortunately, even in the metropolises, not all Bolsheviks were Lenins, and certainly in remote Central Asia the first Bolshevik leaders were not especially distinguished for their revolutionary experience or mastery of the fundamentals of Marxism.

"Before admitting the Moslem masses to social and political activity," maintained some of the local Russian Bolsheviks, "they must first go through a period of development and training in the socialist spirit." And at the Fourth Congress of the Turkestan Soviets which met in November, 1917 (shortly after the Bolshevik Revolution), a certain Tobolin, speaking in the name of the Bolshevik fraction at the Congress, enunciated the following principle: "At present the policy of including Moslems in the regional organs of our Revolutionary government is unacceptable, first, because of the native population's uncertain attitude toward the Soviet Power; second, because of the absence of such native proletarian organizations whose representatives might be welcomed into the higher organs of our Revolutionary government."

Obviously, at the beginning, some of the local Bolsheviks regarded the native masses with a definite feeling of superiority or at least distrust—an attitude which seemed to justify the Emir's assertions that the Bolshevik Revolution in Central Asia was being imposed by a foreign force upon an unwilling population. Even the pro-Soviet organizations of native workers—the Union of Toiling Moslems in Fergana, the Ittafak in Samarkand, the Union of Building Trades in Tashkent—were not sufficiently drawn into the work. It was only in June, 1918, eight months after the Bolshevik Revolution, that the First Congress of the Communist Party in Turkestan adopted a resolution urging "complete confidence in the Moslem workers" and allowing "their admission into the ranks of the Red Army."

The resolution did not come any too soon. The utterly un-Bolshevik and anti-Leninist attitude condemned by the Congress would undoubtedly, if persisted in, have brought about the alienation of the native masses and the ultimate destruction of the Soviet Government in the whole of Central Asia. Certainly it would have precluded the possibility of a Soviet Government in Bokhara for a very long time. Though a grievous mistake was finally corrected, eight months had irretrievably slipped by, and very little had been accomplished in winning over large masses of the native population to the revolution, into the Red Army, into the Bolshevik Party.

Speculating on Difficulties

This brings us to the second reason for the Emir's joy and the Young Bokharans' grief over what they thought was the probable downfall of the Bolsheviks in Central Asia.

The Bolsheviks' initial mistakes—inept approach to the native masses; failure to wreck completely the old governmental machinery and the various nests of their class enemies, fatal alliance with the Left Socialist-Revolutionists, and the failure as a result of these mistakes to gain immediate popular support—encouraged their ubiquitous enemy. Making counter-revolutionary capital out of every Bolshevik misstep and difficulty, the opposition was beginning to put up rival local governments and to wage civil war. Small wonder Kolesov could not keep his promise to the Young Bokharans.

Just at the time when with Kolesov's aid the armed insurrection was to take place in Bokhara, two events occurred which threatened the very existence of Kolesov and the Turkestan Soviets: the loss of contact with the Central Government in Russia, and the formation of an anti-Bolshevik Government in Kokand. Tashkent was in danger, and Kolesov's small and poorly equipped forces suddenly became involved in two major military operations.

The first operation and the most protracted one was against General Dutov. At the head of an army of prosperous Siberian Cossacks and Czarist officers, Dutov had seized the strategic Orenburg station on the Moscow-Tashkent railroad. The seizure is known in the annals of those years as the "Dutov cork" or the "Orenburg cork," Orenburg being the bottle-neck of East-West transport. Dutov's action immediately stopped all communication between the European and Central-Asian centers of the Soviet Government and arrested the transport of grain, arms, or Red forces to Turkestan. Turkestan was isolated, and exposed to starvation. All efforts to dislodge Dutov and liquidate his "cork" proved vain. Worse. Not satisfied with holding Orenburg, Dutov began to press against Turkestan, combining his activities with those of the other White forces in Central Asia and carrying on negotiations with the English interventionists. The task of the Turkestan Soviets on the Tashkent line was to hold back Dutov's armies—a very difficult task which consumed no end of energy and which lasted nearly two years.

Right on the heels of Dutov's capture of Orenburg, about five weeks after the October Revolution, came the organization of an anti-Bolshevik Government in the Old City of Kokand (the New City was under the sway of the Soviets).

As a base for anti-Soviet activities, Kokand was a happy choice. It was a commercial and cotton center, with a relatively large middle-class population and a very small contingent of revolutionary proletarians and Russian railroad workers. Moreover, it was far from Tashkent, i.e., far from the leading revolutionary city in Central Asia, where the main Red forces were located.

While in Bokhara the revolutionists were making ready for the overthrow of the Emir, in Kokand the Fourth All-Turkestan Congress of Moslem Deputies proclaimed Turkestan an autonomous Republic, and proceeded to elect a national government—a council and a ministry—from among the upper industrial and commercial bourgeoisie and its "intellectual" supporters. Judging by its composition, the Kokand government was nothing but the political department of the local cotton kings: "Usuf Davydov, Poteliskhov, Vodyaiev, et al." For the sake of preserving a united front against the Bolsheviks, the reactionary clerical and feudal interests, though relegated to a secondary position, were supporting the progressive bourgeois government.

The Emir of Bokhara was happy—the end of Bolshevism was near! The Russian counter-revolutionists in Central Asia, too, were joyous, becoming suddenly transformed from aggressive imperialists and exponents of the theory of "superior and inferior races" into perfervid upholders of national independence for Turkestan under the hegemony of the native bourgeoisie. Anything was preferable to proletarian dictatorship. And to the credit of the bourgeoisie, both native and Russian, be it said that at the outset it evinced much greater willingness and capacity for class solidarity than did the native and Russian proletarian and peasant masses. One third of the "National" government was made up of representatives of the Russian bourgeoisie.

At the beginning, the Kokand government confined itself to high-sounding declarations and persistent notes demanding recognition from the Soviet Government. At the same time it made hasty preparations for the inevitable struggle. Money was gathered through subscriptions and a government loan. A hired army was organized. Propagandists were sent out to secure the coöperation of other Central-Asian cities. Sympathetic demonstrations were organized throughout the Bokhara Emirate—in Samarkand, Bokhara, and in numerous other towns and villages.

The Turkestan Soviets were at that time engaged in a desperate struggle with Dutov's armies and were quite unable to undertake anything practical to combat the counter-revolutionary government at Kokand. Hence the Soviets, too, were forced to resort to declarations promising an *autonomous Soviet Republic* to the inhabitants of Turkestan. In this battle of declarations the Kokand government had the advantage of being by race, religion, and language closer to the population. It out-maneuvered the Bolsheviks even in its handling of the native workers. In January, 1918 the Kokand Government called a "Moslem Worker's and Warrior's Congress," at which a considerable number of right-wing, petty-bourgeois delegates from the Union of Toiling Moslems and the Ittafak were present. The Congress endorsed the bourgeois government of Kokand. Thus, under the very noses of the Bolsheviks, the native and Russian bourgeoisie in Turkestan were consolidating their forces and gaining the coöperation of those sections of the working population which, but for the myopia of the local Bolsheviks, would naturally be wholly on the side of the Soviets. Soon the Kokand government thought it could afford to adopt more aggressive tactics. It appealed to Dutov for armed aid and Dutov ordered several Cossack detachments to advance along the Central Asian railroad and help the counter-revolution in Kokand.

In Bokhara, the Emir was jubilant. The Young Bokharans, bitterly disappointed by Kolesov's procrastination, were in a state of deep dismay. However, before long friction began to develop in Kokand among the supporters of the bourgeois régime. The feudal and clerical elements, who had the best military force under the able leadership of Irgash, now began to demand greater authority. To rely on them in the struggle against the Bolsheviks meant in the end to yield to them the government, a thing the more progressive bourgeois elements were reluctant to do. The class contradictions between the feudal-agrarian group and the bourgeois commercial-industrial group became sharpened.

The scale began to tip toward the Reds who, secretly represented by the Russian Poltoratsky at the "Worker's and Warrior's Congress," finally realized their advantage and resorted to a decisive measure. Poltoratsky struck at the "holy of holies" of the government, by confiscating the money deposited by the bourgeoisie in the Kokand State Bank. This was equivalent to a declaration of open war.

The bourgeois government was in an unenviable predicament. Too weak to fight the Soviets alone, it yet was too jealous of its power willingly to give *carte blanche* to the feudal and clerical forces (*Ulema*) headed by Irgash. On the other hand, it was too fearful of the possible revolutionary consequences which an appeal to the peasant masses against both Irgash and the Bolsheviks might entail. Reluctantly it turned to Irgash for support. But here the essentially democratic, petty-bourgeois representatives of the workers' organizations bolted—they would not hear of clerical-feudal supremacy. These inner contradictions within the Kokand government spelled its doom. On February 18, Irgash arrested several of the government "ministers," and the rest of the government fled. Meanwhile the Soviets had been rapidly gaining power. The *Ulemists* declared "gazawat"—holy war—against the Soviets, too, carrying their violent propaganda into the mosques and the streets. A mob of several thousand, armed with knives, guns, clubs, tried to seize the Bolshevik fortress in the New City. The same day, however, detachments of Kolesov's army arrived in Kokand. Irgash refused to surrender and disarm. The Red armies launched an offensive against the Old City. Irgash's army was smashed. Irgash himself escaped. The bourgeois government of Kokand was dead.

After the fall of the Kokand government, the influence of the native and Russian bourgeoisie in Central Asia began to decline, and the forces of counter-revolution commenced to flock to the banner of the clerical-feudal elements. Guerrilla detachments, organized by the Ulema, established close contact with various Russian counter-revolutionary organizations, with Dutov, with the Bokharan Emir, and primarily with the English, from whom they obtained arms and financial support.

Another Emir Hoax

With the Kokand menace "liquidated," Kolesov finally turned his attention to Bokhara. It was high time. By February, 1918, conditions in the Khanate rendered the struggle with the Emir exceedingly urgent. The great influx of Whites from Kokand and elsewhere was rapidly rendering Bokhara the most dangerous spot of anti-Soviet activity in Central Asia, especially since it became known that the Emir was in touch with the British intelligence service in Meshed (Persia) and the British Political Resident (George Macartney) in Chinese Turkestan. Macartney, after establishing secret contact with Dutov and various other underground anti-Bolshevik organizations and groups, had approached the Emir; and the Emir naturally expressed great eagerness to join any projected united front of struggle against the Bolsheviks.

However, Kolesov was too intoxicated with his victory in Kokand and he underestimated the Emir's strength. Relying on a small army and the assistance of about three hundred Young Bokharans, he and Faizulla Khodzhaiev, who was then the chairman of the executive committee of the Young Bokharan organization, issued an ultimatum to the Emir. They demanded immediate reforms to be put into effect by a body elected from the central committee of the Young Bokharans and headed by the Emir himself.

The Emir hedged for time. Kolesov refused to wait and ordered his troops, accompanied by the three hundred Young Bokharans, to advance on the city. According to Faizulla Khodzhaiev himself, the resistance offered by the loyal followers of the Emir was genuinely heroic. "The fanatical adherents of the old, the mullahs, though badly armed—with knives, axes, rusty swords—fought desperately. I myself saw how one of them, holding a cudgel in his hand and a long knife in his mouth, advanced unflinchingly against our machine guns and hurled himself against and killed one of our gunners." Still, the revolutionary troops were victorious. Seeing that he was beaten, the Emir sued for peace, granting all the demands of the revolutionists. There was now no reason to doubt his sincerity, and Kolesov ordered the army to return to Kogan, the New City.

The Emir issued a second Manifesto, much more radical than the first. It read:

> In the name of Our great God, We proclaim to Our entire people that a nation can have no greater happiness than the possession of equality and liberty. We fully realize that if Our people be denied its rights and its liberty, if the administration be not reformed in the spirit of the times, We shall fail to attain a happy and peaceful life in Our land. We recognize that the primary cause of the backwardness, darkness, ignorance of Our people is due to the inadequacy of

Our administrative organization and to the people's enslavement.

Having become conscious of these circumstances and having determined to better the lot of Our people and Our country, We had issued a Manifesto eleven months ago, which, thanks to the machinations of a few satraps, remained inoperative.

This brought down great evils upon Our people.

Since Our chief aim is the happiness and freedom of Our people, We, in issuing this second Manifesto, hereby proclaim before Our people that this document represents Our firm decision.

To insure the happiness of Our people, the following measures will be put into effect.

In a long list of reforms, the Emir promised a democratic government, freedom, the abolition of corporal and capital punishment, tax reforms, etc. In the concluding paragraph, the Emir exclaimed: "There are not in this world such satrap forces that could force Us to deviate from these decisions."

Kolesov and the Young Bokharans now demanded immediate disarmament of the enemy's forces. Again the Emir hedged, saying that while he personally should be happy to fulfill this demand, his soldiers and mullahs were so aroused that it would be difficult to persuade them to lay down their arms. The revolutionists were adamant. The Emir begged for three days in which to disarm; Kolesov reduced it to twenty-four hours. According to the arrangement the revolutionists were to send a committee to supervise the disarmament of the Emir's troops, and immediately after that the Young Bokharans were peacefully to occupy the city.

While Kolesov and the Young Bokharans waited in the New City for news from Bokhara, the Emir seized and executed their representatives and hastily reorganized his forces, preparing to attack and wipe out the small forces of the revolutionists. In this he was brilliantly successful.

Conditions favored the Emir. He gained time, not only to concentrate his troops in numbers sufficient to overcome the relatively small contingent of insurgents, but also to take full advantage of the most vulnerable spot in his enemy's ranks, namely, the presence of Russians. His slogan was: Resist the foreign invaders. He declared a holy war against the infidels, the foreigners, and the traitors who had sold out their country and their faith. A mighty outburst of chauvinism and religious fanaticism shook the ancient city, An army, 35,000 strong, rose to the defense of country and faith. Before the revolutionists realized it, they were surrounded. True, they had one advantage, artillery. But even this seemed to work against them. A cannonade which lasted thirty-six hours brought absolutely no results; not one shell struck the city. This circumstance was hailed by the mullahs as proof that Allah and Mohammed protected the holy city against the ravaging weapons of the infidels. When ammunition was almost exhausted, Kolesov smashed through the enemy ranks and beat a hasty retreat toward Tashkent.

Such was the inglorious end of the Young Bokharans' first attempt to overthrow the Emir. Those who could, fled; the rest were massacred. People who had evinced the slightest sympathy with the Young Bokharans were dragged from their homes and clubbed to death. The outrages spread through the entire Khanate. Within the country there was no escape from the bloody vengeance of the Emir.

Barking Jackals

Again the Emir was jubilant. And his joy almost passed all bounds when a couple of months later he learned from Macartney's agents that the English were moving their armies in the direction of Persia and Transcaspia toward the Soviet borders and that in April a special English Mission had been despatched from India to Soviet Turkestan for the purpose of financing and coördinating all the anti-Red operations in Central Asia.

Throughout the summer of 1918, the English were

hastily building railroads and highways to expedite the transport from India of newly formed Anglo-Indian military units. Also in the northern and southeastern sections of Persia, the English military staff, stationed at Meshed, had organized a hired army of natives. Similar military preparations were being made farther west, extending from Mesopotamia through Persian Azerbaidjan to the Caspian. Close contact was established with the counter-revolutionists in Ashkhabad (Turkmenistan).

By July the Emir was in an even happier frame of mind: with the aid of the English the Soviet power in Ashkhabad was overthrown, and an anti-Soviet government was established. Well he knew what a severe blow that was to his formidable foe, Soviet Turkestan. The ring of counter-revolution was tightening. Soon Soviet Turkestan would be crushed by the Ashkhabad armies and at last he would breathe a bit easier. Of one thing he was reasonably certain—the Turkestan Soviets would be too busy on the Transcaspian front to be "meddling" with his affairs in Bokhara.

The organization of the anti-Soviet government at Ashkhabad was preceded by a period of bloody strife and celebrated by the execution of nine Bolshevik leaders on July 15, 1918. Immediately preparations were started for an attack on Tashkent. This, the Emir knew, was in accordance with carefully worked out plans. An uprising against the Soviet power in Turkestan had been plotted in various cities in Central Asia for several months. The Central Committee of the underground anti-Soviet "Military Organization of Turkestan," located in Tashkent, had kept up steady contact with the English in the Caspian region through its Ashkhabad branch. According to the plans, all uprisings against the Soviets in Central Asia were to be synchronized, all anti-Soviet activities were to be coördinated. This was a sound plan. The leaders of the Ashkhabad organization, however, took it into their heads to assume the initiative and to place themselves at the forefront of the entire anti-Soviet movement. They were no doubt encouraged by the proximity of the English forces, as well as by the apparently favorable objective conditions: Dutov was still in Orenburg, the Urals and Siberia were in the hands of Czecho-Slovaks and the Whites; the Emir was still in Bokhara. Exposed to hunger and civil war, Soviet Turkestan, they were certain, could scarcely offer serious resistance. The peace delegates sent by the Soviet Republic of Turkestan, headed by the Bolshevik Poltoratsky who had previously distinguished himself in Kokand, were arrested and Poltoratsky was shot. Newly formed White troops were hurled against Chardjui, on the road to Tashkent. However, at Chardjui the counter-revolution in Transcaspia suffered the first set-back. The workers rose to a man in defense of the city. The White troops were repulsed to Kaakhka, where they reorganized into the formidable and ultimately determining Transcaspian front. In the circle of counter-revolution around Soviet Turkestan, that front, armed, financed and even officered by the English, held out against Bolshevik onslaughts for almost two years.

And from Khiva, too, cheering news was pouring into Bokhara. There was a time when Emir Alim-Khan was greatly worried over the turn events had taken in the neighboring Khanate. Rumors had reached him in the early months of 1918 that a wild revolutionist named Djunaid Khan, at the head of a large army of Turkoman nomads, was leading a bloody insurrection against the real, legitimate, divinely ordained ruler of Khiva. Later he heard that Djunaid Khan had been successful, that while his friend Khan Asfendior and his viziers were the nominal rulers, it was Djunaid Khan who was the real power in the state. It was a bad business, a very bad business! The Emir was grieved not only over the troubles of his friend and fellow-ruler, but also, and chiefly, over the possibility of the Red menace spreading beyond the Khiva borders into his own domain.

Now authentic news arrived that Djunaid Khan was not a Red at all. On the contrary, he was a "rugged individualist," a man with a consuming ambition to become Khan himself. He was behaving like a real ruler, too. Instead of organizing soviets of workers and peasants and thus spoiling the population, he was building his own power and authority, by disciplinary ruthlessness, and, of course, the squeezing of enormous contributions from towns, villages, bazaars, and individuals.

That Djunaid was just the type of ruler who would meet with the enthusiastic approval of Emir Alim-Khan can be judged from the following gruesome account by A. K. Akchurin, an eye-witness of the results of Djunaid's rule:

> The peaceful Uzbek population writhed in the claws of the tyrant. In full daylight the Turkoman hordes raided settlements, slaughtered people like sheep, grabbed their belongings, and what they were unable to take along, they would set on fire. When I was in Khiva in 1919, I had an excellent opportunity to observe the results of Djunaid's rule. Traveling 150 miles in the Chimboi and Zair regions (along the shore of the Aral, where the Amu-Daria falls into the Sea), I did not meet a living soul. The burned and ruined houses, scattered corpses, ravaged homes, charred trees, broken cribs, barking jackals, and nauseating stench gave one a feeling of horror. Many of my companions broke down at the sight of this terrible devastation, some became hysterical. On our way back, we avoided this locality, by taking a much longer roundabout way. The towns of what once was the prosperous Khiva Khanate presented a melancholy picture, indeed. The bazaars were deserted. Rarely, rarely did one stumble upon a ghastly Uzbek roaming through the narrow depopulated streets, or slinking behind the tumble-down clay fences. However, no sooner would a Red Army man appear in the streets than a crowd of Uzbeks would instantaneously gather. They would kiss his hands, his feet, they would grasp at his cloak and rub with it their inflamed eyes, they would lovingly stroke his rifle. Even women would remove their veils and caress him. They did not fear their husbands; for the Red Army man was not simply a man, an ordinary visitor; he was their protector, their savior from violence and ruin.

More than the Uzbeks even suffered the Khiva Kazaks. In certain regions the entire Kazak population was annihilated. Hundreds of young Kazak women were taken by Djunaid Khan into captivity and treated as slaves. The Emir was especially happy to hear that Djunaid was co-operating with the Whites and the English on the Transcaspian front by constantly threatening, annoying, and occasionally attacking the Red Armies from the rear.

The Basmachi

Another source of deep satisfaction to the Emir was the astonishingly quick spread, under his and English patronage, of the so-called Basmach or Brigand movement in Turkestan, especially in Fergana.

Writers on Central Asia often use the term "Basmachi" indiscriminately to describe the numerous lawless bands of distinctly different social origin that had infested the deserts and mountains of the region long before and for a considerable time after the Bolshevik Revolution. On the basis of a purely external similarity, this term has been applied to two social phenomena quite distinct in origin and purpose.

I have mentioned in a previous chapter how the extension of cotton-growing in Central Asia resulted in the impoverishment of the native peasantry and how the Czars' artificial interference with the development of a native industry which might have absorbed the surplus village population caused the appearance of bands of desperate peasants who, having no other outlet, took to brigandage and crime. Those peasant brigands were one type of social phenomenon often referred to as Basmachi. They were not revolutionists. They had no political aims. Their sole purpose was to steal enough money and goods to keep themselves and their families from starvation. Theirs was a purely sporadic, elemental rebellion. Though symptomatic of a profound economic and social maladjustment, their activities had absolutely no conscious political import.

The other social phenomenon covered by the same term is also a form of brigandage, but belongs in its inception to the post-revolutionary period, and is rooted, not in the peasantry, but in a combination of the native bourgeois, feudal and clerical elements disinherited by the Revolution.

Up to the February Revolution, the national liberation movement in Turkestan was essentially a unified movement, despite its motley social composition. Under its nationalist banner were gathered progressive representatives of the native industrial and commercial bourgeoisie, a small number of liberal clergymen, members of the small professional class, and even representatives of the worker, artisan, and peasant classes. The reason for this unity is clear. Each of these classes and social groupings had its own grudge against Russian imperialism, each suffered in its own way. And the consciousness of common suffering welded these essentially antagonistic groups into a revolutionary nationalist entity.

To be sure, within the nationalist liberation movement in Turkestan there were shades of difference with regard to pan-Islamism, with regard to questions of tactics and other points. On the whole, however, those differences were relatively negligible. The leadership accepted also by the workers and peasants was in the hands of the nationalist petty-bourgeois intelligentsia. Potential class antagonisms were temporarily forgotten in the common struggle against the foreign imperialist oppressor.

In Turkestan, as elsewhere in Russia, the February Revolution revealed the gaping chasm between the workers and peasants and the other classes. The majority of the nationalist bourgeoisie, satisfied with having fulfilled its task of national liberation, was ready to withdraw from the battlefield and plunge into an orgy of capitalist expansion and unrestrained exploitation. The illusion of national unity vanished like a puff of smoke. The more advanced workers, artisans and peasants viewed the February events as the beginning rather than the end of revolutionary struggle. This was especially true of those who had had more intimate contact with the imperialist war and the inhuman exploitation in the war industries. Incidentally, in the great war the colonial troops from Central Asia had not been used in active fighting; they had been forced to take, without pay, the most onerous jobs in the rear or in the war industries. Those Central-Asian workers and peasants had been in European Russia, had heard the message, learned the language, and taken to heart the slogans of the revolutionary Russian proletariat. Upon returning home, they, with the few Russian revolutionists, became the inspirers of the class struggle among the native masses. It was they who, shortly after the February overturn, organized in Tashkent the "Soviet of Moslem Workers" in opposition to the bourgeois "Soviet of Moslems" (*Shura-i-Islamia*). It was they, too, who organized the native workers of Tashkent into labor unions, which later played a very significant part in the class struggle in Central Asia. It was they, again, who formed in Fergana the "Union of Toiling Moslems." A similar organization, Ittafak, was organized in Samarkand. At first, all of these organizations were under the influence of the Mensheviks and Socialist-Revolutionists. But as the revolution unfolded, the Bolsheviks began to gain ascendancy, and before long the "Union of Toiling Moslems" formed a political *bloc* with the local Bolshevik organizations and launched a vigorous attack against the nationalist bourgeoisie. So intense was the struggle that on October 12, 1917, a little over a week before the Bolshevik revolution, a small group of *Ulemists* slew five members of the "Union" at a meeting in Kokand.

When the October Revolution broke out, the "Union of Toiling Moslems" in Fergana and the "Soviet of Moslem Workers" in Tashkent were, if not actually, then at least potentially, on the side of the Bolsheviks. Such is the logic of all revolutions. Sham, veneer, superficialities are bound ultimately to vanish in its light. Only the basic realities survive. While the workers of Central Asia were advancing to the revolution, the progressive-liberal bourgeoisie, deprived of its wealth and of its right to exploit, showed its true nature by rapidly degenerating into a violent, bitterly reactionary group of organized counter-revolutionists. The bourgeois government of Kokand was their first counter-revolutionary venture. When that was frustrated, they adopted guerrilla warfare as a method of fighting the Soviets.

Thus a new content was poured into the old form of Basmach brigandage. The class composition of the Basmach bands underwent a radical change. Instead of the poorest peasants disinherited by the Czar's régime, the predominant elements in the Basmach bands of the post-October period were representatives of classes disinherited by the revolution. Also, the Basmach activities lost their purely elemental character: directed by the deposed leaders of the Kokand Republic and by the English representatives stationed in Chinese Turkestan, they now became the coördinated efforts of a political movement—Basmachestvo or Basmachism—with a definite political objective, the overthrow of the Soviet Government.

It is fascinating to study shifts in political alignments, how erstwhile political friends became irreconcilable enemies and how intransigent political opponents became close political allies. We have seen how opposition to Russian imperialism and native reaction united all the progressive elements of Central Asia in one revolutionary movement. We have seen how the fall of the Czar's imperialist government caused the split in the revolutionary ranks. The common objective achieved, the antagonisms among the various groups within the revolutionary movement began to manifest themselves. Within a few months there was a complete reshuffling of forces. The workers, poor peasants, the liberal bourgeoisie, and clergy, once united in their fight upon native reaction and foreign imperialism, found themselves after the establishment of the Soviet régime and the proletarian dictatorship on opposite sides of the barricades. The liberals, the erstwhile "revolutionists," were incensed against the new régime.

They had hailed February, but they were bitter in their denunciation of October. In search of political allies, they discovered the reactionary feudal, clerical, and bureaucratic group, their erstwhile enemies. Though basically opposed to each other, they had one thing in common, a passionate hatred for the Soviets. In the Basmach movement the two united.

These groups formed the upper thin layer of counter-revolution in Central Asia. They supplied the ideological and military leadership. The basic fighting contingents, however, were drawn from the kulaks and, during the first couple of years, from the middle peasants. The kulak's support of the Basmach movement was quite natural; the middle peasant's requires explanation.

The psychology of the middle peasant the world over is dual. Whereas the rich peasant is predominantly a property owner and an exploiter, and the poor peasant predominantly a propertyless toiler, the middle peasant has some of the economic and therefore psychological characteristics of both. He is not an exploiter, but a property owner who works his own fields. As a toiler, he naturally gravitates to the poor peasant, the worker, and the Soviet régime, but as a property owner he is also drawn to the kulak, the bey, the mullah, the Basmachi. Tact, diplomacy, subtle strategy might have won the middle peasant's support of the revolution. Unfortunately, as I have shown, the Bolsheviks in Central Asia were too weak and too inexperienced. The appeal of the counter-revolution to the conservative property-owner in the middle peasant at first proved much stronger than the appeal of the revolution to the dissatisfied toiler in him. Rumors, founded and unfounded, about the nationalization of all property, confiscation of goods, prohibition of worship, unveiling of women, closing of mosques, etc., drove the middle peasant into the ranks of the Basmachi or, at best, made of him a neutral rather than a revolutionary force.

Living conditions, instead of improving, were steadily becoming worse. This naturally was blamed on the revolution. As a result of "Dutov's cork" no grain was being imported into Central Asia. Even the few local industries ceased functioning. The cotton-growing peasant began to feel the horror of literal hunger and wholesale unemployment. Add to this the ignorance, fanaticism, and cultural backwardness of the native masses on the one hand and the inexperience, inefficiency, mistakes, and vacillation of the preponderantly Russian Soviet authorities on the other, and you have a fair notion of the great attraction that the Basmach movement had for the middle peasant at that time.

There were also powerful outside factors that favored the Basmachi. It is noteworthy that though the Basmach leaders of all shades of opinion were unanimously vociferous in their nationalist protestations, they did not spurn the financial help, active coöperation, and occasionally even the leadership of their life-long enemies—the representatives of Russian imperialism and Russian capitalism. Here, too, the unifying force was a common hatred and a common objective. In their determination to crush the Soviets, the native bourgeois nationalists, Moslem clergy, Russian imperialists, Greek Catholic priests and of course the Bokhara Emir were at one.

Perfidious Albion

What threw the Emir and his highest collaborators into veritable raptures, however, was the arrival in Bokhara, some time in November, of Lieutenant-Colonel F. M. Bailey. Bailey brought word of an anti-Bolshevik uprising in Tashkent planned for the middle of January. The Colonel knew whereof he spoke. He was the head of the Special Mission which His Majesty's Government had dispatched to Soviet Turkestan in the spring. The other two in the Mission were Major L. V. S. Blacker, "an officer of ability and resource and well fitted for such an undertaking" and Lieutenant-Colonel P. T. Etherton, a man who had made "a close study of political, economic, and commercial questions affecting Central Asia" and for whom the problems of the East "generally possessed a peculiar fascination."

In his book, *In the Heart of Central Asia,* Lieutenant-Colonel Etherton takes us as much into his confidence concerning the Mission's designs and activities as his official position permits. "The opening of 1918," he writes, "was significant for the developments inimical to Allied interests, not only in Europe, but in Asia, where the safety of our Empire in the East was threatened.... The Bolshevik revolution had created a new set of ideas. These fanatics relied not upon the only feasible machinery of readjustment of international disputes, but upon a worldwide reconstruction which should emancipate every race and tribe and effect a total transformation of human nature. Self-determination was the watchword, a doctrine which if carried to its logical conclusions, must result in anarchy and widespread enmity, jealousy, and chaos.... Such in brief were the dangers confronting us in the Asiatic theater, and it was therefore essential that we should gain and maintain touch with the situation between the Caspian Sea and Chinese Turkestan."

Though ignorant of Bolshevik theory, the agent of British imperialism in the East intuitively felt that the "new set of ideas" of the Bolsheviks was potentially much more of a menace to English domination in the Orient than all of the Czar's armies in the past.

The English government was aware of the "close connection established between Russian Turkestan, the Caucasus, and the states there which had disclosed their ambition for autonomy." It was aware also of certain "overtures" that had been made to Afghanistan with the purpose of creating a Mohammedan State comprising that country plus Central Asia plus the Caucasus, as well as of the creation of a bourgeois-nationalist government in Kokand. The English felt, therefore, that "the moment was opportune for the exploitation of pro-autonomous sentiments" and the "considerable body of opinion well-disposed towards the Allied cause." Hence, "a small British military organization was essential from which the antennæ could radiate for the acquisition of information, and *to exploit whatever appeared favorable."*

In the characteristic euphemisms of the diplomat, Mr. Etherton proceeds to elaborate on the specific tasks of the spying mission. It was designed to place His Majesty's Government "in touch" with the Soviets, to "investigate amongst other matters" (which "other matters" is not indicated) "the cotton question, and to keep *au courant* of the situation as it then was."

Mr. Etherton's innocent reference to "cotton," is somewhat amplified further in the book. "In 1918," relates Mr. Etherton, "vast stocks of cotton were lying in Central Asia.... The fate of those stocks of cotton was a matter of moment ... and I consequently received orders from the Home Government to report as to the possibility of securing and transporting the entire stock to Kashgar."

Though Mr. Etherton does not divulge it, the purpose of this whole scheme was to deprive Soviet Russia of Central Asian cotton. The textile industry in the central regions of Russia, in such revolutionary centers as Moscow and Ivanovo-Voznesensk, subsisted mainly on Central Asian cotton, and only partly on American. With the latter excluded, and Central Asian cotton withdrawn, the Soviet textile industry would be completely paralyzed, unemployment and dissatisfaction in the chief industrial region would increase, and the main industrial product—textiles —for which the city obtained food from the village would be lacking. However, the whole scheme proved chimerical. It would have taken 750,000 camels to move the cotton, and the cost of transport alone "would have totaled twenty-two million rupees." The idea had to be abandoned.

Also, it was the resolution of the Mission "to penetrate to Tashkent, the center of Soviet fanaticism ... where a [Bolshevik] propaganda school was formed for the training of agitators who would go forth to India, Afghanistan, Chinese Turkestan, and all the countries of the Middle and Far East, to preach the gospel of Bolshevism and prepare the way for universal class warfare." To counteract the propaganda of the "ruthless fanatics" and to insure the "safety and welfare of the British Empire," the Mission, too, was "to initiate and put into effective operation a system of propaganda, a powerful weapon that eventually became so potent a factor during the war." By "the war" Mr. Etherton, of course, means subsequent English open intervention in Central Asia and the Caucasus.

Lieutenant-Colonel P. T. Etherton, His Majesty's Consul-General and Political Resident in Chinese Turkestan, remained in Kashgar to continue from the Chinese border the anti-Soviet activities of his predecessor Macartney. His companions, according to plans, made their way to Tashkent. They were soon followed by Macartney.

On August 21, the Tashkent paper *Nasha Gazeta* reported: "An English Mission consisting of two officers and one secretary has just arrived in this city. The Mission left India April 20, and Kashgar July 24. In an interview, the head of the Mission informed the representative of this paper that the Mission has come to Tashkent on the instructions of the English Consul-General in Kashgar with the purpose of studying the state of affairs in the Republic and of dissipating the false rumors about the would-be intention of England to interfere through Afghanistan in the internal affairs of the Turkestan Republic. The Mission protests against these rumors and suggests that they are of German fabrication. The mission plans to remain here indefinitely."

That the Mission's friendly protestations were thoroughly hypocritical, the statements quoted from Mr. Etherton are ample proof. In addition to Etherton's testimony, however, we have the memoirs of General Zaitsev, a Russian White who worked hand in hand with the Mission. According to him, the real purpose and intention of the Mission were: "To prepare and organize armed uprisings against the Soviet Power in Turkestan, and to arrange for the supply of the rebel detachments with arms and money from the nearest English bases, Meshed, Kashgar, Afghanistan."

At that time the English armies had already occupied

Murmansk and Archangel and were engaging the Soviet armies on the Transcaspian front. But the English Mission now joined by George Macartney in Tashkent was all smiles, courtesy, suavity, and amity. They were there only to "study," and to dissipate false rumors!

The work of the Mission in Tashkent was facilitated by the protection it received from the members of the local government who belonged to Left Socialist-Revolutionist organizations which were then on the verge of breaking with the Bolsheviks.

By the middle of September, before Blacker and Macartney left for India, the Mission had succeeded in further strengthening Britain's ties with counter-revolutionary Central Asia—with the leaders of the feudal-clerical forces in the Basmach movement, the bourgeois nationalists, the Bokhara Emir, the Russian Mensheviks, Socialist-Revolutionists, and all the other forces who coalesced around the underground military organizations with headquarters at Tashkent. Colonel Bailey managed to prolong his stay in Tashkent, in a semi-official capacity, as late as November first. Finally, it was proved that he was engaged in plotting against the government. When he was about to be arrested, Bailey fled to the Bokharan Emir, who had by that time become the mainstay of counter-revolution in Central Asia.

Vulture's Feast

It was obvious that things were going from bad to worse for the Reds. And almost every messenger to the Emir from the underground Tashkent branch of the counter-revolutionary "Military Organization of Turkestan" confirmed him in his resolution to hold out—despite the rapid disintegration of Bokhara's economic life.

Severance of relations with Russia deprived Bokhara of its best market. She began to choke with a superabundance of raw materials and starve for the lack of manufactured products. The Emir made a dash for the markets of Afghanistan and India and Persia, but those markets could not take the place of Russia. Cotton-growing and the commercial and industrial enterprises connected with it began to decline with catastrophic rapidity. Bankruptcies began to multiply by the hundred. A sharp financial crisis, a cessation of trade and industry, a febrile enhancement of the military forces, rampant reaction—such were conditions in Bokhara. And the only thing that sustained the morale of the Emir and his feudal and clerical supporters was the news from other parts of Central Asia. This news may be summarized as follows:

December 28:	The rich peasants in the Semirechie region have risen against the Soviets.
January 22, 1919:	A White Guard uprising in Tashkent. Fourteen leading Bolsheviks shot.
April 18:	Red Army defeated near Aktiubinsk, retreats to Kandagach.
May 9:	Red Army at Kandagach suffers colossal defeat, retreats to Kuduk-Emba.
June 23-26:	Red Army suffers another defeat at the Emba station.
July 21:	Annenkov's White armies occupy Semirechie.
July 26:	The White armies are surrounding the Reds who are forced to flee to the Aral Station on the Aral Sea.
August 18:	Annenkov's armies have wrested Cherkask, Petropavlovsk and Antonovo from the Reds in Semirechie.
August 22:	In Fergana, the peasants led by the beys and the mullahs have formed detachments and joined the Basmachi in open war against the Soviets.

September 7:	In Fergana, the peasants and Basmach forces have taken the city Osh, and have completely surrounded the Red Army under Safanov.
October 24:	Flight of Red Army into the Kopala region before the pressure of Annenkov's forces in Semirechie.
October 24:	In Fergana, Mandaminbek and Monstrov, heading the anti-Soviet peasant detachments, formed a "Provisional Government of Fergana."
December 5:	The Red operations against Mandaminbek's Basmach forces in the Garbua Region collapse.
December 30:	Annenkov's armies, after having pressed the Reds all the way to Djarkent and Bogoslovskoie, are now raiding these Red strongholds.

Of course, there were other messages, messages of Soviet victories, of greater and greater numbers of the natives joining the Red forces, but such messages were too few and far between seriously to undermine the Emir's faith in the solidity of his throne.

Altogether, throughout the year 1918 and the larger part of 1919, the Red forces in Central Asia were fighting a bitter and, what most of the time seemed, a hopeless struggle. Tiny detachments of ragged, hungry workers, lacking arms, lacking fuel, lacking means of transportation, lacking experienced leadership, insulated from any contact with the center by a fiery circle of class enemies—monarchists, bourgeois nationalists, counter-revolutionists, English imperialists—carried on a long heroic war in the arid sands, devastated valleys and inaccessible mountains of these remote regions. Blunders, failures, defeats without end.

Take the struggle against Annenkov's White Cossack

Regiments in Semirechie. Surrounded on all sides, the peasantry of Semirechie put up one of the most heroic, stubborn fights in the history of the Civil War. Men, women, children fought in the trenches. There was no food, and worst of all, no salt. Soon, too, all the ammunition was used up. The temporary surrender of the Cherkask region before the superior and well-equipped forces of Annenkov, was followed by wholesale massacres and destruction of property. The peasants and their families fled into the mountains. "It is interesting to recall how we lived at that time," one of the participants of this struggle once told me. "We had no money; so we stamped little pieces of paper which we used as our medium of exchange. Before long, even this proved superfluous. For, forced by necessity, we collectivized everything, forming a primitive kind of military commune. While some fought, the others worked the fields, or repaired the barns, or took care of the stock. We were dressed in raw hides, we had no more cattle, and began to eat our horses for which we had no forage. Everybody worked, everybody fought, including our women and children."

Similar conditions prevailed in the Urdjar region. To fight Annenkov, who had destroyed their villages, the Urdjar peasants organized a detachment that subsequently became famous as the "Mountain Eagles." In the words of the peasant Trofimov, one of the Mountain Eagles, "it was we who finally took the city of Urdjar. We seized most of the equipment and arms that belonged to the general's army, and, after losing only 35 killed and 16 wounded, rapidly retreated. Our families, old and young, followed us into the mountains. It was late autumn. So we dug holes in the ground, and there we lived. It was bitter cold. Soon heavy snow covered the mountains. There was nothing to eat. We simply turned into predatory bandits, raiding settlements and carrying away with us anything we could lay our hands on. Every warrior had four cartridges—two loaded and two empty. While you used the loaded cartridges, the empty ones were being filled in our shop. We had a special shop. You shoot, while the shop fills your empty cartridges. Our women connoitered and smuggled powder from Chuguchak. We also fought with knives, pitch forks, clubs, axes, and what not."

It was the same everywhere else in Central Asia—enemies within, enemies without, enemies all around. For a brief period, in 1918 and part of 1919, it seemed that the centrifugal forces of the Revolution were in ascendancy. The old Empire was disintegrating. Rival governments were sprouting up everywhere. The revolutionary colossus seemed to be prostrate, stretching its bleeding, torn body over two continents. It still swung out its fists in a furious determination to survive. But it seemed hopeless. A little more pressure on the choked throat and all resistance would be gone; the imperialists with the Emirs, Khans, mullahs, beks, beys, and all the other vultures, would croak triumphantly in a sanguinary feast over the dismembered, mangled corpse.

Yes, for a brief period, just about when Lieutenant-Colonel Bailey was visiting Alim Khan, it seemed that the grandiose plans of British Imperialism would soon be realized. The fertile valleys, the large spaces, the mineral-laden mountains, the multitudinous peoples of Central Asia and the Caucasus would at last be sucked into the English Empire. The prospects were indeed excellent. Turkey was beaten, crushed. The Arab East had already become an English possession. Persia lay helpless under the tramping feet of the British armies. Caucasia was shackled hand and foot by the Scotch battalions and the English Fleet in the Black and Caspian Seas. In Cabul, the Afghan capital, sat a spineless government completely under English sway. Germany had surrendered. The British army and navy could now be hurled full force against the Bolsheviks—in Siberia, in Murmansk, in the Far East, in the South....

But to the amazement of the whole world and the deep chagrin of the Emir and his supporters the Revolution held out. In desperate struggles, in the fire of intervention and civil war, the originally weak, inexperienced, and ideologically amorphous local organizations gradually hammered themselves into sharp, invincible weapons that ultimately insured the Bolshevik triumph in Central Asia. It was by tenacity, daring, devotion to the revolutionary cause that, as we shall see in the next chapter, the Bolsheviks finally won their victories. This has been acknowledged even by the bitterest detractors of the Revolution. "It is sufficient to point out," wrote the White émigré Potekhin in 1921, "the incredible fact of the existence in 1918-1919 of the Turkestan Soviet Republic. Completely cut off from Moscow, surrounded on all sides by Dutov's, Kolchak's, Annenkov's, Denikin's, and the English armies, deprived of transport, fuel, grain, the Turkestan Bolsheviks managed to hold their own even in those most difficult years!"

VII

ANOTHER VICTORIOUS PAGE

> "O ye rich and bloated ones!"
>   The Leader speaks—
> "Cast your gold away and riches...
>   "Your house's ablaze!
> "The flames of time encircle you....
>   "Your house's ablaze!"
> In the thunder-voice of storm!
>   The Leader speaks.
>
> Through rain and sleet, o'er mountains and
>   deep valleys
>   The Leader speaks,
> 'Neath scorching sun, 'neath gleam of distant
>   stars
>   The Leader speaks,
> To rising masses in Bombay
>   The Leader speaks,
> In the thunder-voice of storm
>   The Leader speaks.
>   —From Uzbek Worker Song.

Britain's Outraged Dignity

THE Emir was so engrossed in celebrating the succession of Bolshevik failures in his own Khanate, in Transcaspia, in Caucasia, in Khiva, in Semirechie, and in the Urals, that he failed to notice that immediately around him things were rapidly heading toward a crisis. He did not realize that even his victory over the Young Bokharans in the spring of 1918 was illusory, that the blood of the Bokharan and Russian revolutionists, flowing in a common stream, had predetermined the path which the revolution would follow, that common struggle and common sacrifice would ultimately make the tie between the masses of Bokhara and the Russian revolutionary proletariat well-nigh indissoluble. In the words of a Young Bokharan who had participated in that struggle, "Our common errors, credulity, and failure had their historical justification and revolutionary compensation. It taught us to work together. It taught us not to be credulous. It stirred the indignation of vast masses of people who had never before been touched by our propaganda. It tore the halo from the Emir's head."

To be sure, outwardly it seemed that the Young Bokharans were still languishing in inactivity, most of them refugees in Tashkent, the rest lying quietly "underground" in Bokhara. But what the Emir failed to understand was that time was on their side, that with the increased taxes, the lack of manufactured products, the catastrophic decline in trade, and the spread of unemployment, life itself was preparing the soil for the revolution.

The humble, pious peasants, the mainstay of the Emir's power, were beginning to heed the revolutionary slogans which, despite all of the Emir's precautions, charged the atmosphere. They were turning in growing numbers to the left. And his soldiers, too, irregularly paid, undernourished, ill-clad, ill-housed, decimated by epidemics, were beginning to grumble and desert.

The Emir knew little of the powerful fermentation that was developing in the lower strata of his subjects. The revolutionary movement was gaining a mass base. From the liberal middle-class elements which had been frightened away by the extremism of the Turkestan Soviets, the center of gravity of the revolution was shifting to the peasant masses who had nothing to lose but their poverty. Concurrently, the Young Bokharan organization in Tashkent was shedding the last vestiges of liberal bourgeois-nationalism and adopting the militant, revolutionary program of the Bolsheviks. There was a reshuffling of forces. Many of the less fervid revolutionists dropped out, while the Young Bokharans who remained were enlisting in the Red Army.

However, in the earlier part of 1919, the Emir still felt relatively secure under England's protecting wings. The Turkestan Soviets, he knew, were as yet in no position to help the Young Bokharans to fight him—to quote Colonel Etherton's innocent boast—"they were confronted by the British in northeast Russia, and were meeting with strong opposition in Semirechie and Fergana, *with all of whom I was in touch.*" And at home the Emir could not yet decipher the writing on the wall: he did not know that the underground revolutionary groupings in the Khanate were being revitalized and that the Young Bokharans in Tashkent had finally succeeded in reëstablishing contact with them.

The first major shock the Emir received was in June, 1919, when he learned that England was withdrawing her forces from Transcaspia, leaving only a small detachment in Krasnovodsk. At first he refused to believe it. England could not afford to do it! She could not and would not allow Bolshevism to gain a permanent foothold on the boundaries of her Asiatic Empire. Bolshevism would be a perpetual threat to her position in the Orient. Such a step would damage her prestige in the East irreparably. England could not do such a thing.

The reason the Emir was so stunned by the news was his inadequate grasp of the world situation. England's withdrawal from Transcaspia was not a matter of conscience or of free choice. She needed her armies elsewhere. Her position in India was in peril. The Bolshevik anti-imperialist slogans were beginning to bear fruit.

As early as February, 1919, the bourgeois revolution in Afghanistan, stimulated by the anti-imperialist pronouncements of the Soviets, had developed into an open war against England. The bourgeois progressive group that had come into power with Amanulla Khan had dared to challenge the British lion. The Afghans, of course, did not rely merely on their tiny military forces. They knew that back of them was the entire Orient and that in front was an embittered India straining at the Imperial chain. The calculation was eminently justified. Afghanistan's blow at England sent a thrill of joy through the colonial and semi-colonial East. Already the Afghan tribes in the north-western part of India were becoming more "insolent" in their struggle with the British troops. Already one hundred and twenty thousand Indian workers were out on strike, and the strike was spreading. Already Punjab was in the throes of a peasant revolt. In Persia, in the Arab East, in Egypt, the anti-British movement was gaining momentum. Under the terrific pressure of the surge for national emancipation in her colonies and dependencies Great Britain was straining her last resources to hold out, to save her prestige.

What the Emir did not yet know, Colonel Etherton (we judge from his book) knew only too well. It is from Mr. Etherton's story, indeed, that we gather the reasons for England's retirement from Transcaspia. "The huge force of 300,000 men massed on and near the Afghan frontier," he complains, "was unable to achieve anything, nor did we exact the retribution to which we were so justly entitled...." Typical spokesman of imperialist Britain, Colonel Etherton blames everybody but England for England's troubles. The Afghan "attack" was "unprovoked" and "scandalous"! "Amanulla," he confides, "had for some time been coquetting with the Bolsheviks; he saw in them a means to free himself from the restriction under which the foreign relations of Afghanistan were controlled by the British government.... My information clearly proved that the Bolsheviks had promised him assistance in men, money, and *material*...." Colonel Etherton's comments on the Afghan War are classic revelations of the imperialist mind. "At the close of the Afghan War," he wails, "and the conclusion of a treaty devoid of compensatory advantage to ourselves, or any punishment for our outraged dignity, we were left in a parlous condition as regards prestige in Central Asia. Immense difficulty was experienced by myself and my colleague ... in counteracting the violent Bolshevik propaganda which ensued as the outcome of this campaign and its unfortunate ending."

In 1919 the Orient was seething with revolt. While the Soviets were denied contact with the West, Moscow became the Mecca of numerous missions, delegations and individuals from the oppressed peoples of the East. And in December, 1919, the People's Commissar for Foreign Affairs was in a position to report to the Seventh Congress of Soviets that

> We addressed the Governments of North and South China, the Mongolian Government, the Persian Government and the revolutionary organization of Korea, stating our concrete program and giving up the entire legacy of the Czarist régime and its continuation by the Kerensky government. We solemnly announced to the Turkish and the rest of the Moslem world our desire to help the Moslem peoples in their fight for their lost liberties.... To whatever Eastern country we turn our eyes, whether Persia, China, Turkey, or Egypt we observe a deep fermentation which is assuming more and more of a movement against European and American capitalism. This movement has for its ultimate object the attainment of our ideals.

It was the coincidence of the national liberation war in Afghanistan and the ominous rise of the national liberation movement throughout the East, especially in India, that forced England to withdraw her troops from Transcaspia. Her position and her prestige in the Orient were seriously impaired, her safety was threatened. She had to mass her soldiers in the most dangerous spot, on and near the Afghan frontier. That is why only a small detachment was left in the city of Krasnovodsk, on the Transcaspian front. Though the retirement of the troops had not brought about the cessation of British intrigue, it had marked the end of England's military intervention in Central Asia.

The Emir is Disconsolate

A pall of gloom hung now over the Emir's "Ark." As 1919 was drawing to an end, the messages from the various anti-Soviet fronts were increasingly alarming.

On September 13, the Red forces of Turkestan, under the leadership of Frunze, all but demolished Dutov's crack army by the Aral Sea railroad station. Dutov was driven into Semirechie. The famous "Dutov cork" was blown into fragments. The Red Armies of Turkestan at last joined forces with the Red Armies from the Center. The isolation of the Turkestan Soviets was at an end.

Then came the distressing news that Kolchak's armies were wiped out in Siberia, Denikin's in South Russia. Red regiments smashed their way into the Caucasus.

On January 6, 1920, the Bolsheviks began the new year by capturing Krasnovodsk, the last stronghold of the anti-Soviet forces on the Transcaspian front.

Every new message increased the Emir's anxiety. In the spring the news came that in Semirechie, the Reds had annihilated Annenkov's and the last remnants of Dutov's armies, and that Annenkov and Dutov, with several hundred officers, had fled to Chinese Turkestan.

The most crushing news, however, came from Khiva. Djunaid Khan was meeting with serious military reverses, and was losing his authority. Many of the Turkoman chieftains and their personal followers were deserting him. The Young Khivans, political cousins of the Emir's enemies in Bokhara, were coming out into the open, brazenly setting up revolutionary headquarters in all the larger cities of the Khiva Khanate. They were carrying their subversive propaganda into the very heart of the Khivan population. They were winning support not only among the workmen, the peasants, and the petty tradesmen, but even among the clergy and the more prosperous classes, all of whom were eager to throw off Djunaid's yoke. The strange thing was that those Young Khivans, though they styled themselves "Bolsheviks," were not really Bolsheviks. They were middle class nationalists, Uzbeks, who were appealing to the Uzbek masses to rise against the Turkoman usurper and his Turkoman hordes. Why, the Emir wondered, did they call themselves Bolsheviks and popularize the name among the masses, when they were religious Moslems, when, according to reliable reports, the last meeting of the Central Committee and the Presidium of their party was preceded by fervent prayers in the mosque?

Nonplused, worried, harried by a great dread, the Emir followed the cheerless news from Khiva. Finally, the worst happened. Djunaid Khan was overthrown. He and his bands fled to Persia. The Young Khivans organized a revolutionary government. The Bolsheviks organized a branch of the Bolshevik party. The Khivan government was under the direct influence of the Bolsheviks. . . .

The fiery ring of revolution around Bokhara was tightening. In a last, despairing spurt of energy, the Emir resolved to give battle. He started to swell still further his already burdensome and untrustworthy army by hysterically ordering four mobilizations within a short time. He increased the taxes, purchased ammunition, and agitated for a holy war. He financed the counter-revolutionary guerrilla bands in Fergana and, needless to say, repressed the slightest sign of disaffection.

Above all the Emir now tried very assiduously to strike up a friendship with the new Afghan ruler—Amanulla Khan. Embassies were exchanged. Assurances of eternal friendship and rich gifts were showered on both sides, Amanulla presenting the Bokhara Emir with several cannon and four or five war elephants.

It was suggested that in flirting with Alim Khan, Amanulla cherished the hope of ultimately uniting all the Moslem peoples under the holy banner of Pan-Islamism carried by a mighty Afghanistan. Whether or not Amanulla really entertained such grandiose hopes is difficult to determine. What he undoubtedly dreamt of was territorial expansion in the direction of Eastern Bokhara, now Tadjikistan. The victories of his armies over England had gone to Amanulla's head, and he thought that the hour for creating a greater Afghanistan had struck.

However, Amanulla's policies were cautious. While encouraging the Emir's overtures, he at the same time took pains not to antagonize seriously the Soviet Government. Indeed, he was among the first to grant official recognition to the Soviet régime. Obviously, Emir Alim Khan could not rely on Afghanistan too much. Nor could he place any faith in his subjects, who were greatly stirred by what had happened in Khiva and was now happening in Soviet Turkestan. In Turkestan a special commission, consisting of three very able Bolsheviks—Frunze, Kuibyshev and Eliaev—sent by the Central Executive Committee of the Russian Socialist Federation of Soviet Republics, was introducing better order in the revolutionary organizations of Turkestan, rehabilitating the economy of the country, and, what was of supreme importance, drawing into this work of reorganization and rehabilitation large numbers of native workers and peasants. As a result of the Committee's energetic action, the government and Party organizations in Soviet Turkestan had quickly and basically changed their national composition.

The work of the Commission in improving economic conditions and creating a genuinely national Soviet Government in Turkestan had an immediate and salutary effect on the neighboring Khanate. The peasants in Bokhara were growing more and more impatient with the despotic régime of the Emir. No walls, no executions, no floggings could stop the wave of enthusiasm that was generating in Turkestan from spreading in all directions. Khiva, where the old régime was weakest and where the population was groaning under the savage Djunaid-Khan, had felt the impact first. Now it began to be felt in Bokhara. Affected by events in Turkestan and Khiva the masses in Bokhara became even more susceptible to revolutionary propaganda. The anti-Emir movement was growing. By August, 1920, conditions were ripe for a second revolutionary advance against the Emirate.

The Bokharan refugees in Tashkent and the Turkestan Central Bureau of the Young Bokharan organization launched a furious propaganda campaign among the peasants and the Emir's army.

"Fellow countrymen," they wrote, "be not afraid, justice and power is on your side.... Bloody Nicholas is no more. The Czarist friends of the Emir who might have taken sides with him and sent the Russian army against you have long since been hurled out of Russia. There is now only the Workers' and Peasants' Red Army which is wholly on our side, and which is always ready to come to our aid.... Long live the union of the liberty loving Russian Red fighters and the revolutionary army of Bokhara!"

The Emir finally realized that he could not stem the revolutionary tide, that the day of judgment was inexorably drawing closer. He hastened to make secret preparations to save the vast treasures amassed by himself and his predecessors, which lay in the vaults of the palace. "To secure the safety of his wealth," reports Lieutenant-Colonel Etherton, "he offered to confide it to our care, and requested us to take charge of it pending the dawn of brighter days and a return to normal conditions." The Emir offered to relieve the British agent of all responsibility during transport. All he wanted for his thirty-five million pounds sterling in gold and silver coins and ingots was a "receipt for the sum in question." Though greatly touched by this "remarkable offer" and by this beautiful demonstration of "how high our credit stood even in remote Bokhara," Colonel Etherton, because of the "isolated nature of Bokhara," and the "warring elements" that surrounded it, was unfortunately unable to take custody of the treasure. "Certainly, so far as Kashgar was concerned," he explains, "I could not have accommodated so large an amount in my treasury without special arrangements, and moreover, the difficulties of getting there would have been insuperable."

Poor Alim-Khan was left trembling over his gold, while the Young Bokharans were preparing for the revolution.

On August 18 a congress of the Young Bokharan Communists met in Chardjui. The selection of Chardjui was not accidental. Chardjui was an important station with a considerable number of revolutionary railway workers; also the peasant population in the Chardjui region was the poorest and most exploited in Bokhara. Finally, the majority of the population was Turkoman, inimical to the Bokhara Emir and his preponderantly Uzbek officials.

STRUGGLE FOR POWER 121

The Congress at Chardjui decided upon an armed uprising. Propagandists and organizers were thrown into the districts. On August 23rd, the Sakor-Bazar revolutionary organization seized that city. On August 30th, the appointed day, the armed peasantry supported by armed contingents of the Young Bokharans and the Russian railway workers at Chardjui occupied the city encountering no resistance and shedding not a drop of blood. Simultaneously, Kermin, Shakhriziab, and a number of other cities fell into the hands of the revolutionists. Immediately a proclamation was issued to the people of the Bokhara Khanate stating the aims of the revolution.

All the lands, wells and irrigation canals were declared to be the property of the people of Bokhara. The real and personal property of the Emir's officials, of the reactionary sections of the clergy, and of all active counter-revolutionists was pronounced subject to immediate confiscation by the state. A congress of the people's representatives was promised which congress would directly proceed to carry out the task of land and water reforms and of taking over all enterprises for the benefit of the state. Also an appeal was addressed to the government, proletariat, and the Red Army of Russia, wherein the Young Bokharans, speaking in the name of the workers and peasants of Bokhara, asked that the comrades of the Russian Soviet Republic help them in the struggle against the armed forces of the Emir.

The appeal was, of course, calculated to appease the nationalist elements in Bokhara by removing the suspicion of a Russian invasion. Naturally, too, the response to the appeal was immediate. In his order to the Red Armies on the Turkestan front, Frunze wrote: "In various places in Bokhara there have broken out revolutionary uprisings. The hour has struck for the final struggle of the oppressed and enslaved toiling masses of Bokhara against the bloodthirsty government of the Emir and his Beks. The regiments of the newly-born Red Army of Bokhara are advancing to help their people. It is the duty of the Red regiment of worker and peasant Russia to take its place by their side. I order all our armed forces to go to the aid of the people of Bokhara in their hour of need. ... Red Army men, fighters, commissars, the eyes of the whole of the Soviet Union are turned toward you in the faith that each and every one of you will fulfill his revolutionary duty. Forward, to battle for the interests of the toilers of Bokhara and Russia. Long live the awakened people of Bokhara. Long live the emerging Soviet Republic of Bokhara!"

Under the Walls of Bokhara

(From the Memoirs of G. Omeliusty.)

It was the thirtieth of August, towards evening. The streets of New Bokhara, swathed in darkness, were quiet, deserted. Only now and then a rider would gallop by, a Red patrol would pass with measured step. From the city's outskirts one could hear the cries of the Emir's guards.

Nothing seemed to disturb the usual martial-law atmosphere of the period—the outer tranquillity, the inner tension.

Nothing seemed to betray the excitement behind the curtain-drawn windows, where the Party Committee and the Military Staff were in session. Yet the excitement was great—news had just arrived of uprisings in Chardjui and Karshi. The insurgents seized Old Chardjui. In Karshi the battle was still raging. The revolutionary detachments were supported by the city poor. The henchmen of the doomed régime were offering furious resistance. ...

The situation was crucial, dangerous. It called for decisive steps. The uprisings must get vigorous support. The fate of the Bokharan revolution was at stake. Success in Chardjui and Karshi was not enough. The enemy had to be struck in the very heart.

Harsh conditions of revolutionary struggle and underground work had forged bold, resolute characters, had taught them to make decisions on the spot and act instantly. It took no more than one hour to call together all the organizations and Worker Red Guards from the surrounding settlements. Fighting detachments were organized forthwith. Those who had no arms were armed—rifles, cartridges, etc. A proclamation was issued, calling on the labor population of Bokhara to support the insurgents. Another proclamation to the Red Army, urging its aid to overthrow the Emir and establish the Soviet Power.

The plan of action was simple. The revolutionary detachments to advance toward Old Bokhara in two columns—one along the highway from Kogan, the other from the railway through the Karakul Gates. On the way the detachments must draw in the rising population in the villages. The Red Army contingents to be in back. Object—to take Bokhara. Military activities to begin at dawn—four o'clock sharp. Meanwhile, a concentration of forces in all strategic points. Absolute secrecy. The enemy must not be warned. Strong patrols at all city exits. Signal for action—the firing of a cannon.

At four o'clock, to the minute, the first cannon shot burst forth and reverberated through the clear morning air. The Bokharan revolution announced its arrival.

Cutting the air with a whiz, the missile shot up, flew over the city, descended, and struck the clay wall of the yard where the Emir's cavalry was stationed. Immediately, at the northern end of the city, on both sides of the highway, a battery of machine guns burst out, followed by the crackling of rifles. The Red detachments went forth to storm the stronghold of savage tyranny.

The attack was launched abruptly and conducted fiercely. The Emir's hirelings could not withstand the shock, and, abandoning their provision trains, shedding their guns and cartridges, started a hasty and disorderly retreat into Old Bokhara.

Several cannons, boxes of ammunition, wagons, a few captives, rifles, cartridges were our first spoils.

The twelve kilometers between the Old and the New Bokhara were covered in no time. By noon our contingents were fighting in the suburbs nearest to the city.

At a distance loomed the embrasured city walls. They had been there for six centuries, rising seventy feet above the ground and so thick that wagons could travel on top of them. Our cannon balls made only slight impressions on them. It was difficult to take those walls. They offered firm protection to the enemy. Yet they had to be taken at any price. Final victory could be won only within those walls.

The enemy understood it, and it was behind those walls that he was preparing to put up the real fight. The walls of the city, the adjacent cemeteries, the houses, the streets, everything was adapted for defense.

The Russian White Guards, the Emir's officials, the beys, the bourgeoisie, all were mobilized for the counter-attack.

Clutching Korans in their hands, tearing their clothes, issuing frenzied cries, the mullahs incited the city mob. "Death to the Djadids," came from behind the walls. "Long Live the Revolution," came the answer from our side.

A desperate battle developed at the very walls of the city. Both sides fought tenaciously. The cemetery changed hands several times; several times the Red warriors came up to the very walls, but, sprayed with a shower of bullets and rocks, they were forced to retreat with considerable losses. Several times they vainly hurled themselves at the walls. Now and then the city gates were flung open and the infuriated mobs, exhorted by mullahs and officials, supported by a steady fire from the walls, yelling "Allah," advanced against our machine guns, throwing themselves at our gunners with bare hands.

Utilizing their numerous cavalry, the Emir and his generals, by sudden attacks against our flanks, tried to upset our battle array at the city walls.

Twice our left column penetrated the Karakul Gates into the old city, but, met by superior forces, pelted with grenades in the narrow streets, it had to withdraw, leaving many dead behind.

Neither that night nor the following day did the battle abate even for one moment. Flames, the roar of artillery, the clatter of machine guns, yells, curses, cries, all mingled together in the weird night.

The ranks of our fighters were thinning. In that struggle many a comrade gave his blood or his life for the cause of the Revolution. Our ammunition was almost used up, yet the citadel of counter-revolution was holding out. The fury of desperation added strength to the enemy.

Then came the third day. The fighting, somewhat abated during the night, broke out with even greater violence and seethed along the whole line. One thought bored through the consciousness of all of us—the thought of the crucial importance of that day. If we did not hold out, if we retreated from the walls, the question of the Bokharan revolution would be postponed for many years, and the uprising would be ruthlessly quelled.

We made a last attempt. Everything that could in some way injure the enemy was thrown into this attack. At the price of the lives of our bravest comrades we managed to make a breach in the city walls. They dragged the cannons right to the very walls and shot into them.

With shouts of triumph the first two groups of daredevils dashed into the city. They were soon followed by the others. Street fighting started, and it was bloodier than the fighting outside the walls. Under a shower of bullets, hand grenades, under streams of boiling water from the roofs and the windows, enveloped in flame, the revolutionary Bokhara detachments, the Red guards, and the Red Army were pushing ahead. The narrow, crooked streets, the thick clay walls offered obstacles at every step. We had to fight for each house, for each square. The neighborhood of the Emir's "Ark" was all in flames.

However, the crucial moment was over. As we advanced, the enemy's resistance began to weaken, and at the "Ark" it was finally broken. Here our two columns met. A few more sporadic clashes, a few more victims, and the Red detachments reached the northern part of the city. The smashed remnants of the Bokharan counter-revolution were scattering in all directions. The Emir and his little group of henchmen fled. To the history of the proletarian revolution another victorious page was added.

Epilogue and Prologue

Colonel Etherton, who obtained interesting information about the Emir's last days in Bokhara from one of the Emir's ministers who had visited him in Kashgar, tells us that the revolutionists' attack on Bokhara "was so well planned that the Emir only escaped by the merest good luck. He left the palace disguised as a carter and actually passed through the city gates whilst the insurgents were searching the palace for him."

The same source provides us with another very illuminating and characteristic detail:

"From Hissar the Emir dispatched a mission to Kashgar, headed by one of the ministers who had escaped with him, conveying letters to the King-Emperor, the Viceroy of India, and myself. In them the Emir recounted his overthrow by the Bolsheviks and subsequent plight, and begged that his state, which he placed unconditionally at our disposal, might be incorporated within the British Empire."

Pleased by this fine "tribute to British integrity and power," Colonel Etherton, nevertheless, had to decline, because "there could, of course, be no question of further extension of territory on our part."

On the very day the Emir fled, a Revolutionary Committee and a Soviet of People's Commissars had been organized in Bokhara. As the names indicate, almost the entire government was made up of natives: Abdusaidov, Aminov, Akchurin, Arifov, Yusupov, Imburkhanov, Khodzhi-Khasan Ibrahimov, Faizulla Khodzhaiev, Kul Mukhamedov, Pulatov, Abdul Mukhidinov, Mukhtar Saidzhanov, Ussman Khodzhaiev, Khusainov, Burkhanov, Shegabutdinov. Shortly after, a Congress of representatives of the peoples of Bokhara met and declared Bokhara a People's Soviet Republic. And six months later, on March 4, 1921, the new Soviet Republic of Bokhara (BSR) entered into a series of military, political and economic agreements with the Russian Socialist Federation of Soviet Republics (RSFSR—there was no USSR then; the Union of Socialist Soviet Republics was formed in December, 1922) according to which the RSFSR, guided by the principle of self-determination of peoples, renounced "the colonial policy of the former capitalist governments of Russia for which the laboring masses of Bokhara, like other nations of the East, have always been an object of exploitation" and recognized, "without reservation, the self-government and complete independence of the Bokharan Soviet Republic, with all the consequences deriving therefrom." . . . One of the consequences was, of course, the unconditional right of Bokhara not to join the RSFSR, or to secede from it after it had joined. Soviet Bokhara chose *not* to join.

However, to quote the preamble to the agreement:

> Deriving from the profound consciousness that, not only can there be no conflict of interests among the toiling masses of all countries, but also that the betterment of the workers' existence is rendered possible solely by their struggles in common and uniting their forces against the imperialist bourgeoisie of the world; deriving also from the necessity of elaborating common plans in the struggle for independence and for the coördination of forces, as well as of introducing uniformity into their preparation; and, furthermore, from the conviction that the working masses, after having eliminated any possibility of exploiting each other, are interested in the strengthening of the productive forces; and believing, finally, that only a close union of the toilers of the East and West will secure for them victory and that all Soviet Republics must proceed along the road of fraternal union—the RSFSR and BSR have decided to conclude this treaty of alliance. . . .

In conformity with the sentiments expressed in the preamble, the two republics, in addition to settling all questions of boundaries, mutual military aid in defense "against the unceasing attacks of the world bourgeoisie and its agents," and the coördination of their economic and commercial policies and plans, agreed, in true fraternal spirit, that "the RSFSR shall lend its assistance to the BSR for the establishment and development of its industrial and other economic enterprises by putting at the disposal of the latter all necessary materials, implements of production, and the like..." also "the necessary contingents of engineers, technicians, hydro-technicians, and other experts for prospecting as well as for organizing mining and manufacturing industries of the BSR and for irrigation works..." also "instructors, including military instructors with a knowledge of the native languages, teachers, school-manuals, literature, material for equipment of printing offices, etc." Furthermore, "in order to give the BSR immediate assistance in respect to current necessities, the RSFSR lends to the BSR an unredeemable subsidy," *that is, a subsidy which will not have to be repaid.*

Such was the spirit of the agreement—a complete reversal of the imperialist policies of the Czar. Instead of keeping subject Bokhara industrially backward, the revolutionary government of Russia was eager to help the newly liberated republic, now not as a subject but as an ally, to develop its national economy and productive forces; instead of keeping the Bokharan masses in ignorance, the government of the victorious revolutionary proletariat of the more advanced Soviet Republic offered instructors, teachers, textbooks, literature, printing presses; instead of exploiting the Bokharan masses, the RSFSR offered them "unredeemable subsidies" so that they might develop their industries and yet be spared the necessity of going through the stage of capitalism.

VIII

RECEDING VERSUS EMERGENT

> ...*I glory in the great hour*
> *When the triumphant storm*
> *Crashed down upon the foe.*
> *It smashed our yokes,*
> *And freed the slaves to swarm*
> *As clouds upon their nest,*
> *And raised the flag of battle....*
> *I glory in that day supreme—*
> *The Beginning of October....*
> *O land of mine...*
> *I stand your daylong watch.*
> —ALI ROKEMBAYEV, Kirghiz poet.

Revolution in a Quandary

THE overthrow of the Emir was only one of the more spectacular episodes in the fierce social drama that has been unfolding in Central Asia during the last eighteen years. The revolutionary explosion, by removing the Emir, removed the lid that had pressed down and held together a population perpetually seething with national and class antagonisms. The result was a period of turmoil and violent readjustment, the echoes of which still reverberate through the distant hills and valleys of Eastern Bokhara (now Tadjikistan).

The fundamental problem facing the new Government was that of direction. Whither was the revolution to go? The local Bolsheviks were themselves not clear as to the basic theories of Communism or the specific character of the Bokharan revolution. Yet without a clear theoretical line, there could be no effective action. The antiquated social structure had collapsed. The débris had to be cleared away: some of it destroyed, but more saved for the new edifice. It was a matter of proper selection. But no selection was possible before the builders had an approximate notion of what they wanted to build. A plan, however tentative, was needed. Yet no plan could be suggested without first having the question as to the proletarian or bourgeois nature of the Bokharan revolution adequately answered.

To many the whole question seemed rather baffling: How could one attach a proletarian or bourgeois label to a revolution which had in back of it neither a proletariat nor a bourgeoisie? Under the Emir, capitalism in Bokhara had been in its earliest infancy. The relatively recent introduction of Russian finance capital had not fundamentally changed the ancient social structure. Bokhara was essentially a feudal, peasant land, and the revolution was primarily the uprising of the village masses against the socially and economically undifferentiated upper class—the richest landlords, the richest mullahs, the richest merchants and bankers and state functionaries. What sense was there in speaking of a bourgeois revolution without a real bourgeoisie or a proletarian revolution without a real proletariat? Furthermore, the Russian Bolsheviks often pressed the adjective *socialist* as the correct term to apply to the Revolution. To many of the skeptics, however, that too did not seem satisfactory. Like the Mensheviks, like the members of the Second International, like our own American Socialists, these Bokharans tended to deny the socialist character of the revolution even in Russia, let alone in Bokhara. The socialist order, maintained those of them who had a smattering of Marx, could not be established in a country of backward industrial development. The few scholiasts never wearied of citing the famous sentence from Marx's *Introduction* to the *Critique of Political Economy:* "No social order ever disappears before all the productive forces for which there is room in it have been developed; and new higher relations of production never appeared before the material conditions of their existence have matured in the womb of the old society." Even Czarist Russia, despite several decades of capitalism, had not developed all its potential productive forces to a stage even remotely approximating maturity, so what point was there in expecting semi-feudal Bokhara to skip the stage of capitalist development and to plunge into a drive for new, higher, *socialist* relations of production? Any attempt to give the revolution in backward Bokhara and even in more advanced Russia a socialist character would do unpardonable violence to historically ineluctable economic trends and would prove abortive. Needless pain. Needless suffering. Needless bloodshed. You cannot skip a whole social and economic epoch. Why follow a will-o'-the-wisp?

The objections were for the most part passionately sincere. Few of the people who advanced them, Russian and native middle-class intellectuals, realized that they were rationalizing a profound fear of being hurled into the untried, the utterly unknown. They were not opposed to socialism in the abstract, as a concept. They flinched when it began to be spoken of as a reality for which one had to struggle.

The answer urged by the Bolsheviks was substantially as follows: They granted that the revolution in Bokhara was neither purely proletarian nor purely bourgeois, that it was primarily the upsurge of the poor working population of the villages. In the words of Lenin: "If a definite level of culture is necessary for the establishment of socialism (although no one can say what this definite 'level of culture' is), then why should it be impossible for us to begin first of all by attaining in a revolutionary way the prerequisites for this definite level, and *afterwards,* on the basis of the workers' and peasants' power and the Soviet system, proceed to overtake the other peoples? You say that a definite state of civilization is required for the establishment of socialism. Very well. But why could we not first of all create the prerequisites for such a state of civilization in our country by banishing the landlords and capitalists and then starting our advance toward socialism? Wherein is it written that such variations in the usual historical order are inadmissible or impossible?"

It was said that the capitalist stage of development was inevitable, especially in the case of the extremely backward nationalities liberated by the revolution. The Bolsheviks refused to accept that. If the victorious revolutionary proletariat of the more advanced countries in the Soviet Federation carried on systematic propaganda in a country like Bokhara, and if the Soviet Government made available to Bokhara all the means at its disposal, it would be incorrect to suppose that the capitalist stage of development was inevitable here. With the aid of the proletariat of the most advanced Soviet countries and the leadership of the Communist Party, there was no reason, the more mature Bolsheviks felt, why Bokhara could not avoid the pain of capitalist exploitation, why it could not complete the bourgeois revolution, especially the redistribution of land, under the rule of the Workers' and Peasants' Soviets.

The lack of theoretical clarity and the wavering attitude of most of the local leaders, including some would-be Bolsheviks, resulted, however, in numerous mistakes, and interferences with the accelerated development of the bourgeois-democratic revolution. Only the richest merchants, mullahs, and ex-officials of the Emir were not allowed to vote or be candidates in the elections for the first All-Bokhara Congress of Soviets. The word socialist had not been incorporated in the name of the Republic. No move had been made to enter the Russian Socialist Federation of Soviet Republics. Except for the confiscation of the property of the Emir and his highest officials and the abolition of the old taxes, little had been done of a revolutionary nature to stir the imagination or better the lot of the working masses. The one major thing attempted was the formation of a state monopoly for the buying and selling of agricultural products and improving the exchange of commodities with Soviet Russia. Also half-hearted efforts were made to break up the old administrative machine of the Emirate and to replace it by central and local revolutionary committees comprising government appointees, some members of the Communist

Party, and elected representatives of the people. Most of the attempts had proved futile.

Bolshevik ideology demanded unqualified orientation toward the poorest elements in the village and the city. Had those been encouraged to enter the Soviets, the Soviets would have soon become genuine revolutionary organs, effectively guiding the revolution in a socialist direction. An ideologically clear, thoroughly welded and disciplined Bolshevik organization, even though small numerically, might have accomplished much despite the difficulties which alienation of the petty-bourgeoisie would have inevitably entailed. Revolutionary daring was needed, bold policy, measures that would activize the city workers, the handicraftsmen, and the poor and middle peasants and draw them closely around the Party and the Soviets. A sweeping agrarian revolution, the nationalization of *all* lands and their transfer to the impoverished peasants— that was what the masses craved, only such an act would have elicited enthusiastic support from the ruined peasantry. But the complex nature of the revolution and the lack of Bolshevik training among the local leaders precluded such a course; hence, excessive caution and ceaseless vacillation. Even the moderate program adopted at the outset remained a paper program. Characteristically, the Constitution of Soviet Bokhara, ratified as late as August 18, 1922, guaranteed all citizens "the right freely to dispose of their movable and immovable property." In Soviet Bokhara people could buy and sell and bequeath to others their lands and their other belongings just as unrestrainedly as in any bourgeois country!

The lack of theoretical clarity accounts also for the unwholesomely swollen ranks of the local Communist Party —a membership of 14,000 within a few weeks after the fall of the Emir. True, in the 1922 purge the membership was rapidly reduced from 10,000 to 6,000, then to 3,000, and finally to 1,000! But even that scarcely improved matters.

The situation was tragically aggravated by the fact that Soviet Bokhara possessed neither the trained executives nor the experienced organizers for the colossal tasks confronting the Government. The native progressive intelligentsia, scant at best, had been largely destroyed by the Emir or decimated by the exigencies of war and revolution. Among those who survived, not many were ready to work with the revolutionary government. Few administrators could be drawn from the illiterate masses. Administrators are not trained over night. Willy-nilly, members of the new administration, whether appointed or elected, were often drawn from the old bureaucracy—venal, corrupt politicians bitterly opposed to the revolution and its purposes. Abuse, sabotage, treason, provocation and deliberate distortion of Party policies were the usual thing. Styling themselves "revolutionary," these vestiges of the Emir's bureaucratic machine were always guarding the interests of the exploiting groups. The presence of such elements in the ranks of the Party precluded concentrated effort or unified policy. Even among the leaders there were fundamental disagreements and serious "left" and "right" deviations. On the left, particularly among the local Russian Communists, there was an effort to propagate, without a proper evaluation of immediate conditions, the emergency measures of Russia's war-time communism: forced contribution of food, prohibition of all private trading, closing of bazaars (which measure was bound to hurt not only the antagonistic commercial bourgeoisie but the potentially friendly middle peasants as well), conscription of labor and mobilization in the Red Army. On the right, there were tendencies toward bourgeois nationalism, local chauvinism, pan-Islamism. Even revolutionary leaders—Muhamed Khodzhaiev, Usman Khodzhaiev, Arefov, and many others—were subsequently discovered to have been traitors working hand in hand with the beys, the mullahs and the forces of reaction.

The worker and peasant masses were becoming disillusioned. Popular disaffection was growing. The Basmach movement was gathering momentum. Counter-revolution was raising its head. Destruction, arson and murder held the country in their grip.

The Thief and the Unique Rose

By the time the revolutionary tide reached Bokhara, Basmachism in Turkestan—now an autonomous republic in the RSFSR—had begun to disintegrate. The removal of "Dutov's cork," the triumph of the Red Armies on all fronts, the improved revolutionary technique of the Turkestan Bolsheviks, as well as the general trend toward economic recovery after the introduction of the New Economic Policy (NEP), had their effect. The middle peasantry, numerically the most potent factor in the Basmach movement, began to desert the ranks of the counter-revolution. With the middle peasants' support in Turkestan gone, the Basmach leaders began to cast about in search for new places of activity.

They turned their eyes to Soviet Bokhara where the weakness of the new Bokharan government had caused a succession of economic and political convulsions and created an atmosphere favorable to the dissemination of Basmach propaganda.

To lend their anti-Soviet activities the appearance of a popular revolt and thus to secure the support of the disillusioned masses, the Basmach leaders proclaimed the slogan "Fight for our People's Rights." Reactionary to the core, they made every effort to conceal their true nature behind a smokescreen of high-sounding nationalist and democratic pronouncements. A considerable portion of the population accepted their leadership and fought for their slogans. They received assistance from abroad. From Afghanistan, whither he had fled on March 5, 1920, Emir Alim Khan kept on sending financial help and stirring appeals to the faithful.

The Basmach movement in Bokhara started in the Lokai valley, located in the Hissar Bekdom and populated by semi-nomadic Uzbek tribes—Lokai, Mongyt, etc. It was here that the Basmach bands in Bokhara first took on a political coloring, playing the rôle of defenders of Moslem tradition and the ancient economic and social structure of their tribes. The tribal chieftains sensed that their economic domination, political power, and social prestige were menaced by the Bolsheviks. They assumed therefore from the outset a position antagonistic to the new government, and used their tremendous influence among their tribesmen to lure them into joining the counter-revolution. Held firmly by family, clan, and tribal ties, noted throughout Central Asia for their splendid horsemanship and military prowess, the Uzbeks of the Lokai valley formed the most powerful Basmach bands and produced the best Basmach leaders.

The largest and most efficiently organized band was that of the notorious chieftain Dualet-Monbei. Of only slightly lesser importance were the Basmach detachments under the leadership of Sultan-Ishan, especially ferocious in their treatment of people suspected of revolutionary sympathies. Smaller Basmach bands under the command of the brigand Djabar began to percolate into Western Bokhara and menaced the center of the Republic. The most gifted and daring of all the Basmach leaders in Eastern Bokhara, indeed, the whole of Central Asia, was Ibrahim Bek, a member of Issa-Khodza, one of the Lokai tribes.

The son of a rich kulak, Ibrahim, while still a youth, had squandered his father's wealth and had gone into horse-stealing as a means of replenishing his fortunes. But horse-stealing was too piddling a business for the ambitious Ibrahim. Seeking military glory, he entered the service of the Hinos Bek, where he soon attained the rank of captaincy. It was at this time, according to romantic legend, that Ibrahim fell in love with the rich widow Dona Gul, Unique Rose. But the Unique One declined his fervent suit, saying that she would consider him only if he became Bek. Ibrahim resolved to become Bek. The revolution provided him with the great opportunity. Demoniacally ambitious, an extraordinarily gifted organizer and military leader, he proceeded, as soon as the Revolution broke out, to gather around himself a large band of devoted and well-armed followers. Within a short time his band attracted wide attention. Because of his great services to the Emir, the young chieftain of this valorous band soon became, legend tells us, a candidate for the high office of "Keeper of the Royal Stables." When, however, the wise counselors of the Emir pointed out that the appointment of a notorious horse-thief to such a post was susceptible to humorous comment and likely to reflect upon the dignity of his Royal Highness himself, the Emir began to waver. Ibrahim's tribe resented the aspersion cast on his character. Who had ever said, they challenged, that horse-thieving was prohibited among the faithful followers of the Prophet? Recognizing the justice of their challenge, the Emir gave the job to Ibrahim. After the Emir's departure for Kabul, Ibrahim's star continued to rise and his and his band's fame to spread. The tribal chieftains acclaimed him as their leader, signifying their great admiration by tossing him (according to tradition) into the air on a white woolen carpet and proclaiming him Bek.

On the day when thousands of motley horsemen, arrayed in colored caftans and gay turbans and armed with every kind of ancient and modern weapon, paraded before him, Ibrahim Bek called for Dona Gul. His quest was satisfied, his love was requited, and the Unique Rose brought her fragrance into Ibrahim's growing harem.

Ibrahim Bek quickly extended his authority over other Uzbek tribes. Under his banner, heretofore scattered and disunited Uzbek bands in Lokai and even in Kuliab consolidated into a formidable anti-Soviet force.

The Emir, aware of the developments in Bokhara, began to have happy dreams of a restoration. He hailed the rise of Ibrahim Bek, showering honors and presents upon him. Financed, it is asserted, by the English, he kept Ibrahim well supplied with money and ammunition. Through a host of emissaries, Alim-Khan conducted an intensive campaign of agitation and propaganda against the Soviets.

The movement spread. District after district joined the Basmachi. Remote from the center, remote from Tashkent or even Bokhara proper, protected by the absence of roads, assisted by the majority of the village population, the Basmachi were almost impregnable.

The number of the Basmachi increased.

On the other hand the Red Army detachments were few. They were not used to the climate, nor familiar with the terrain. They were being killed off by malaria and other local diseases. In certain sections 95 per cent of the Red Army were sick with malaria. They were being betrayed at each step. By December, 1921, there were about twenty thousand active Basmachi. Led by Ibrahim, they were sufficiently strong to besiege and finally take Dushambe. The Red Army was forced to retreat along the Baisun-Shirobad-Termez line.

The weakness of the Basmach movement lay in its internal national and class rivalries. The Uzbek bands often clashed with the Tadjik bands, and the Turkoman bands with both. The Kazaks introduced further complications. Among the Basmach leaders, too, there was no coherent program. The exponents of feudal and clerical aspiration were on top but they were often balked by the opposition of the more liberal bourgeois democratic elements. Though all of them were engaged in the common struggle against the Bolsheviks, they nevertheless distrusted one another, and as a result failed to evolve a united program, a solid organization, an authoritative, universally accepted leadership. Ibrahim Bek was a bold warrior and splendid organizer, but he was an Uzbek whom the other nationalities distrusted, and so ignorant as to be utterly unfit to give political guidance.

Moslems of the World Unite!

The chances of the Basmachi were considerably improved with the appearance of the Turkish adventurer Enver Pasha on the troubled Bokharan scene. In comparison with the provincial small-fry, Enver was a world figure. He had been active in the Young-Turk movement ever since 1908 and had been an important personage in the Turkish nationalist party "Unity and Progress." He had achieved no small fame in the Turkish army. He had been responsible for the bloody Armenian massacres in 1914-1915, and was partly instrumental in entangling Turkey in the Bulgarian war and then in the World War.

During the World War he had been one of the most powerful men in Turkey, and, together with Djemal Pasha and Tolant Pasha, had formed the dictatorial triumvirate that ruled the country. Handsome, brilliant, magnetic, unscrupulous, daring and imaginative, Enver Pasha had been renowned throughout the Moslem world—in Persia, Afghanistan, India, Central Asia, and even China. His personality had made itself felt on the European stage as well. At home, the Caliph-Sultan, his kinsman, had been a tool in his hands.

But his success was meteoric. He soon began to meet with reverses. His rivalry with the rapidly rising Mustapha Kemal and the thorough defeat of his armies in the Caucasus had culminated in his being accused of causing Turkey's débâcle and being condemned to death in 1919. Enver had fled, trying to reach Odessa. When that attempt failed, he escaped to Germany, and from there, secretly, in his own aeropane, took off for Moscow. But Nemesis was on his trail: the plane crashed. And it was only after he had spent some anxious days in Kovno and Riga prisons, that he had finally found his way to Moscow. The grandiose ambitions that Enver Pasha cherished when he came to Moscow he never divulged. On the face of it, it seemed, there was a solid basis for Bolshevik friendship— Enver Pasha cordially hated the British, so did the Bolsheviks; the Bolsheviks were suspicious of Germany, so, professedly, was Enver. Indeed, at the Baku Congress of Eastern Peoples, Enver declared that he "hated and cursed German imperialism and German imperialists as much as he did British imperialism and British imperialists." In his declaration of faith, Enver sounded ultra-revolutionary—he was for the Soviet Government, he fully subscribed to the ideas of the Bolsheviks, he hoped for the day when the oppressed people of the world would finally see that salvation lay in revolution.

Enver protested a little too much; in view of his past, his sudden conversion failed to impress the Bolsheviks. Furthermore, in Turkey, Mustapha Kemal was in power; he was friendly toward the Soviet Union, why speculate too much on Enver? They were extremely courteous to Enver, of course; but their orientation was toward Kemal, who, though less vehement in his protestations, was in a better position to make relatively modest promises good. When Enver tried to act as intermediary between the Soviets and Turkey, his kindly offices were firmly declined. Enver was restless and impatient, but he hid his resentment deep in his breast. His greatest disappointment came when on March 16, 1921, the Bolsheviks actually signed the peace treaty with his bitterest enemy—Mustapha Kemal. Seeing his hopes of displacing Kemal with Bolshevik help go to smash, Enver resolved to leave the Soviet Union. He went to Batum, where a secret Enverist Conference planning an uprising against the Kemal Government had been called. The Bolsheviks, not aware of Enver's machinations and reluctant to violate the rules of hospitality, did not interfere with his freedom of movement. However, when a protest came from Kemal, directing the Soviet Government's attention to the secret conference in Batum, a close watch over Enver was instituted, and when, shortly after the Conference, Enver tried to escape to Turkey, he was gently intercepted and detained by the Soviet authorities.

But Enver proved too slippery even for Bolshevik vigilance. Ostensibly he was resigned to his fate. He did not even appear angry. Of course he understood the awkward position in which the Soviet Government found itself; of course he still had nothing but admiration for the Soviet principles, and particularly for the Soviet manner of handling the Moslem national minorities. Indeed, since it was impossible for him to serve his co-religionists at home, he should be happy to help them in the Soviet Union, especially in Central Asia where he was sure he could do a great deal towards exposing Britain's imperialistic schemes. Wasn't his friend Djemal Pasha useful to the Bolsheviks in Afghanistan where he had organized Amanulla Khan's army against Britain? Well, he would like to go to Transcaspia to meet Djemal Pasha, who was returning from Kabul, and then to Bokhara for a rest, for a hunting trip, perhaps. His bland manner and his apparent approval of their handling of the national minority problem deceived the authorities, and he was permitted to follow his heart's desire.

He came to Central Asia in the guise of a warm friend and admirer of the new People's Soviet Republic of Bokhara. However, three days after he accepted from the Bokharan Government the post of directing the formation of a National Red Army, he suddenly vanished. As it turned out later, he made his way to Eastern Bokhara, together with Khasanov, a Bolshevik war commissar suddenly turned renegade, to the remote Kurgan-Tepi Bekdom, where he joined the powerful Basmach chieftain Daniar-Bek.

But before leaving for Kurgan-Tepi, Enver Pasha had entered into a secret agreement with Usman Khodzhaiev, the Chairman of the Central Executive Committee of the Bokhara Republic. Soon afterwards, Usman, at the head of 600 men, deserted the revolution and joined Enver Pasha. The "allies" issued a proclamation to the people wherein they accused the Bolsheviks of nationalizing women, destroying religion, and similar horrendous crimes. The concluding paragraph was an almost hysterical call to the "Faithful" to "stand guard over Islam."

Enver Pasha's kinship with the Turkish Chalif, a personage holy in the eyes of every good Moslem, his sympathy with the Afghan pan-Islamists, and the cordial reception accorded him by the Bokharan intelligentsia, enabled the reactionary clergy to focus popular attention on him as a "savior of Islam," a leader of the "Moslem War of Liberation."

Before long, Enver established relations with the Emir, from whom he received the exalted title of "Commander in Chief of All the Forces of Islam, Son-in-Law of the Chalif, and Representative of Mohammed." He plunged enthusiastically into the work of uniting all the Moslem bands—Uzbek, Tadjik, Turkoman, Kazak, etc. He played a subtle game. Pretending to work hand in hand with the Emir (who was spreading leaflets with promises of generous treatment to all revolutionists who would join the Basmachi) and with Ibrahim Bek who was winning numerous battles in various parts of Eastern Bokhara, he secretly nurtured his own ambitious plan of organizing a vast "Central Asian Modern State." Dreaming the sweet dream of recreating, under his rule, the great glory of ancient Maverannger, he entered into communication with Fergana, Samarkand, Khiva, in an attempt to induce the Basmach bands operating in those regions to coöperate in a unified plan of action. He appealed to the chauvinism of the upper classes and the religious fanaticism of the masses by urging the principle of Central Asia for the Central Asians and by evoking visions of "A Great Central-Asian Moslem State." As against the Communist slogan: "Workers of the World Unite," Enver ingeniously coined the analogous slogan: "Moslems of the World Unite."

His ultimate ambition was, by uniting Bokhara, Russian and Chinese Turkestan, Afghanistan, and Kazakstan, to create a vast Pan-Turanian Empire that would deliver a final death blow to the British Empire. Feeling his growing strength, Enver Pasha became contemptuous of the Red Army, and overbearing in his attitude toward the Soviet Régime. He began to make political demands and issue ultimata. In a message to T. Akchurin, who then served in Baisun as the representative of the Soviet Government of Bokhara, Enver demanded the immediate withdrawal of the Red Army. The message, signed by "Said Enver the Vice-Chalif," by Ibrahim Bek and two other Basmach leaders, read as follows:

> To the Representative of the Bolsheviks in the City of Baisun.
> We, the representatives of the peoples inhabiting the territory of the real independent Bokhara, declare

to you, that after crossing the Baisun river, we have reached the unanimous decision to keep up our fight until we have forced you to evacuate our country. To avoid unnecessary bloodshed, we, moved by humanitarian reasons, are hereby proposing that you immediately leave our land. If you comply with our demand, we shall be your friends and we shall help you to escape starvation. If not, you shall perish as your families are perishing in your starving country. We hesitate to spill human blood. But we deem it our sacred duty to fight those who have broken into our country against the wishes of our people. We shall be happy to shed our own blood and to die as martyrs fighting for our cause.

Enver's inspiring leadership sent a thrill of joy through the Basmach forces. The chieftains everywhere were becoming ever more defiant, ever more aggressive. Echoes of his slogans are discernible in every Basmach proclamation of that period. Here is a fascinating, though wretchedly written, Basmach document sent as a reply to the representative of the Bokharan Government, by three important Basmach leaders, one of whom had at one time been a prominent Djadid and a valiant fighter against the Emir's régime:

Accept our greetings. The Lord be praised, we are in good health.

We have received your senseless letter, and are quite surprised by your strange attention. In your letter you write: "Since the beginning you had worked mightily for the Bokharan Revolution, but just as we were considering advancing you to a very important military post, you, misled by the presentations of certain unscrupulous people, deserted us. Come back. Your mistakes shall be forgiven." Such consideration from you is indeed surprising; for was it not you who, with the aid of your Bolshevik brothers from Russia, invaded the land of Bokhara, shed the blood of the people (nation) and forever destroyed the gold and the bread, in short, the entire necessary wealth of the people, trampled upon our holy places, such as our mosques and our *mederesse,* taken, with the aid of the *Cheka,* from the poor population both property and lives, calling them bureaucrats, counter-revolutionists, kulaks, and *burjuis?* Was it not you who undertook the carrying out of the idea of Bolshevism and Communism?

For a mere piece of bread you have sold out to the cursed Russians your religion, your faith, your conscience. The Russian Bolsheviks have brought oppression and suffering upon Bokhara. There was much talk about Bokharan independence, but in reality there was no such thing in fact. That was why one of the old Bokharan revolutionists, the hero Usman Khodzhaiev, despite his having been President of the Bokharan Republic, declared open war against the Russian consul and you. He could not bear the yoke. I, one of the sons of our country, in the name of the welfare and progress of our land, have heroically fought and shall continue to fight the Russian Bolsheviks and traitors like yourselves.

Not one of the sons of Noble Bokhara—the real heroes of our nation—will ever accept your vile ideas, will ever sell his honor and his conscience.

To-day we behold the people of Bokhara, one and a half million strong, within city walls and in the mountains, passionately wielding their swords, fighting the enemies of our nation. And we, side by side with the true sons of our sweet fatherland, will fight against you, Communists, for independence and prosperity. We are not brigands, but true and humble servants of our nation. We shall drive the Russian enemies from our country, and shall rid ourselves from them forever. Our ideas and our paths are, blessed be God, genuine; and our work is hourly unfolding without a hitch. Arms in their hands, from all sides, Moslems are voluntarily joining us, eager to take part in the holy war, zealous in the struggle to liberate Islam and the Moslems. Everything favors the victory of Islam, and we are confident that soon we shall purge our sweet fatherland by destroying the faithless and ignominious ones.

You also write in your letter: "If you fail to heed our proposal, we shall show you our strength and our ability to fight." This assertion of yours is precisely what we earnestly wish. We are always ready to battle against you; for all the guns and cannons of your comrades, victory depends on God. Whomever He chooses, he is the victor. Never and under no circumstances shall we evade battle with you; we shall ever advance.

Dear ones! Forgive our advice. Before it is too late, join us and earn our nation's gratitude, work in the ranks of the soldiers of Islam, so that history may record the popularity of your names.

We wish you good health.

If you wish to be at one with the soldiers of Islam, chase the Russians out of our sweet land. Then we shall work together for the glory of our fatherland. This is our only wish.

      Respectfully,
THE BOKHARA REVOLUTIONIST KARRY ABDULLA
NURKUL BATYR
DANIAL—BEK OLLIKBASHI.

The confusion of nationalist and pan-Islamist aspirations which their epistle reveals is typical. Even more typical is the insistence on Bolshevik and Russian identity. In view of the support the Basmachi willingly received from the Russian counter-revolutionists, the sincerity of the Basmach leaders is open to serious doubt.

Here a Moslem Saint is Buried

But to return to the principal heroes of our narrative. Enver's phenomenal success in unifying the Basmach forces began to overshadow the achievements of Ibrahim Bek. This made Ibrahim feel rather resentful. Moreover, Enver's strength was such that he had become the veritable ruler of Eastern Bokhara. This, naturally, made the Emir feel rather uneasy. Personal ambition, jealousy, intrigue began to undermine the unity that seemed to have been attained. Ibrahim Bek kept on complaining to the Emir about his rival, while the Emir, distrusting yet fearing Enver, pursued a double-faced policy. On the one hand, in his official communications to Enver he was ordering Ibrahim's unqualified submission to the "Commander in Chief"; on the other, he was issuing secret orders to Ibrahim to keep close watch over Enver Pasha's activities and to hinder him from gaining excessive power. Continuous friction between the two leaders finally resulted in an open clash. At one time Enver seized Ibrahim and kept him under arrest for five days.

As everywhere else in the Soviet Union, in Bokhara, too, counter-revolution, devoid of constructive ideas, always retrospective, always dreaming of a resuscitated feudal and religious past, could not for long retain the loyalty of the masses. Their phrases about Moslem unity, about "our people," about national independence, etc., etc., were bound to reveal their hopeless unreality when exposed to the acid test of actual practice.

In spite of themselves, often completely unaware of it, the masses are inevitably affected by the impact of revolution. What seemed unquestionable, is challenged and exposed. What seemed eternal, lies shattered in the dust. What in ordinary times would take them decades to learn, the masses now discover in a flash, a few weeks, in a few days. What appeared tolerable, even desirable, for centuries, suddenly begins to appear monstrous and absurd. In the glare of the revolution lies are exploded, tinsel ripped off, sham exposed. Revolution brings untold suffering, but it also brings luminous hope. And herein lies its strength. Revolution may be temporarily put down; it cannot permanently be crushed. The seeds it throws into the souls of men germinate, expand and finally burst forth into the open once more.

The spirit of revolution had swept over Central Asia, and no power on earth could permanently arrest its revivifying influence. Enver Pasha, for all his daring and brilliance, was ultimately powerless against it. Where fundamentals were concerned, he was not much above his associates and rivals. Essentially a dyed-in-the-wool reactionary, in the long run he proved impotent in the face of the revolution. He could not, even if he had wished to, free himself from the fetters of his class and the obsolete social and economic ideas of his adherents. Wherever he went, all the evils of the Emir's régime sprang back to life. The same old officials, the same old corruption. Despotism as cruel and stupid as that of the Emir. High-handed treatment of the peasants in the villages. Requisitions, seizures of property, abduction of women. But things that the poor and middle peasant had once viewed as normal, they now, unconsciously responsive to the spirit of the times, began to consider travesties. The striking contrast between the comradely, honest, conciliatory behavior of the Soviet authorities and the Red Army, and the supercilious, provocative, and lawless conduct of the Basmach leaders and Basmach troops could not but result in a change of the peasant's heart. Village after village began to turn against the Basmachi. Peasant delegations begging for the immediate liquidation of the Basmachi in their localities were by now a usual occurrence at Soviet headquarters. Peasant coöperation with the Red Army was almost the rule. The Basmach movement was cracking on all sides. The once irresistible Enver Pasha was meeting with reverses. His Basmach bands were losing battle after battle. The Red Army was advancing on all fronts. The "Commander in Chief" of the Moslem forces began to lose his prestige. Wholesale desertions started. Ibrahim Bek now broke with Enver Pasha and withdrew to Lokai where he organized an uprising against his erstwhile chief. Another important chieftain, Maxum-Faizula, withdrew his forces to Karategin. Enver Pasha was isolated. Pressed by the Red Army, he retreated to Kuliab, where he had hoped to recuperate and make his last stand. But seeing his forces melt away and sensing impending disaster, Enver Pasha hastily retreated toward the Afghan border.

There, in one of the mountain defiles between Baljuan and Khovaling, Enver, on the eve of his departure, met in secret conclave the more important chieftains and their followers who were still loyal to him. It was August 4, 1922—a little over a year since Enver had first appeared in Central Asia lured by a glowing vision of a pan-Turanian

Empire and driven by a great thirst to avenge himself upon Kemal, the British, the Bolsheviks and all his other enemies. He was reluctant to admit even to himself the extent of his defeat. He would go to Afghanistan, he would arouse the Moslem world, he would come back at the head of a great Moslem crusade against the Bolsheviks. Meanwhile let his chieftains fight on; woe to him who betrayed the cause!

And just as Enver, in the midst of his men, was reaching the height of his eloquence in depicting the glorious Moslem future, he espied a Red Army detachment winding its way down the narrow mountain pass. A fierce battle ensued. Both sides fought desperately. Enver, distinguished from the loose-gowned native chieftains by his snappy military outfit and his fine bearing, behaved like a real hero. He fought to the very last, shouting commands, rallying his men. But it was to no avail.

When the battle was over, Enver's body, riddled with bullets, was found lying under his wounded horse. His personal possessions can now be seen in the military museum at Tashkent. His body, according to the natives, is buried on top of a lonely mountain. But this is apocryphal. Actually his grave is unknown. "Some queer fellow," remarks Khodzhibaiev in his book on Tadjikistan, "has placed in Sarikhosorom on the spot where Enver was killed, a tall pole with a little white flag attached to it," which means here a Moslem saint is buried. . . .

Thus came to an end the turbulent career of one of the most spectacular adventurers of modern times.

A Ticket to Heaven

After the death of Enver Pasha, the Emir began to look around for some one of equal stature to take charge of the Basmach movement. His choice finally fell on Khadzha-Samibey, better known as Selim-Pasha, one of Enver Pasha's friends and colleagues. But Selim-Pasha had neither the magnetic personality, nor the prestige, nor the military talents of his predecessor. The Basmach chieftains, especially Ibrahim Bek, refused to accept him as their Commander-in-Chief. His military plans were ignored, his orders disobeyed, and he himself, deserted by the rank and file Basmachi who were too busy gathering in their harvest from the fields, was hard pressed by the Red forces to the River Pianj. There on the steep shore of the turbulent Pianj, addressing a vast crowd of Tadjik peasants—men, women, and children—gathered from the surrounding villages, Selim-Pasha, mounted on his beautiful white horse, delivered, according to legend, the following impassioned message:

"Oh, brave and good Tadjik people! Enver Pasha and I were the messengers of Allah. You know not why you have lost your pious Emir. Nor do you know why we were the victors before, and are the vanquished now. The reason is that men of evil spirit have appeared in your midst, men who submit not to authority, men who attack the very foundation of the holy law. Angered with you, Allah has taken from you the good Emir and has cursed you with a host of infidel Djadids and Bolsheviks. We were victorious when you obeyed our call and followed the ways of Islam. We are being beaten, because your sons are being lured away by those evil people who scoff at our holy shariat and at ancient rights of property. I am going now to join Enver, who is among the faithful, in heaven, surrounded by houris and ineffable pleasures. I am going there. And if you too wish to join us in heaven, bridle your sons, respect the holy law, fight for the sheriat against the Bolsheviks, the Djadids, the infidels."

On concluding his speech, Selim spurred his white horse and hurled himself into the abyss below, into the roaring, gray waters of the Pianj. For a moment his head appeared above the water, and then it was gone.

The deaths of Enver Pasha and Selim-Pasha, and the Red Army's occupation of three important Basmach strongholds in Matchi, Karategin, and Darvaz, forced the frightened Emir and his chieftains to exert every ounce of energy to consolidate their forces for further resistance and for regaining the confidence of the peasant masses without whose active support no serious struggle against the Bolsheviks was possible.

No one was more aware of the need of winning the masses than Ibrahim Bek, who had by this time become the leader, not only of the Uzbek, but also of the Tadjik Basmach forces. Adopting and distorting the Bolshevik method of agitation and propaganda among the masses, Ibrahim, with the fervid assistance of the clergy and the counter-revolutionary intelligentsia, showered the country with proclamations, manifestoes, promises, threats, imprecations.

Heroic slogans such as "Death at the hands of a Red Army man is a ticket to Heaven," or "Fight the Infidels: If you die, you die a martyr-hero; if you live, you remain a saint" were shouted in the streets, from the roofs of mosques, in the market places.

Letters from Emir Alim Khan, genuine and forged, promising money, promising arms, promising heaven on earth if he came back to his people, were spread by the thousands.

In one of such letters, perhaps forged, the Emir wrote:

> My Monarchical greetings to all My military officers and fighters in the ranks, as well as to all the plain residents—be they Nogais, Uzbeks, Tadjiks, or Soviet employees. Finding Ourselves against Our will far away from Our fatherland and Our people, I and My friends are greatly grieved and are doing everything in Our power to lighten the burdens of the terrible misfortune that has befallen you and to help you in your struggle against the Bolsheviks.
>
> However, the Commission I had sent out to inspect Our Moslem troops, has brought back tidings that rob Me of My sleep. It has reached Me that My people have lost faith in Our final victory, and are receiving the Russians with a great show of cordiality. Impress this on every one—such behavior is arch treason, and those guilty of it will meet with dire punishment. It has also reached Me that some of My fighters in the holy war are unfaithful to their sacred

vows and are deserting to the enemy. These traitors are leading Our people away from victory, are leading them to destruction.

There is no reason to doubt Our final victory. I have had conversations with the Europeans who live in Kabul and who have taken an interest in Our affairs. They have promised to sell Me rifles at the price of one sheep per old rifle and two sheep per new one. They also promised to aid Our armies by sending five hundred airplanes which are due to arrive here any moment. Also inform My people that the Soviet Government is at present in very bad straits. It has been attacked by the English, French and Chinese armies, which are already near Moscow. Just hold out a little while longer. The end of the Bolsheviks is near. Let every one join the armies of Islam, always bearing in mind that the field of a holy battle lies on the road to paradise. Believe that everything I say is the holy truth.

Emir of Bokhara Said-Mir-Alim-Khan. Kabul, 1343, Shoval 26.

Ibrahim also organized an excellent system of espionage. Everywhere, in each city, in each village he had agents—kulaks, mullahs, traitorous Soviet officials—who kept him informed of every intention or plan of the Soviet authorities. The population of Eastern Bokhara, the peasantry, was paying for all this. Recalcitrant tax-payers were brutally punished. In such cases Ibrahim Bek resorted to wholesale executions. The reign of terror instituted by Ibrahim in Eastern Bokhara lasted with varying degrees of intensity well into the year 1925.

Consolidating Forces

The protracted military struggle against the Basmachi consumed so much of the young Republic's energy that relatively little strength was left for attempting anything else. Ambitious programs, and plans, and resolutions were proposed and adopted, but these were for the most part only excellent intentions, registered on official paper, and made to appear important by the application of the government seal. Still, by the end of 1922—after the Party purge—systematic efforts at economic rehabilitation were actually on the way: the exchange of commodities between the city and the village was considerably improved; state trading centers were at work; a number of commercial enterprises with the participation of private capital were launched; both the export to Russia of raw products—cotton, wool, caracul, silk—and the import from Russia of some manufactured products were definitely on the increase; the Bokharan State Bank was opened; an apparatus for the collection of taxes was devised and was already in operation; the first practical steps toward regulating currency emission and establishing a fixed state budget were made.

Towards the middle of 1923, two more banks, in addition to the Bokharan State Bank, were doing a brisk business—the Central Asian Commercial and Agricultural Banks. The total capital of the three banks was then about 10,000,000 gold rubles.

State revenues, insignificant in 1921, had grown to slightly over 2,000,000 rubles in 1922, and to 8,000,000 in 1923. In 1923 the Bokhara-Termez Railroad, which had been destroyed by the Basmachi, was rebuilt. Telegraph and telephone communications were reëstablished. Over 1,000,000 gold rubles were spent in repairing the damages done by the Basmachi in the cities of Bokhara, Kermin, Karshi, Denau, etc. Also, a great deal was done during this period in reconstructing irrigation canals in districts not exposed to Basmach ravages, and in stimulating cotton-growing and cattle-raising.

Considering the difficulties, an enormous amount of work was accomplished also in the fields of education and sanitation. In education the policy was to open as many Soviet schools as possible. More than illiteracy (96 per cent of Bokharans were illiterate) the new government feared the influence of the old schools conducted by the mullahs. To stimulate interest in the new education, the government found it necessary to grant privileges, exemptions, and even monetary compensations to parents who agreed to send their children to Soviet schools. A few teachers' training schools were opened. Also courses were organized to train natives for various political, economic, and cultural jobs. Two million rubles, i.e., 28 per cent of the State revenues, were spent on education in 1923. During the same year, the USSR asigned 24 medical specialists, 136 general practitioners, and 154 nurses to Bokhara. A number of medical clinics and pharmacies was opened. Large quantities of drugs were imported from Russia and Germany. The most remarkable achievement in the field of sanitation was the opening of the now famous Institute of Tropical Medicine. (It is due to the work of this Institute that malaria, the bane of Bokhara's existence, has been practically eliminated in the city and considerably reduced throughout the country.)

The work of the Government took a sharp turn toward greater effectiveness immediately after the first joint Conference of the Central Asian Republics in 1923. One result of that Conference was the thoroughgoing inspection of all the State and Party bureaus with the consequent intensification in the weeding out of hundreds of saboteurs, traitors, provocateurs, and other dubious characters who had clogged the governmental machine. Another result was the reorganization of all the economic departments of Bokhara with the aid of some of the best and most experienced workers brought in from Turkestan. Chaos began to be harnessed. Economic and political life was entering upon its normal course.

The most significant result of three years of fighting the Basmachi was the inexorable and ever-accelerating process of class differentiation in the cities and villages of Western and Central Bokhara. From an attitude of antagonism or neutrality, the poor and middle peasants, disillusioned in the Basmachi and their nationalist and religious slogans, were gradually swinging into an attitude of active sympathy with the revolution and its purposes. More and more they were drawn into the revolutionary ranks, coöperating with the Red Army, organizing their own fighting detachments, arming themselves with clubs when better weapons were not available, and scouring the mountains in pursuit of the Basmachi. By 1923 there was a large and well-functioning organization of poor and middle peasants—the Peasants' Union—that was doing a great deal of work in crystallizing the peasants' hatred for the beys, the kulaks, the reactionary mullahs. Counter-revolution, despite its fierce resistance, was beginning to retreat, to yield ground.

In the cities, too, a similar process was taking place. A country that had scarcely known of organized labor had within three years created a number of labor unions, unions of builders, teachers, weavers, unskilled workers, and artisans. In 1923 there were only about 12,000 members in these unions. But their members were the most advanced and respected in the laboring population of the country. Their influence in revolutionizing the masses was enormous.

Bolshevik Technique

At last the government was in a position to pay a little more attention to the Basmach-ridden sections in the East, along the Afghan and Indian borders. But because of the absence of roads and other means of communication, segregating it from the rest of the Soviet Union, Eastern Bokhara was not only exposed to Basmach operations generated within the country but also to the ravages of brigand bands organized across the borders. It was no accident that Enver Pasha, Selim-Pasha, and a host of other adventurers chose Eastern Bokhara as the center of their anti-Soviet activities.

Life in Eastern Bokhara was so precarious that whole regions had become completely depopulated. Peasants abandoned their homes and sought refuge in the mountains. About 43,000 peasant families with stock, cattle and implements fled to Afghanistan. As a result of the disturbed conditions, the sown area in Eastern Bokhara was reduced by 72 per cent, the cattle by 60 per cent, the population by 25 per cent. The country was ruined and starving.

Everything was in a state of chaos. Nominally Soviet territory, Eastern Bokhara had no Soviet or any other kind of government. Revolutionary committees, composed almost exclusively of Russians not sufficiently familiar with local conditions, existed only where detachments of the Red Army were stationed. Under such circumstances little if anything could be done by the committees in establishing contacts with the population, in spreading the revolutionary message, in winning over the peasantry by wise economic, political, and cultural measures.

The position of the revolutionists in Eastern Bokhara was indeed difficult. To attempt anything constructive, they had to eliminate the Basmachi; to eliminate the Basmachi, they had to win the masses; and to win the masses, they had to do something constructive.

Refusing to be confounded, the Bokharan government finally (July, 1923) took the bull by both horns. Fighting the Basmachi and constructive work, it was decided, must be done simultaneously. The task was entrusted to an especially appointed Revolutionary Council consisting of a Military Chief and a Political Adviser, and presided over by a leading Bokharan Communist, Faizulla Khodzhaiev. The main problem was the Sovietization of this heretofore neglected region. Concomitantly with a succession of well-considered military strokes, the Council proceeded to lay the foundations of Civil Government. The entire region was divided into central and local administrative units, each unit under the control of a Revolutionary Committee.

The task of organizing those administrative units was an onerous one. Even under the Emir there were fewer capable administrators and executives in the Eastern section of the Khanate than in Bokhara proper. The revolution further depleted their numbers. Of those that remained, an infinitesimal minority could be relied on to fit the inchoate will of the masses into the clear purposes of the Bolsheviks. Most of the old and experienced officials were definitely anti-Soviet. Those few who were not wholly inimical were too ignorant of the theory and practice of Communism and insufficiently attuned to the pulse of the revolution. To be sure, there were some Russians available. But if not contrary to Bolshevik principles, the putting of Russians into conspicuous places in Bokhara, and particularly in the troubled Eastern section, would be highly impolitic. It would expose to misinterpretation the Russians' motives. Accordingly, all the lime-light posts on the Revolutionary Committees were therefore given to natives believed to be in sympathy with the revolution. To prevent serious distortions of policy, members of the Communist Party, generally tried revolutionists from more highly cultivated Moslem peoples—Tartars from the Volga, Turkomans from Baku—were placed in unostentatious, but highly strategic positions. This had the desired effect. In addition to insuring relatively consistent Bolshevik policies, it gave the natives a sense of self-government and removed the possible suspicion of Russian chauvinism. The presence of Tartars and Turkomans in the government was salutary also in that such officials, being themselves members of minority Moslem peoples, were more apt to grasp the problems and enter into the psychology of the natives.

A great deal was done to improve the economic life of Eastern Bokhara. Bazaars were revived, manufactured products imported, agricultural products purchased by the government. Branches of all the departments of the government of Bokhara were established in Dushambe. From Turkestan and the Caucasus contingents of experienced organizers of labor and peasant unions, of coöperatives, of industry and commerce were despatched to Eastern Bokhara. In recognition of old attachments and loyalties, a series of local, tribal (Lokai, etc.), and national (Tadjik, Uzbek, Kirghiz, etc.) congresses was called, where current economic, administrative, and cultural problems were taken up and thrashed out. In September, 1923, the first modern Soviet School opened in Dushambe, and shortly after a Soviet school was started in Karatag and then in Kuliab.

The government was so determined to rally the entire people against the Basmachi that it took every care to neutralize the opposition of the rich by respecting their property rights and to win the support of the clergy by sparing their religious sensibilities. The mosque was not touched. The mullahs were not criticized. Religion was either left severely alone or shown every sign of deference. Bolshevik tolerance finally reached such a point here that the Moslem divines were actually drawn into making pro-Soviet declarations and assailing the Basmachi.

After several months of intensive work, the situation in Eastern Bokhara underwent a basic change. The peasants, weary of lawlessness and bloodshed, were glad to return to a settled life. They were coming back from the mountains in hordes. Assured of the government's readiness to overlook past sins, Basmach bands, one after another, began to surrender their arms and return to peaceful labor. Ibrahim Bek's prestige fell so low that he adopted trickery and magic to preserve a semblance of authority with the masses. A Tadjik collective farmer, who in 1924 had been a basmach under Ibrahim Bek, told me the following story: "Once when things appeared particularly hopeless for our band, Ibrahim Bek in the presence of a couple of hundred mutinous followers, rose from his gold-embroidered carpet and slowly and solemnly advanced toward a tall lonely tree. He fell on his knees and pronounced a long and devout prayer. Then he rose and, muttering something to himself, put his ear to the trunk of the innocently rustling tree. The performance lasted about half an hour. The face of Ibrahim was so austere and so concentrated that a great awe fell upon the people. When everything was wrapped in dead silence, Ibrahim, his eyes burning with an intense flame, turned to his men and in a ringing voice announced: 'I have just spoken to the Emir and the head of the English army. They have given me their word of honor that within a few days they will send here a countless number of cavalry and infantry.' The mutinous brigands were subdued."

Nothing but desperation could have driven Ibrahim to such dangerous tricks. Seeing that the Tadjik masses were turning definitely against him, he was hoping against hope that a miracle would happen, and that "countless numbers of cavalry and infantry" would come from the hills of Afghanistan and save him from his plight. To raise funds, he tried to sell all kinds of high-sounding titles; but the naïve Tadjiks would not be lured. The villagers now became adamant in refusing Ibrahim provisions. Enraged, he would swoop down upon a village, seize everything he could lay his hands on, slay any one who dared to object, and flee back into the hills. But neither magic, nor titles, nor murder could help him. He was doomed. Counterrevolution in Eastern Bokhara, though not entirely wiped out, was now definitely on the decline.

Showing Way to Millions

The years 1924-1925 brought to a close the second phase of the Bokharan Revolution. It is not within the province of this book to detail the progress of Soviet Bokhara year by year. Perhaps a few figures taken from the report submitted by the Government before the Fifth All-Bokharan Congress, will help the reader in forming some idea of Bokhara's achievements during this period. The cotton area was increased 100 per cent in comparison with 1923. The total sown area jumped from 380,000 to 425,000 hectares. The value of agricultural production in 1924 was 45,000,000 rubles, of cattle-raising, 7,000,000. Over 2,180,000 rubles were spent restoring the system of irrigation. In 1923-1924, the imports amounted to 7,500,000 and exports to 10,500,000; in 1924-1925 it was planned to increase imports to 15,000,000, and exports to 20,000,000. The number of branches of government commercial enterprises increased from 25 in 1923 to 98 in 1924.

After citing similarly striking figures with regard to

banking, road building, education, sanitation, social insurance, etc., the government report concludes as follows:

> Such are the results of the government's activities. The results, though noteworthy, cannot of course satisfy us except as a beginning. We took hold of a country that had been devastated by the Emir. What the Emir's régime bequeathed to us was all-pervading economic decay, a pauperized peasantry, universal illiteracy, backwardness, bigotry. That we are the first to begin to build this country may under the circumstances be considered a just cause for pride. It is difficult. In spite of the difficulties and the incessant fighting, we have managed to carry out, in part at least, the task laid upon us—to build, to organize, to defeat the enemy, and, what is most important, to steadily lay the foundation of the country's prosperity, to improve our economic structure and better the conditions of the workers and peasants. Under the leadership of the Communist Party of Bokhara our toiling masses in their recent victories have not only shown their strength to their former oppressors but have also pointed out a way to the millions of the oppressed peoples in the East.

It was clear that, on the whole, Soviet Bokhara, helped by the proletariat of the other Soviet Republics and guided by Marxist-Leninist theory, was pursuing more or less a socialist course.

In evaluating the work of the government, the delegates to the Congress had to answer for themselves these questions: Had the government been creating some of the prerequisites for building a socialist order in Bokhara? Had the growth of the productive forces of the country been accelerated? Who had been molding and directing the Republic's economic and cultural policies—the capitalists and landlords and imperialists for their own profit, or the vanguard of the workers and poor peasants for the benefit of the whole working population? Whose were the Soviets? Whose the courts? Whose the schools? Whose the militia (police)? Whose the army?

The answers were obvious. Indeed, the delegates were

so impressed with the constructive achievements of the government that they moved that the word "Socialist" be added to the official name of the Republic. By a unanimous vote, the Congress declared Bokhara a Socialist Soviet Republic.

A Wrong Made Right

The addition of the word "Socialist" to the name of the relatively primitive, industrially backward Soviet Republic of Bokhara was exceedingly significant. It marked the ideological growth of the native leaders, their acceptance of the basic thesis of the Bolshevik Party as to the socialist character of the Bolshevik Revolution and their readiness finally to join the Union of Socialist Soviet Republics.

Besides the liberation of labor, however, and the struggle for a coöperative commonwealth, the word "Socialist" also stands for the end of all national oppression. It has been previously pointed out that Bokhara's relations with what was once Great Russia—the backbone of Czarist imperialism—had been amicably settled by the agreements of 1921.

Those agreements were derived from the basic Marxist propositions that national inequality is a result of historically conditioned economic inequality and that the essence of the national question consists in the minority nationalities' overcoming the backwardness they inherited from the past and catching up with the more advanced countries in a political, cultural, economic, and every other sense.

Accordingly, instead of enhancing Great Russian domination, the Russian Bolsheviks have always regarded it their task to help the working masses of the other, the non-Great Russian nations, to overtake Central Russia which, owing to historical causes, had gone ahead of them. The first step in that direction was "to organize industrial centers in the republics of the formerly oppressed nations and to attract the greatest possible number of *local* workers to these industries." The prerequisite, the real carrier of a socialist revolution anywhere is the proletariat, and the only way to have a growing native proletariat in Bokhara was to accelerate the development of native industries. The ultimate solution of the national problem, the Russian and Bokharan Bolsheviks knew, would be in developing the productive forces of the country under the hegemony, not of the bourgeoisie, but of the proletariat, i.e., under a proletarian dictatorship.

But in 1924 the national problem in Bokhara had another, purely local, aspect: the strained relations among the various peoples who had for centuries lived in mutual antagonism under the Emir.

The Bokharan revolution for instance did not immediately remove the dangerous signs of Uzbek chauvinism bequeathed by the old régime. "We are all Bokharans," reiterated the Uzbek revolutionists enthusiastically. By insisting on this all-inclusive "Bokharans," which to them was synonymous with "Uzbeks," they were obviously yielding to the temptation of attenuating national differences by denying their existence. However, the national minorities who had for centuries been oppressed by the Uzbek Emir declined to view the matter in the same light. The slogan of self-determination of peoples had burned itself into the souls of men. The revolution had promised self-determination of peoples, and the Kazaks, Tadjiks, Turkomans and Kirghiz had taken these promises seriously. Rather than attenuate, they tended to exaggerate national distinctions. They resented Uzbek supremacy and clamored for national autonomy, national governments.

The problem was further complicated by the fact that the individual nationalities comprising Bokhara inhabited not only Bokhara but the other Central Asian Soviet Republics. The majority of the Khorezm (Khiva) Republic, for instance, was Uzbek. Some sections of the Turkestan Republic were settled by Uzbeks, others by Tadjiks, still others by Turkomans, and still others by Kirghiz. This was the evil legacy of Central Asia's past.

Throughout the first period Soviet Bokhara made perennial attempts to adjust the growing national tangle within its borders. In 1923, the Bokharan government had called special congresses to discuss the economic and cultural problems of the various national minorities living within the confines of the Bokharan Republic. There was a Kirghiz Congress, and a Kazak Congress, and a Turkoman Congress. The government had organized special regional and district departments to carry on work among these peoples. The Central Executive Committee of the Republic had formed a special Turkoman section which, besides attending to the economic and cultural needs of the Turkomans in Bokhara, was also engaged in administrative and representational work. As to the Tadjiks, they were too busy fighting with or against the Basmachi to attempt anything constructive along the lines of national self-determination.

The vain efforts of the government to maintain peace among the various nationalities inhabiting Bokhara proved definitely that the only efficacious remedy for the evil of chauvinism would be the breaking up of Bokhara, as well as the other Central Asian Soviet states, into small national units, and the reassembling of those units into distinct national Republics, on the basis of ethnic, cultural, and national kinship. The idea of National Soviet Republics met with the enthusiastic approval of the vast majority of the population in Central Asia. Since however such reorganization would involve large sections belonging to the Soviet Union (Turkestan for instance), it became imperative that Bokhara too become a part of the USSR. The fact that she declared herself a Socialist Soviet Republic made her eligible for membership.

Accordingly, the same All-Bokhara Congress (September 20, 1924) which declared Bokhara a Socialist Republic passed the following historic decision:

> National development on soviet principles demands the union of the laboring classes of all nations on a united soviet territory in order to secure their economic and political development and to promote cultural-national construction.

The national movement in this spirit and for such purposes has spread throughout Bokhara, embracing the largest part of the laboring masses. A single will is manifest here: to unite the separate parts into one national unit, to give to the nations the soviet state formation.

These aims are expressed also by the fraternal peoples outside of the frontiers of the Bokhara People's Soviet Republic. A united general impulse embraces the laboring population of Bokhara, Turkestan, and Khorezm.

The will of the laboring people is the law of the soviet state. By virtue of this, the Fifth All-Bokhara Congress of Soviets solemnly declares:

(1) The supreme will of the peoples of Bokhara—the Uzbeks and Tadjiks—is the creation by them, together with the Uzbeks of Turkestan and Khorezm, of the Uzbek Socialist Soviet Republic, a part of which is formed by the Autonomous Region of Tadjiks.

(2) Fraternal agreement on the entering of the Turkoman people of Bokhara into the composition of the Turkoman Socialist Soviet Republic.

(3) States the absolute necessity for Socialist Uzbekistan and Turkmenistan to join the Union of Soviet Socialist Republics for the purpose of socialist construction, protection against imperialism, and in virtue of international fraternity of the laboring masses.

Go ahead, brothers and comrades, against the national hostility and subjugation by the bourgeoisie, for the liberation of Eastern peoples, for the dictatorship of the proletariat, and for communism!

For the Congress: Presidium of the Fifth All-Bokhara Congress of Soviets.

After similar resolutions had been passed by the other Republics involved—Khorezm (Khiva) and Turkestan—the Central Executive Committee of the USSR, recognizing "that the free expression of the will of the toiling peoples is the supreme law," decreed the formation of the Uzbek and Turkoman states and their admission as constituent members into the Soviet Union, with Samarkand as the capital of the first and Ashkhabad of the second. Eastern

Bokhara was declared to be the Autonomous Soviet Republic of the Tadjiks, with Dushambe, subsequently renamed Stalinabad, as the capital city. Tadjikistan was to remain within the framework of the Uzbek Republic.

Bokhara went through its final transmutation. Disintegration was immediately followed by the reintegration of its national elements into the Uzbek and Tadjik states, each embracing those sections of Central Asia where the majority of the population was respectively either Uzbek or Tadjik. By a process of fission Old Bokhara formed the nuclei of two new states, and by a process of accretion each nucleus grew larger at the expense of old Khiva and Turkestan. Incidentally, there is no more Turkestan or Khiva. After the Tadjik sections of the two Republics were absorbed into Tadjikistan and the Uzbek sections into Uzbekistan, the remainder went partly into Kazakstan and partly into Turkmenistan.

Thus an ancient wrong was made right. "This act," boasts a Soviet geographer, "has had no parallel in history, and has been made possible only in the land of the Soviets, where all nationalities have equal rights and where in perfect conformity with the great principles of the Soviet Government each people is allowed to determine its own destiny."

To the Tadjiks, especially, this change was the realization of a long cherished dream—to develop their own nationality and their own culture within the framework of their own state. "Greetings to Tadjikistan," wired Stalin on that occasion, "greetings to the new toilers' Soviet Republic at the gates of Hindustan. I wish you every success in making your Republic a model for the countries in the East.... Comrades in Tadjikistan, raise the culture of your country, develop your country's economy, help the city and village toilers, draw to yourselves the finest sons of your fatherland, and show to the entire East that you are the best offspring of an ancestry that held steadily to the banner of liberation!"

The announcement of their national liberation and Stalin's warm greetings were received with a tremendous outburst of enthusiasm throughout the land.

> *Do you hear the happy shouting, Tadjikistan?*
> *Your glorious day has come, Tadjikistan!*
>
> *Your day has come! Your day of joy has come,*
> *My wild, rocky, young Tadjikistan!*
>
> *One of a mighty family of peoples,*
> *Your chains are smashed, my land Tadjikistan!*
>
> *For centuries enslaved, now your own master,*
> *Your former rulers gone, Tadjikistan!*
>
> *To the peoples of the East your key has opened*
> *The doors to a new life, O great Tadjikistan!*

PART THREE

COMPLETING THE BOURGEOIS REVOLUTION

"Formerly, the national question was regarded from the reformist point of view; it was regarded as an independent question entirely separated from the general question of capitalist rule, of the overthrow of imperialism and the proletarian revolution. It was tacitly understood that the victory of the proletariat in Europe was possible without a close alliance with the liberation movement in the colonies, that the national colonial question could be solved quietly, "automatically," off the beaten track of the proletarian revolution, entirely separate from the revolutionary struggle with imperialism. To-day we can say that this anti-revolutionary outlook has been exposed. Leninism has proved, and the imperialist war and the revolution in Russia have confirmed it, that the national question can be solved only in connection with and on the basis of the proletarian revolution, and that the road to victory in the West leads through the revolutionary alliance with the liberation movement of the colonies and dependent countries against imperialism. The national question is part and parcel of the general question of the proletarian revolution and of the question of the dictatorship of the proletariat."

—JOSEPH STALIN, *"The National Question," Foundations of Leninism.*

IX

WHERE COTTON IS KING

Tender the gold of the white atlas boon,
Green is the sheen of its robe iridescent
Under the hot gleaming sun of high noon.
—AIDIN SABIROVA, Uzbek Poetess.

White Gold

WHETHER one reads local papers, or listens to orators, or converses with workers, or visits schools, movies, unions, coöperatives, the first word or derivation from that word one is likely to see or hear is *khlopok*—cotton—the "white gold" of Central Asia. People here talk cotton, sing cotton, play cotton, work cotton, study cotton, dream cotton. If you see a Central Asian's face clouded, you may be certain that the sky is clouded, for there is nothing that he fears more than rain in the summer months—rain is the enemy of cotton.

Even the struggle with the counter-revolutionary *Basmachi*, until recently of intense concern to the people of Central Asia, has now receded to a place of secondary importance. And the attention that is still given to the Basmach movement is primarily due to the possible effect it may ultimately have on the cotton crop.

Considerably more than fifty per cent of the agricultural produce of Uzbekistan and Tadjikistan is cotton. The major part of the local industries is in some way connected with cotton. It must not be thought, however, that this consecration to the growing of cotton is true only of these Republics. It is true of the whole of Central Asia. The cotton campaign in these countries is part of a larger plan embracing also the territories of Turkmenistan, Kazakstan, Transcaucasia, and even the Southern section of the Ukraine.

I have before me a pile of Central Asian papers for the year 1931. Nearly every headline and every editorial deals with cotton. I pick at random a few papers, arrange them in chronological sequence, and the whole struggle for cotton unfolds before me. Here is a paper dated June 16th. June is the month of weeding, hilling and digging. Accordingly, a huge headline streaming across five columns announces: "The Comsomol Is the Trusty Sentinel of the Bolshevik Cotton Harvest." Immediately below this headline, in smaller type: "Youth, form into detachments and regiments and join the weeding campaign, place guards and supervisors over each canal, be the foremost fighter and commander in the struggle for a bumper cotton crop." And then: "Time is short. The harvest is in danger. All forces must concentrate on the cotton fields!" Among the other items on the front page: "Failure to appreciate the importance of scientific research in cotton hampers the cotton campaign." "Destroy the winged enemy—the locust." "More attention to our cotton sovkhozy (state farms)!" Needless to say, the two-column editorial is also devoted to cotton.

On July 7th—a similar picture: "The Cotton Plan in Danger." "Our Collectives Show the Best Results." "Shakhrinoy Is Disgracefully Slow." "Banner Handed to Heroes of Bolshevik Spring." "Cotton Independence for the Soviet Union."

August 19th: In August cultivation continues but preparations must be made for picking, transporting, and storing the cotton. Naturally the front pages reflect this: "Not All the Links Are Ready for the Strain of the Cotton Harvest Campaign." "No Preparation for the Cotton Harvest at the Vakhsh." "Kanibadom Leads in Making Ready for the Cotton Harvest." "Railroads Have No Cotton Transport Plan."

September 5th: Gathering in of the harvest has begun. The paper is hysterical. "Within two days everything must be mobilized for cotton harvest—labor, government and

COMPLETING BOURGEOIS REVOLUTION

party machine, store-houses and transport." "The Cotton Plan of the Third Decisive Year of the Piatiletka Must Be Fulfilled!" "Show Bolshevik Tempo!" "To-day, at the Home of the Red Army to Discuss Problems of Cotton Harvest." "The Planters of Aral Adopt a New Cotton-Picking System."

October 20th: Autumn rains are approaching. Haste. Haste. A screaming headline across the entire page: "Throw the Entire Able-Bodied Population into the Cotton Fields." "Six Districts Are Still on the Black List." "Women in the Collective Farms Are Forming Shock Brigades." "The Creeping Pace Must Come to an End!" "The Manager of the State Cotton Farm at Regar must Be Thrown Out."

November 18th: "The Struggle for Cotton Is a Struggle for Socialism." "End the Slow, Irresponsible, Lackadaisical Work at the Cotton Mills." "More Shock-Brigades and Socialist Competition in Our Struggle for the Cotton Plan." "Individual Responsibility for Failure To Join in the Cotton-Picking Campaign." "Agronomist Dolgov Is a Deserter."

Except for the various political, international and cultural items in the inside pages, the newspapers, with all their graphs, figures, calculations, and screaming front page headlines which daily record achievements, losses, and prospects on the cotton front, appear like a queer combination of trade papers and war bulletins.

Though tremendously stimulated by the Soviet Government, the Central Asian's interest in cotton is not new. Cotton of inferior sorts has been grown here for centuries. One of the chief incentives of the czars for extending their imperial power to remote Central Asia was the determination to obtain cotton for Russia. Most of the Russian colonizers of Central Asia were people who in some direct or indirect way were connected with cotton. Central Asian cotton was the basis of the rapid growth of the textile industries in the Northern capitals, and the source of immense private fortunes in Russia.

After 1914, Russia's hunger for cotton increased a hundredfold. Years of war and revolution left millions of people without wearing apparel. Old clothes were worn to shreds, and nothing new was being produced. Imports had been reduced to zero. And when trading with the outside world was resumed, comparatively little gold could be spared for the purchase of clothes. The Soviet Union was determined to build up its industries, and it spent the lion's share of its revenues on production rather than consumption goods. Moreover, the revolution aroused appetites. The workers and peasants of Soviet Russia began to clamor for textiles more loudly than they would have clamored if they had suffered similar privations under the old régime. Again, in the midst of an antagonistic world, the Soviet Union needed an adequate and uninterrupted cotton supply, for in the event of war Russia without cotton would be helpless. Small wonder that the Soviet Union cherishes the ambitious hope of achieving complete independence of the cotton markets of the rest of the world. Small wonder, too, that it puts no end of study and planning and money into cotton. It endeavors to extend the cotton area through vast irrigation and reclamation projects, it induces cotton-growing by lowering taxes on cotton lands, by granting the cotton grower special credits for seed and implements and family maintenance, by selling him bread grains below wholesale cost, by building machine and tractor stations, by building vast government-owned cotton plantations, by encouraging cotton growers' coöperatives and collectives, and so on without end.

White Plague

But just as the Soviet Government is intent on accelerating the development of cotton, so are its enemies set on retarding it. The reader will recall the famous Industrial Party trial held in Moscow in the winter of 1930. He will recall that one of the crucial points in the strategy of those experts, engineers, professors, and economists was to wreck the cotton industry of the Soviet Union. The kulaks and

COMPLETING BOURGEOIS REVOLUTION 173

the beys fought cotton in the villages. The engineers fought it in their offices, concocting absurd irrigation, reclamation, and electrification schemes. The experts, the professors fought it in the State Planning Commission, in the universities, and in the learned journals. For years there raged a ruthless war on the cotton front, war with all its concomitant evils—treason, espionage, sabotage, subtle ideological camouflage. Read such books and articles as *Cotton Cultivation in Turkestan* by V. I. Uferev, or *Agricultural Economy* by N. M. Kozhanov, or *The Hungry Steppe As a Cotton Region* by Yaroshevitch, or *The Technique of Cotton Cultivation* by S. Grigoriev, and finally *Cotton as a Monoculture* by A. A. Fedotov—what a remarkable mélange of insincerity, ambiguity, innuendo, false reasoning, misinformation and cant, all dished out in a sauce of scientific objectivity!

Here is citizen Fedotov, the gray-headed, dignified gentleman who shed bitter tears on the trial stand entreating the proletarian court for mercy, for a chance to live and atone his sins. In 1925 when he was still considered one of the leading cotton experts in the Union and was honored and trusted by the workers' government, the same gentleman, in an effort to cool the Bolsheviks' zeal for cotton, wrote:

"The beautiful sunny South of the United States suffers from the white plague. This is a well-established fact involving the whole population of the South, a region predominantly agricultural. Indeed, cotton, instead of being a blessing, has now become a curse; it certainly has reduced the people's vitality, and every one in that region, old and young, has become the slave of cotton.... Cotton-growing has brought about the pauperization of the agricultural population, it has aggravated the race problem, it has exhausted the best soil in America, it has increased the number of tenant farmers and reduced the number of farm proprietors, and, also, it has led to perennial clashes between the creditors and the soil-tillers. That is not all—we should add spiritual impoverishment. Cotton-growing limits one's interests, limits one's agricultural technique, cramps one's spiritual growth; it renders one narrow, helpless; it makes one a slave...."

Not a word about the surviving feudalism, the cotton plantations, the share-cropping system, the virtual disfranchisement of Negroes in our South. Not a word about capitalism and its concomitant evils. Fedotov attributes all the real and imaginary evils in our South to cotton—cotton is a white plague! But Fedotov would not rely on mere suggestion. He must clinch his argument. He must underscore the lesson:

"The picture I have drawn has meaning also for us.... In our Union, the cotton-grower, however impoverished he may become, can still hope to retain the right to his land; but all the other evils attendant on cotton are quite liable to occur here too.... In Turkestan cotton-growing has been progressing by leaps and bounds. We are justly proud of our achievements when we speak of cotton. But should we have as much reason to be proud were we to examine the situation from another point of view, from the point of view of the well-being of the cotton grower? Since 1921 cotton production in our Union has increased ten-fold. It is reasonable to inquire—has the condition of the cotton grower become ten times better than before? Of course not...."

Similar "subtle" anti-cotton propaganda is found in the other "expert" studies. When, in its fight for cotton, the Soviet Government began to introduce modern machinery into Central Asia, the publishing houses were deluged with "scientific" monographs proving that cotton-growing was incompatible with modern machinery. "Agriculture," wrote one of these authorities—N. M. Kozhanov—"contains a stable, conservative kernel which can never be ground under the wheels of an advancing machine technique—this holds particularly true of an intensive culture, such as cotton."

Another flood of learned treatises was let loose upon an unsuspecting reading public, when the Soviets, further to accelerate their march toward cotton independence, started to build and encourage State and collective cotton farms.

Figures were worked out, graphs drawn, examples adduced —all tending to prove that cotton could be successfully cultivated only on the basis of small-scale farming.

So powerful and all-pervading were these ideological saboteurs that even the Five Year Plan, particularly the first draft, bore unmistakable traces of their influence.

For Cotton—For Socialism!

It has always been a source of wonderment to me how the Soviet Government, in face of the concerted opposition and constant sabotage of the leading cotton experts, has managed to advance so rapidly toward cotton independence.

While at Tashkent, I had had occasion to acquaint myself with the activities of the Central Asian Bureau, a powerful organization whose function it is to plan and coördinate the economic and cultural activities which are of common interest to all the Central Asian Republics— water, cotton, transportation, silk, coal, grain, health. Every phase of the work is directed by a special committee. The cotton committee is the most important of all, being one of the largest and most modern business organizations in the world. Functioning in many ways like any capitalistic business enterprise, its distinguishing feature is the fact that it is Soviet owned. As the cotton monopoly of the Soviet Government, the Committee wields tremendous influence and power. It contracts for all the cotton grown in Central Asia; it owns and controls all the cotton-ginning plants and cottonseed oil factories in the region. It has its own scientific research stations, where methods of irrigation, fertilization, and seed selections are studied and on which more than a million dollars a year is spent. It conducts its own gigantic farms where the selected seed for the peasants is produced. It has an experimental factory for trying out new machines and methods of cotton manufactures, cotton-ginning, etc. It has its own large plant for the production of cotton gins, and its own construction department for putting up new factories. It has training schools for cotton experts, and it teaches the peasants to grow cotton of a higher and more standardized quality than we are growing in America. Subject to the revision of the Economic Council of the Soviet Union, the Cotton Committee, in agreement with the growers' coöperatives, fixes the prices which the government, the sole purchaser of cotton in the entire Union, pays to the Central Asian peasants.

The several Central Asian Republics, working hand in hand with the Cotton Committee, carry on a ceaseless barrage of cotton propaganda. As a result of this propaganda and of the numerous measures calculated to stimulate cotton-growing, the Soviet Union can show the following figures: In 1924 the whole cotton area in the Soviet Union measured 447,000 hectares; in 1925, 591,000; in 1926, 654,000; in 1927, 765,000; in 1928, 925,000; in 1929, 1,055,000; in 1930, 1,632,000. In 1931 the plan was to exceed the 2 million mark, and for 1933 to reach the 3 million mark.

Every worker and peasant has the slogan "Cotton Independence" continually dinned into his ears. "The imperialists are raising barriers against our export trade. The imperialists are trying to interfere with the realization of our Five-Year Plan. They are arming to the teeth plotting another war against our Socialist Fatherland. Our answer is: 'Cotton Independence!' "

There are other reasons. The sowing and picking of cotton, as well as the steady attention it requires throughout the entire summer, make cotton culture an excellent absorbent of labor power. A ton of raw cotton probably represents more human labor power than a ton of any other farm product. Clearly, in Central Asia, with its great scarcity of land, cotton planting offers the most economical way of utilizing a possible labor surplus.

Another consideration is the economic benefits resulting from what may be termed "regional specialization," i.e., regions that are most adapted to the growing of a certain product must specialize in that product, duplication must be eliminated—this is rational and economical. The Turksib and the Termez-Stalinabad railroads have been built to facilitate the exchange of commodities—grain and lumber to flow into Central Asia from Siberia and Central Russia; cotton to travel from the South to the grain regions in the North.

Not only is such territorial specialization economical and rational—it is also highly politic. It makes the several National Republics economically interdependent and renders less likely any excessive tendencies toward local nationalism which may degenerate into chauvinism and even into separatism.

Furthermore, a considerable increase in the cultivation of cotton in Central Asia creates an economic base for industrializing a heretofore purely agricultural region. This, from the communist's viewpoint, is exceedingly desirable. An increase in the number of native proletarians brings the communist dream closer to realization. That that is so, can be gathered from the decision of the Communist Party in the Soviet Union henceforth to build textile factories only in cotton-growing regions.

Then again, territorial specialization makes not only for national interdependence, but also for class interdependence, thus welding the Union horizontally as well as vertically. When the peasant, together with his patch of cotton, raises enough grain and vegetables to supply his personal needs, he is more or less immune to proletarian influence. He is, relatively speaking, lord in his own domain. Specialization entails dependence on the market. And since in the Soviet Union the market is completely controlled by the Workers' government, crop specialization means greater dependence of the peasant on the proletariat and vice versa.

In view of all this, it is no exaggeration to say that cotton is the magic key to the maze of economic, political, and cultural inroads the Bolsheviks have made into the age-long immutability of Central Asian existence. I do not wish to simplify unduly. In the final analysis, the Bolsheviks are more interested in socialism than in cotton.

But in the conditions of Central Asia, cotton is the natural medium through which the Bolshevik ideal can be realized. It is indeed highly significant that *For Cotton—For Socialism* is the title of a book written by one of the leading communists in Central Asia. "For Cotton—For Socialism"—this is the underlying motive of nearly every act and measure of the local government. This phrase must be held in mind with especial vividness when we come to discuss the sweeping agricultural revolution which resulted from the great Land and Water Reform and the Collectivization Campaign that have shaken Central Asia during the last ten years.

X

LAND AND WATER

> ...*And we only received in reward*
> *The master's hard blows with the knout.*
> *But here now, to-day, look, my comrade,*
> *Our great happiness overflows.*
> *For the best of the country's sweet waters*
> *And the soil now to us have returned.*
> —ALI TOKOMBAIEV, Kirghiz Poet.

THE land and water situation in Central Asia was long in crying need of reform. Harrowed by civil war and the Basmachi, the local Soviet authorities could do little more than express their good intentions by pious resolutions and sweeping decrees adopted annually and deposited in the archives. Between the years 1918 and 1925, every conference, every Soviet and Party Congress in Central Asia stressed the immediate importance of basic land and water reforms. But lacking an adequate administrative apparatus, particularly in the villages, the Soviets were unable to carry most of these measures into effect.

On the other hand, it was impossible to create a strong net of rural soviets in face of the persisting old economic and social relations in the villages. The agrarian revolution which in Russia had taken place simultaneously with the political revolution, was slow in developing here. By 1925 the beys were still in the saddle. They still held their lands, and their influence, though slightly shaken, was still extensive. The agricultural workers and the tenant farmers depended on them for a chance to earn a livelihood and for loans, at usurious interest. Owing to their influence and power, the beys managed to insinuate themselves everywhere. The village soviets and the peasant unions were honeycombed with them and their henchmen. I knew of an Uzbek Soviet that was entirely made up of beys, mullahs, and their followers. This was not by any means an isolated case. Poor and even middle peasants were not admitted into the organization. When a "cleansing" was instituted, it was discovered that among the 122 members there was not one poor peasant. The soviet was disbanded, and a new unit consisting of 750 poor and middle peasants was organized in its stead. The beys even managed to worm themselves into the village Party nuclei. In the Samarkand and Tashkent districts numerous Party nuclei dominated by beys consistently sabotaged every progressive land measure.

The hope of the government and the Party lay with the poor and middle peasants. The only way to create a solid soviet apparatus was to have the village organizations under the complete control of those who represented the poor and exploited sections of the village population. The poor peasant had to be activized. The middle peasant had to be won over or at least neutralized. A situation had to be created whereby the agricultural workers, the tenant farmers, and the less prosperous middle peasants could be aroused to aggressive action against the beys. This would create for the Soviets a firm social base in the villages. Sharpening class conflict and ruthless revolutionary actions would purge the village organizations of class enemies and saboteurs. The peasants were tired of fighting. Fine words and ringing promises could not move them to action. Something definite, tangible had to be offered. The poor peasant had to be convinced that the Soviet government really meant to improve his lot—to give him land, to give him water, to give him stock, to give him credit. If to achieve this the bey had to be expropriated, the poor peasant would scarcely object to that. For centuries he had been hungry for land and thirsty for water, and he certainly would not be squeamish as to the manner of quenching his ancient hunger and thirst. Would the bey fight? So much the worse for the bey. Would the mullah fulminate? So much the worse for the mullah.

I recall a characteristic story told me by Ikramov. He was at a meeting of poor peasants in a village in the Tashkent district. Someone came and reported that the local bey and his family, when notified that 97 acres of their land and a part of their live stock and agricultural implements were to be confiscated, started an awful hullabaloo, crying, tearing their hair, cursing. Upon hearing the report, the peasants burst into laughter; one shouted: "We and our fathers cried for decades because we had no land; it won't harm the bey if he cries one day."

Thus the urgent need for strengthening Soviet authority in the village was one consideration that made the land and water reform in Central Asia imperative. Another consideration, no less cogent, was the pressing necessity of increasing the productive forces of the country. Antiquated implements, obsolete methods, wasteful handling of land and water resources, frightfully low efficiency—all these evils could not be remedied without a veritable agricultural revolution. In many localities, for instance, there still existed the old custom of annual land redistribution, a custom that precluded sound planning and rational management, and resulted in the temporary owner's barbarous abuse and neglect of the soil. Where, as a result of land shortages, communal ownership existed, the lands were used in annual rotation by different parts of the communes. Each year one part worked and received the product of its work, while the other parts loafed and received nothing. In communes where the land was distributed among individual families, there were innumerable cases of families owning five or six different strips of land scattered through various sections of the communal possessions. As a result, the remote strips often would not be cultivated at all.

The utilization of the limited water supply was also highly irrational, the water having been in many cases distributed on the basis of ancient tribal and clan arrangements. In the course of time some tribes had increased while others had declined, but the amount of water granted to each remained unchanged. Thus it often happened that small tribes had much more water than large tribes. Similar incongruities existed within the individual tribes. In some instances clans of one hundred families got as much water as those counting one thousand families. Some tribes and clans had too much water, others did not have enough. But this was not all. In many localities, married men were entitled to a greater share of the water supply. Accordingly, fathers hastened to buy wives for their sons. And since buying a wife was an expensive proposition, it was the richer peasants and the beys who could afford to purchase wives for all their sons, including the infants. The poor peasants could rarely obtain wives even for their mature sons. Among the latter, protracted bachelorhood was the usual thing. They had to hire themselves out for years in an effort to accumulate a sum large enough to pay for a spouse.

Inequitable and irrational distribution of water and land was largely, though not solely or even mainly, responsible for the evils besetting Central Asian agriculture. The main cause, it seems, was the general shortage of good, irrigated, arable land. The official speeches and documents of the period indicate that the Soviet authorities had known long before the launching of the reform that mere confiscation of the beys' lands would not half satisfy the needs of the poor peasantry. They had seen from the very outset that besides a more equitable distribution of the existing lands, waters and stocks, the solution of the problem ultimately lay in a vast extension of cultivable areas. Indeed, there had been some who felt that the energy and funds expended in fighting beys and confiscating their old lands might be more advantageously utilized in obtaining new lands. These objections, however, were quickly dismissed when the proponents of the official plan pointed out that far-reaching irrigation, reclamation, and amelioration projects could scarcely be carried out without the sympathetic coöperation and the actual physical labor of the native peasantry, and that confiscation of the beys' lands and abolition of some of the outmoded customs pertaining to land and water were to be regarded simply as

COMPLETING BOURGEOIS REVOLUTION 183

the initial steps in the agrarian reforms. In the words of a local Bolshevik, "It would have been impossible to rouse the village masses, especially the landless peasants, to struggle for the development of new lands at a time when they beheld available lands still in the possession of the rich, the usurers, the landlords, the beys. It was absolutely essential that the peasants, the poorer peasants, should be thoroughly convinced that we were actually trying to free them from serfdom. And to protect them from the beys it was absolutely essential for us that the poor peasants themselves take active part in carrying out the reforms, in confiscating and distributing the lands. Only then, only after the reform had been accomplished and the great necessity for extending the arable lands had become apparent, would it be possible for the government to enlist the collaboration of the village masses in large reclamation and irrigation projects."

The Soviet authorities regarded the seizure and division of the beys' property as a means to a greater end, as a step the political effects of which were expected immeasurably to outweigh the economic ones. Here exceeding caution was required. Glowing promises of an economic paradise would have resulted in sanguine expectations which, owing to the shortage of lands, might have ultimately redounded against the promisors. The delicate balance between promising enough to arouse enthusiasm yet not so much as to entail disappointment was deliberately maintained. In this affair the Government played intermittently the rôle of incendiary and that of fireman, now setting passions aflame, now turning a hose of cold water upon them.

Art and Propaganda

The Land and Water Reform in Uzbekistan was nothing less than an agrarian revolution, a change incomparably more fundamental than anything the Bolsheviks had heretofore attempted in the one-time Emirate of Bokhara.

The method which the Party and the government employed in carrying out the land reform offers a classical illustration of the workings of the Soviet system: Perfect control from the top combined with colossal initiative from the bottom. The Party, the entire Soviet apparatus, and the vast peasant masses were mobilized for the great task.

The campaign technique, evolved by the Bolsheviks in Russia and avidly taken over by the countries on the periphery, is simple and effective. The impulse for any economic, political or cultural campaign usually comes from the top, though not infrequently the first vague demands for it emanate from the bottom. When a campaign is decided upon, its underlying ideas and method of procedure are thoroughly thrashed out at Party meetings, Soviet meetings, Young Communist gatherings, etc. Since almost every form of activity in the Soviet Union is organized, and since it is the policy of the Party to have a Party nucleus in every organization, it is obvious that once a campaign is launched, it is the duty of each Party nucleus to popularize the objectives of the campaign in the organization in which it works. Accordingly, in each factory, office, school, village, newspaper, and theater, meetings are called, reports made, suggestions and criticisms called for, coöperation solicited. Good suggestions are immediately communicated to the directing staff and often fitted into the general plan. In this way the mass is drawn into the work. When the work is well done, the mass is made to feel that it, rather than the Party leadership, is the initiator of the campaign. At all times a good campaign implies complete coöperation between the leadership and the mass.

The first step after the idea of the reform had been accepted was a tremendous propaganda campaign. The country was covered with placards, printed slogans, leaflets and popularly written pamphlets explaining the proposed measures. More effective even was the use of the spoken word. Hundreds of specially trained speakers were thrown into the villages. Students from the universities, Young

Communists, Pioneers, were mobilized for the purpose. Dozens of "agitation trucks" decorated with posters and slogans and carrying a native orchestra, native singers and agitators dashed along the country roads, stopping at fairs, before Chai-Khanahs, before mosques, organizing meetings, explaining, answering questions, arousing the population. Amateur theatrical companies, hastily brought together for the purpose, went from village to village presenting a primitive propaganda playlet, "The Bey on Trial." Soon, too, the Uzbek-kino released special moving pictures prepared for the occasion. Within a couple of months the Land and Water Reform was on every tongue.

While the propaganda campaign was at its height, preparations were made to organize an efficient administrative machine for putting the reform into effect. It was a gigantic task. For instance, to carry out the reform in a strictly scientific manner, Fergana alone would have required about 1,500 surveyors. I don't know how many thousands of surveyors would have been needed for the whole of Uzbekistan. But since the reform had to be instituted immediately, surveyors were out of the question; the inadequate information supplied by the local peasants had to be relied on. Similar difficulties sprang up at every step.

As the plan finally crystallized, the administrative apparatus was to be composed of specially appointed central, regional, and local commissions, with members selected from the best workers in the Party and in other economic and labor union organizations, and subjected to an intensive course of preliminary training. The appointed commissions were to work hand in hand in each village with "Commissions of Peasant Coöperation," consisting of from ten to fifteen members *elected* by the general assembly of all the local middle, poor, and tenant peasants.

Service on the Peasant Commissions was to be voluntary, involving no remuneration; the duties were manifold —examining itemized property lists filled out by beys, tenant farmers, agricultural laborers, middle peasants; aiding the appointed Commission to uncover undeclared property, illegal transfers, sales, temporary "gifts"; calling meetings; posting announcements and proclamations; and in general safeguarding the interests of the village poor and serving as a link between the commissions and the peasants.

By the time the appointed and elected commissions were ready to begin work, the various class attitudes toward the momentous reform had become fully manifest.

Poor Beys

Needless to say, the rich property owners were bitterly opposed. In their subterranean propaganda, they resorted to every possible misrepresentation and calumny. They played on the peasant's fear of the unknown, on his religious prejudices and old loyalties. They spread rumors that "the land was being confiscated for the purpose of transferring it to the Soviet employees," or that the land was being "taken away from the Uzbeks to be given to the Russians." The middle peasant was told: "To-day the Soviet is seizing our lands, to-morrow it will grab yours." Referring to former land decrees which had not been enforced, the beys whispered that the whole thing was a hoax, that the "Government will toy for a while with the poor peasants, but the lands will remain in the possession of the present owners." This argument had a powerful effect on the poor peasants, who hesitated to reveal their sympathies with the reform for fear that they might later be deprived of their means of earning a livelihood.

In many cases the beys attempted to evade confiscation by not declaring their full possessions. They tried every possible trick. They hastened to cancel contracts with their tenants so that they might claim that they were themselves engaged in working the land. Taking advantage of the poor peasants' fear, they often introduced their tenants as their sons or grandsons. Some even voluntarily divided their lands among their tenants, accompanying the procedure with a warning: "Now remember, this is not for

COMPLETING BOURGEOIS REVOLUTION 187

long. Justice will triumph in the end, and then woe to those of you who will have made use of my property." Others divided their property among their "toiling" sons. Still others managed to obtain signatures from local peasants testifying to the "fact" that they were not beys. There were some foolhardy beys who actually succeeded in organizing armed detachments of farm hands to "defend our property."

Bribery, intrigue, terror—the beys shunned nothing. Not a few Bolsheviks were slain by, or at the instigation of, the beys. This continued long after the reform had been carried through. Uzbek papers of that period are filled with weird tales of treachery and terror.

However, as the agitation for the reform unfolded and its success became assured, a number of the more farsighted beys sought recourse in a more conciliatory position. Threatened with losing everything, they tried to salvage something by voluntary renunciation of their property rights. Many even feigned enthusiasm for the reform, hoping thus to placate the revolutionary forces and to get on the right side of the government. In their statements one meets with such expressions as "the Soviet Government is to be congratulated on its land reforms which are destined to enhance the might of the toiling peasantry" or "realizing the usefulness of the reform, and in an effort to meet it half-way, I hereby voluntarily surrender all my real property . . ." or ". . . we have come to the conclusion that further to exploit the benighted village peasantry which gives its last strength in return for a miserable one-fourth of the land's yield and lives in a state of semi-starvation, is criminal. We therefore gladly surrender our lands to the Soviet Government, a government that has until now settled every one of life's problems in an equitable manner and that will no doubt be as just in distributing our lands among the poor peasants." Some of the statements sound violently revolutionary; one even concludes with the slogans, "Down with the exploitation of peasant labor! May the toiling peasant be the rightful owner of our land!" Nor was there a lack of histrionics. In the village of Uch-Kurgan, nine beys appeared before a large peasant meeting and dramatically yielded their 415 *desiatins* to their tenants. And on the eighth anniversary of the Bolshevik Revolution twenty rich beys in the Rishtan district publicly transferred their five hundred *desiatins* to the poor peasants.

It may be worth noting, though, that in most cases these "benefactors," while voluntarily surrendering to the "toiling peasants" such lands as were either entirely unfit for cultivation or required heavy expenditures, tried to retain the most fertile and best irrigated lands for themselves. In many other cases they were moved by a desire not to pay taxes on relatively worthless land, or by the hope that an ostensibly magnanimous gesture might blind the authorities to the vast tracts of good land they had withheld for themselves.

Poor Mullahs

At one with the beys was the upper land-owning Moslem clergy. When news of the reform first appeared, the clergy got busy scanning the Koran and other holy books for passages that might be appropriately used in confuting all arguments favoring the new measures. Basing themselves on the Sheriat, some mullahs maintained that "if the land of one man is taken from him and given to another, the latter exposes himself to the wrath of Mohammed if he either consumes or sells the products of that land." Other mullahs proved by citations from the Prophet that confiscated cattle would "turn blind," that confiscated land would "yield worms instead of bread" and that he who tilled such land would be "cursed by God himself." One mullah in agitating among his farm hands and tenants resorted to this argument: "If Allah has not given you anything, how can you expect mere man to give you?" Other mullahs appealed to the poor peasants' sense of honor: "How could you bear feeding on robbed land?" And there is a case on record where a group of poor peasants were so affected by the appeal of an ishan that they actually passed a resolution declaring that "they would sooner die than live on iniquitously gotten land."

On the whole, however, the clergy, for all its prestige, proved quite unable to convince the poor peasants that the punishment that awaited them in the world to come would outweigh the benefits they would derive in this world. The peasants were inclined to take their chances.

In fighting the ishans and the mullahs, the Soviet authorities exercised extraordinary care and patience, biding their time, waiting for developments.

One vulnerable spot in the position of the mosque was the conflict of interests between the upper and lower clergy: the first, rich, powerful, and economically allied with the beys; the second, relatively poor, weak, and economically more closely connected with the wretched peasant masses. This conflict of interests was taken advantage of by the Bolsheviks; without attempting direct attacks on the mosque, they proceeded to assail the reactionary clergy by exposing before the masses its greed and selfishness.

What made the position of the upper clergy especially vulnerable was the possession of much fertile land coveted by the peasants. The land reform, crystallizing as it did the conflicting class interests in the village, succeeded in smashing the already shaken front of the clergy—the upper clergy siding with the landlords, the beys; the lower with the peasants, the government. The village mullah knew that opposition to the reform meant the implacable hatred of the land-hungry masses. As to the upper clergy, its intransigence succeeded in almost irretrievably alienating the majority of the population.

Sensing danger, and having finally come to realize the inevitability of the reform, the less myopic of the upper clergy began to beat a hasty retreat. The Soviet authorities refrained from gloating or vindictiveness. When the recalcitrants called upon the faithful to resist the redistribution of lands, a group of prominent "penitents," encouraged by the Government, issued a proclamation in favor of such redistribution. Rather than quixotically oppose religion and fight the Koran and thus antagonize the masses, the Bolsheviks availed themselves of the opportunity to utilize the proclamation issued by the mullahs. The document was printed in the Bolshevik press and given the widest publicity. It was long and abstruse, citing innumerable chapters and verses from the Koran and other holy books, and proving beyond the shadow of a doubt that, according to Islam, "the owner of land must himself till his land" and that "if the owner is himself unable to do it, he must renounce his land in favor of him who is able." The concluding paragraphs read: "Hence, the measures directed by the Soviet Government towards supplying the landless peasants with the surplus lands (which it is a sin to keep!—*Haram*) and towards freeing the serf from age-long humiliation and bondage—such measures shall never be unlawful according to the Islamic religion.... On the basis of the above proof, the beys who have many lands must themselves transfer their property to the landless peasant. Should they fail to surrender their land, gotten through iniquity and deceit, it would not be against the law of Islam for the government to seize and for the peasants to use such lands."

Like the beys, and for the same reason, many of the rich clergy began to renounce their lands. The famous ishan Fakhritdin Vali-Khodzhaiev was among the first voluntarily to surrender his vast land holdings and in a much hailed epistle "blessed" the land reform and the Soviet Government. "In my message of benediction," he wrote, "I wish to point out that the Government which has brought peace into our land is satisfying the needs of the poor and the hungry who look to it for support. The Government has found it necessary to distribute land among the poor. Gratified with the Government's action, I bless its magnanimity. Generous gifts of bread and clothing to the poor and hungry are in accord with the conduct of our Prophet Mohammed who, following the ways of our Lord God, even borrowed from the Jews in order to feed the hungry and clothe the needy. Moreover, four of Mohammed's apostles (Vizirs-Chakhariars) had actually sold themselves into slavery so as to pay the debts of some poor and hungry people."

The statements of the "progressive" Fergana and Tashkent clergy, as well as of the renowned ishan Vali-Khodzhaiev, created a furore among the intransigents who accused the "progressives" of wilfully misinterpreting the teachings of Mohammed and deliberately distorting passages from the Koran. They made every effort to prevent these statements, published in thousands of leaflets, from reaching the masses. They destroyed every bundle of leaflets they managed to lay hands on. Of course, their efforts were futile. The news spread like wildfire. Within a few weeks the religious front was completely shattered. Even the most rabidly reactionary mullahs were finally forced to an attitude of pretended "neutrality."

What is more, there suddenly broke out, for the first time in the history of Islam, desertions of the Holy Orders and conversions to Bolshevism and atheism.

From a score of similar documents, taken at random, the following statement of one disillusioned village divine is illustrative:

"Deceived by the beys and the clergy, I, Babo-Abad Sharipov, at the Mosque of Khadzhi-Abad, had for decades been pouring nonsense into the heads of our benighted toiling peasantry. I now see the truth. Having read the statement issued by our upper clergy, I have come to the realization that our entire clergy has used the Sheriat and the Koran for economic ends. I solemnly swear before the whole people and the Soviet Government that henceforth I shall not be the servant of a faith which I have ceased to recognize or believe in, which is calculated to deceive the people. I shall henceforth do honest work, till the soil, like all other peasants. I, therefore, ask the Soviet Government to grant me a plot of land in accordance with the established labor norm."

And here is part of another typical document showing the manner in which the village poor received the sudden ideological about-face of the mullahs:

"We and our fathers have for many years been under

the yoke of our beys and our lying clergy. The latter, by means of religious deception, sowed hatred amongst us, and we attacked one another. And all the while the beys and the mullahs were happy and jubilant. Now we see our upper clergy littering Uzbekistan with proclamations culled from holy books. But we, the farm hands of Maslagad-Tepe, would like to answer these proclamations. And where were you before with your proclamations? Have you, our spiritual guides, been fooling us, and refused to open our eyes? We, the farm hands of Maslagad-Tepe see through your deception, and we trust only our workers' government...."

Poor mullahs! No anti-religious Bolshevik propaganda could possibly have been more disastrous to the prestige of the mosque than the stupid, selfish, and undignified behavior of the mosque's servants. Intrigue, hypocrisy, obsequiousness, compromise, opportunism—they shunned nothing as long as there was the least hope of retaining a vestige of influence and power. The land reform gave the Mohammedan religion in Central Asia a blow from which it never recovered.

The Intelligentsia Too!

Another Soviet victory resulting from the triumphant march of the agrarian revolution was the gradual winning over of the best elements of the Uzbek intelligentsia. The first bid for educated support was made by Akhan-Babriev, the chairman of the Central Executive Committee of Uzbekistan. Addressing a conference of teachers at Andijan, he described in glowing terms the nature of the land reform and what it meant to the long-suffering Uzbek people, and made an impassioned plea to the teachers and to all Uzbek intellectuals to join the government and the Party in the great task of rehabilitating the country. This, in a sense, was an appeal to national pride and patriotism, an attempt to utilize the emotional dynamite contained in old loyalties.

COMPLETING BOURGEOIS REVOLUTION

Akhan-Babriev's appeal met with a warm response. Immediately a conference of several hundred progressive leaders of the native intelligentsia was called at Kokand to discuss a number of important questions pertaining to the economic and cultural life of Uzbekistan. The most important point on the agenda was the land reform. Here was the flower of the national intellect: teachers of the old and the new schools, religious luminaries and scholars, writers, etc. Most of them had been either definitely antagonistic to the new régime or proudly indifferent. After the purposes of the land reform had been explained by a member of the local government, heated discussions began, but their general tenor was favorable to the government. Naturally, there was grumbling too. Some of the older men seemed to take special pleasure in pointing out the inefficiency and abuse of power of some of the government commissions. Then sprang up the well-known Uzbek writer Fazid-Bek. "Where have you been until now?" he shouted. "Why have you been sleeping until now? When the Soviet Government launched the reform, you said: 'This is a very difficult question,' and you washed your hands, and remained standing aloof. And now you come here and complain that certain commissions don't work well. You consider yourselves a cultural force, so why in the name of culture don't you help the commissions to do their work?"

Fazid-Bek's outburst was greeted with loud applause. The Conference passed a resolution promising the intelligentsia's coöperation and support in carrying the land reform into effect. Like the declaration of the mullahs, this resolution was given the widest publicity in the Soviet press.

Like a Dream Come True

To the Government, more important than the attitude of the beys, the clergy, and the intellectuals, was that of the middle peasant. Neither rich nor poor, neither kulak nor farmhand, the middle peasant was the central political and economic figure in the Uzbek village. His support was essential to the success of the reform. His opposition would have been fatal. Small wonder most of the pro and con propaganda was primarily directed at him. Placed centrally and pulled in diametrically opposed directions, the middle peasant oscillated between the two extremes. At first the reactionaries seemed to have the upper hand. As a property owner, the middle peasant was naturally apprehensive of any policy that involved confiscation of property, even if not his property. The bey's argument "To-day they are expropriating me; to-morrow they will rob you" had struck a sympathetic chord. At best the middle peasant assumed a position of watchful waiting or neutrality, at worst he coöperated with the beys and mullahs. It took no end of promising and reassuring and cajoling to finally draw the middle peasant toward the government. Only when he was confident that his property would remain intact did he begin to take an active part in the work of the Commission of Coöperation, fighting side by side with the poor peasants. His slogan now was, "Let us be middle peasants all!" The middle peasant's change of heart was a triumph of Bolshevik diplomacy and tact. With him on the side of the reform, the agricultural revolution in Uzbekistan was secure.

We now come to the one class that was the most direct and immediate beneficiary of the reform—the poor peasant, the tenant farmer, the agricultural laborer. As regards the reaction of this class, there come to mind several characteristic episodes I heard told by various people who had been active in instituting the change.

On the way to a meeting of the Central Executive Committee of Uzbekistan, a few members of the Government—Akhan-Babriev, Ikramov, and others—stopped off at a little station to greet the assembled peasants. That was in the early days of October, 1925. The land reform was as yet only a vague rumor. To feel out the peasants, the government representatives tackled the question of water and land. The peasants listened, nodded, scratched their heads, posed questions, and before the train started asked the visitors to urge upon the session at Andijan the necessity of land redistribution. "But are you ready to help us in putting it through? Aren't you afraid that the beys and the kulaks will do everything possible to balk us?" "How?" answered an old peasant. "They can't hide their lands in their pockets!"

That the overwhelming majority of the poor peasants favored redistribution of land is not surprising. For them, the whole period of agitation for the reform and of putting it into effect was one grand, unforgettable holiday—festivities, celebrations, parades, bands, speeches, cheers. They flocked to meetings. They listened to reports, asked endless questions about the extent of the financial aid the Government proposed to give them, about seed, tractors, and, almost invariably, about schools. They exposed the tricks of the beys, and worked enthusiastically with the Commission of Peasant Coöperation which they had themselves elected. Where the Commission did not function well or rapidly enough, the peasants, impatient, their appetites whetted, on occasions took the initiative and, *on more than one occasion,* perpetrated acts of such cruel violence that they had to be stopped by the Government. Often when the land commission went about inspecting the beys' estates, all the poor and middle peasants of the village, carrying banners, singing songs, would break out into spontaneous demonstrations and would follow the commissions from house to house seeing to it that "justice be done."

The joy of the average farmhand or tenant farmer when he got a plot of land, some implements, and, occasionally, even some live-stock can well be imagined.

In 1931, an Uzbek peasant, a chairman of a collective farm, told me of the great happiness the reform had brought into his household. "I had been a farmhand, working for a rich bey. During the reform I was given a part of the bey's land and a fine ox. When I first saw the great, big, handsome ox, it looked like a dream come true. I was so happy, I rushed over to him and began to kiss him. When I came back home, I was told that my wife had just given birth to a boy. Was there anything else a man could desire—two joys in succession! And I called my son Er-Islokhaty—Land Reform. I wanted my son to remember that he was born on the happiest day of my life...."

> *We shan't forget the bey's oppression,*
> *His cruelties and violence—*
> *The bey ruined the peasant's home.*
> *The hour of retribution is here.*
> *I shall tell you the story of the bey's crimes,*
> *Of his shamelessness:*
> *For a hundred rubles he would ask*
> *A thousand ruble security. And the*
> *Judge would say: Correct.*
> *To whom could the poor man*
> *With three children complain?*
> *Who had the power to complain against the bey?*
> *The poor man had only one remedy*
> *That remedy was—bitter tears.*

XI

TOWARD SOCIALISM

Free peasant, does not your heart throb with the desire
Sooner to behold our beautiful valleys, our fields?
Have you not been lifted on the wing of a sweet dream—
To work on the open breast of Spring,
To work not with an omach, but with a great, great machine?
Peasant, you have become the master of happiness.
With the strength of your will shall you transform
The face of the free earth.
The tractor—your friend. You—on the heights of freedom.
The lands your very own.... You in the midst of joy!...
           —Uzbek Peasant Song about Land Reform.

Fear of the Unknown

BY THE spring of 1926, 56,830 peasant households in Uzbekistan were provided with land taken from the beys, and 19,790 more with plots obtained from newly irrigated government territory. Thus within a few months 76,620 propertyless peasants were transformed into petty proprietors. Of these only 35% had their own live-stock and only 27% their own, although primitive, agricultural implements. Expropriation of the beys, forced sales of surplus farm stocks and modest government credits granted to about 47% of the newly settled peasants remedied the situation somewhat. Moreover, during the spring sowing, the government threw 412 tractors of its own into the newly irrigated fields. Fifty-five thousand households were provided with cotton seed. In addition to 567,000 rubles credit, the Uzbek government distributed among the peasants 153,000 *poods* of wheat and 8,500 of alfalfa seeds for sowing and 100,000 *poods* of wheat for consumption.

By and large the effects of the land reform were as anticipated. The prestige of the Soviet state was enhanced. The Party and government apparatus in the rural districts was strengthened. Relations between the poor peasants and the Government were firmly cemented. The passive neutrality or antagonism of the middle peasant was overcome. The position of the beys and the mullahs was definitely undermined. The native intelligentsia was partly persuaded to coöperate with the new régime. The need for irrigation, reclamation, and amelioration was made manifest. Although, even after the reform, 50% of the landless peasants remained without land, agriculture was made more productive.

The main danger, from the communist viewpoint, was the numerical growth of the individual peasant-proprietor class. Left unchecked, the more unscrupulous and predatory peasants would become kulaks, and would within a short time again achieve economic supremacy. Indications of such a possibility were not wanting. There were cases where farmhands and tenant farmers, unable to manage their newly acquired lands, voluntarily returned them to the original owners, the beys. Where government credits or live-stock or implements proved inadequate, the poor peasant again fell into the claws of the usurer, the bey, the kulak. Furthermore, in view of the fact that about 50% of the landless peasants were still unprovided for, there was a basis for continued exploitation of labor and private enrichment. Finally, an increased number of small peasant holdings would not be conducive to effective central planning or to a full utilization of modern mechanical improvements, or, what is even more important, to the growth and development of a collectivist psychology.

The Land and Water reform was actually only the first, the bourgeois phase of the agrarian revolution in Central Asia. The second, the socialist, phase started only with the collectivization campaign of 1929-1930, in the midst of the first Five-Year Plan. The principal objective of that plan was to lay the foundation for the "building of Socialism" in the Soviet Union. But the building of Socialism in one country—in the midst of an inimical capitalist world

—posited the attainment of a large degree of economic independence. The USSR had to become economically self-sufficient. Among many other things, that meant also "Cotton Independence."

That natural conditions in Soviet Central Asia were favorable to a rapid development of cotton-growing was clear. What was lacking were scientific method and mechanization. The question then came up as to the possibility of introducing the machines and tractors and scientific control demanded by the Five-Year Plan on tiny plots of land owned and cultivated individually by poor and ignorant peasants. And the answer was, that it was impossible, that altogether no real planning could be effected in the presence of a vast, chaotic, petty, individual economy, and that, therefore, any attempt to carry out the Five-Year Plan in Central Asia would necessitate rapid collectivization of the cotton lands.

The basis for such a move was present. As elsewhere in the Soviet Union, here, too, one of the most powerful missionaries of collectivization was the modern machine. A small number of collective farms had been organized here shortly after the Civil War; during the Land Reform of 1925-1927 a few more had been formed; by 1929, 3.5% of the peasant households of Central Asia were in collectives. Still, as compared with the rest of the Union, Central Asia was "disgracefully" delinquent. Then the order was issued, and the collectivization campaign was rapidly set in motion. The technique was very similar to that of the Land Reform campaign. Again agitation, again propaganda, again bands and theatrical troupes and orators, again attacks on the "mullahs, the beys, and the kulaks," again appeals to the individual and class interests of the poor and middle peasants. But considering the difficulty of demonstrating the advantages of collective ownership and management, the period of preliminary propaganda was too short; the training of special organizers, inadequate; and the voluntary principle of collectivization, not sufficiently popularized. In 1925-1927 the landless peasant and the tenant farmer had readily, in most cases enthusiastically, acclaimed the confiscation of the rich man's property. At that time no involved arguments were necessary. The poor peasant had grasped the idea immediately. Why not? He was always ready to get something for nothing. But now it was a different matter. On the face of it, collectivization meant not getting but giving. The benefits, even when understood, which was not yet the case with most peasants, were remote and problematical; the loss of ownership and personal control was immediately and painfully tangible. The Land Reform scarcely involved a psychological adjustment; the transfer of some lands from the feudal landlords to the poor peasants had not seriously affected either the institution or the psychology of private ownership. If anything, it had created a vast number of new petty proprietors. But collectivization, despite the lure of the tractor and the influence of the few state farms, machine and tractor stations, and cotton-growers' coöperatives, still meant a definite break with the past, a leap into the unknown, and economic and psychological revolution.

Dizziness from Success

Yet the struggle for cotton and socialism demanded collectivization, and the Bolsheviks were not the people to flinch before difficulties. Next to the Civil War, the spring sowing campaigns of 1930 in Uzbekistan and of 1931 in Tadjikistan were probably the most intensely dramatic and lurid periods in the whole history of Central Asia. The class struggle in the village flared up with unprecedented violence. The surviving kulaks and the beys fought tooth and nail against collectivization. Now their propaganda was falling on more hospitable soil. "We told you so," was their refrain to the middle peasants. "Before it was we, now it is you, and the end is not yet." Even the onetime landless peasant was dubious. Nor can it be said that most of the local authorities were distinguishing themselves by efficient and diplomatic handling of the situation. Eager to show results, over-confident of their ability to control the peasant masses, many of them followed the line of least resistance: instead of patient suasion, coercion; instead of revolutionary elasticity, bureaucratic rigidity.

Collectivization was an exciting game; and the overzealous players rivaled one another in their headlong rush for the goal. In one region the local officials declared four districts one hundred per cent collectivized, and to make reality conform to their boast, they used force to drag the peasants into the collectives. In the village of Donjor, a poor peasant told me of how a certain Abdulaiev, a local communist, had handled the job of "strengthening the kolkhoz (collective) movement." At a meeting of Kolkhozniks addressed by Abdulaiev, eight poor and middle peasants, including the man who told me the story, expressed their unwillingness to remain in the collective. Abdulaiev jumped up, and, shaking his fists, delivered himself of an harangue full of objurgations and threats. He announced that peasants deserting the kolkhoz would receive no credit and no bread. "If that's the case," replied the eight, "we'd rather stay in the kolkhoz." But Abdulaiev's ire was aroused, and he decided to frustrate the "clever trick" of the "class enemies." "Now it is too late. Now we won't take you back. If you apply eight times, if you prove that you are sincerely anxious to join the kolkhoz, then perhaps we'll consider you again. Meanwhile, to those who have withdrawn we'll return neither their lands, nor their horses, nor their wagons; for we are in the majority. We'll give you back your horses only upon receiving 100 rubles in cash from each of you. As to the land, you may get some in May, if we have any land to spare." In a resolution formulated by Abdulaiev the peasants were denounced as "enemies of collectivization."

In their exuberance, some kolkhoz organizers made reckless promises. One fellow declared that the Soviet Government would give 500 rubles and a horse to every peasant entering a kolkhoz. Another organizer went to the length of saying that the Soviet Government would provide all the farmhands and poor peasants with wives.

There were organizers whose conduct in the villages bordered on lunacy. I recall the case of the "communist" Aliman Djandarbekov—a gay old chap, and quite a toper. When under the weather he used to "talk big" to the peasants. "Well, comrades," he would say to the awed villagers, "with the help of Allah, we have got your cattle already. Now we shall collectivize your wives and daughters, and make them sleep with us, and we'll have a perfect Commune."

In a Kokand village, ten middle peasants were denied membership in a kolkhoz because they had been seen praying in the mosque. In the village of Kodja Yakshabo, a kolkhoz was dissolved because the members insisted on going to the mosque. In the Bokhara districts some overzealous officials declared that in the kolkhozi cremation of the dead would be compulsory. And in the district of Kashka-Daria one "learned" native communist expelled a few peasants from a kolkhoz because they were unable to answer his questions: "What is Socialism?" "When did Darwin live?" In the village of Mazor, the native Communist Buribikov became so irritated with the four hundred peasants who refused to join a kolkhoz that he called out the military and chased the peasants 20 kilometers away from the village.

Many officials became, in the words of Stalin, "dizzy from success." Not satisfied with the simpler forms of collective farming, they attempted to foist upon an unprepared peasantry full-fledged communes. They were deterred by nothing. Does the Party hold that collectivization must be voluntary? Well, party instructions must be interpreted "liberally"; the peasant doesn't know what's good for him—he must be forced into a kolkhoz. Does the peasant object to parting with his horse? Nonsense. We break into his house, into his stable, into his barn, into his chicken coop, and collectivize his horses, calves, sheep, chickens. Is the peasant who refuses to join a kolkhoz a middle peasant? That, too, is a minor detail. We'll confiscate his property, deprive him of his legal rights, and brand him a kulak. In certain Central Asian villages, twenty per cent of the inhabitants were arbitrarily stigmatized as "kulaks," and their properties confiscated.

At a village meeting reported in the Moscow *Pravda*, the peasants of Djon Aryk complained against the highhanded methods of the local organizer Ablaiev. One peasant shouted: "To me my ox is dearer than my wife. To me my horse is dearer than my children. I will gladly join the kolkhoz, but leave me my ox and my horse.... We are all for collectivization, we are all for the Soviet Government, but we are all against what Ablaiev is doing. *Togre*—correct?" "*Togre!*" echoed the meeting in unison.

The peasants were so vague on the subject, that there were numerous cases of individual peasants joining simultaneously several collectives.

The sowing campaign was threatened. Many were afraid to plow their land for fear that it might be taken away from them. Others who had been administratively inducted into collective farms were too resentful to work. Even voluntarily organized collectives had not the faintest notion of the extent of their lands, of the amount of cattle or implements in their possession, or of how to proceed with their collective labors. The cotton plan was in danger. Yet so busy were some of the local Soviet bureaucrats with writing up long lists of *kolkhozniks,* that they did not heed the ominous signs. "The peasants here have been so busy joining the collectives," boasted one official telegram from a Khorezm village, "that they have done nothing to prepare for the spring sowing; they have not even carted the fertilizer to the fields." Success! A few more weeks of such overwhelming success, and the Soviet Union would have faced a cotton famine in 1930, and Central Asia would have faced appalling economic disorganization and ruin.

Anti-Soviet elements speculated on those "successes." Surreptitiously they agitated against collectivization: "Allah is against collectives. This is certain. Behold how the new collectives fall apart as soon as pressure from the outside is removed"; or "They say our women will be forced to remove their veils and will be collectivized by the Government"; or "The collectives will be forced to raise only cotton. No bread-grains or rice will be permitted to be sown. The Government will starve us to death"; or "The only ones who will benefit from a collective will be the lazy-bones, the loafers, the shiftless, the ne'er-do-wells. They will do nothing, while the industrious peasant will have to do all the work." In the Fergana, Tashkent, and Samarkand districts, the kulaks, ignoring the commandments of the Islam faith, began to "work" among the women. Secret meetings of women were organized. The women were urged to do only one thing—scream, scream that they would have no kolkhozi.

But it is easy to over-emphasize the pig-headedness of the local officials, the infernal cleverness of the kulaks, and the universality of poor and middle peasants' objections to the kolkhoz. These things existed to a large extent, they made the task of the Bolsheviks in Central Asia exceedingly difficult. Yet the fact that the cotton area in the whole of the Soviet Union increased from 1,055,000 hectares in 1929 to 1,632,000 hectares in 1930, and that in the Fall of 1930, 29% of all the peasants in Central Asia were solidly joined in collectives—an increase of 25.5% in one year—suggests that the obstacles were not insurmountable.

Fascination of Tractors

The question arises: what were the factors in the economic and political situation in Central Asia that made the triumph of collectivization possible, despite the tactlessness and inefficiency of many organizers, the doubt or reluctance of many peasants, and the intensive anti-collectivization propaganda of the united forces of the kulaks, the beys, and the mullahs?

In the Soviet Union, especially in its more distant sections in Central Asia, the people had lived for centuries in unchanging primitive conditions. The only means of locomotion was the ass or the camel. In some of the mountainous regions even the principle of the wheel was unknown. The people scratched the surface of their fields with crude heavy sticks (omach) pulled by the ox. In the villages even kerosene lamps were unheard of; they used candles and more often a bit of cotton floating in a small dish of oil. Ventilation, sanitation, hygiene were unknown. The ancient system of irrigation was miserably inadequate. The Central Asian village was the symbol of darkness, filth, and disease.

One can well imagine the tremendous fascination that a tractor, a motor truck, an airplane, a hydro-electric plant, or a locomotive holds for the Central Asian peasant. He is awed by it, but he is drawn to it. He is suspicious of its novelty, but lured by the advantages it offers. All the Bolshevik had to do was to bring these things to the attention of the peasant, and they spoke for themselves. All that was necessary was to organize a couple of modern state farms, several machine and tractor stations, and to electrify a few villages, and no amount of political bungling could counteract the power of such propaganda.

The moment the poor peasant discovered that working the soil with a tractor was easier, better, cheaper, and faster than struggling with an *omach*, he became excellent potential material for a kolkhoz.

In 1930 the elements seemed to coöperate with the Bolsheviks. The spring was late in coming. The peasant who had only one ox was in danger of not getting through with his sowing on time. Every day was precious. Plodding behind the *omach*, perspiration running down his face, the peasant could not but be powerfully impressed by the tractor on the neighboring state farm which, working twenty-four hours a day, accomplished ten times as much as he was accomplishing. If he could only get a tractor, his anxiety over the lateness of the spring would vanish, he would gain several days in the race. And what a wonderful Bolshevik contraption that was! Mind you, when the tractor was not working on the field, it supplied motor power for the water pump, or the mill! It was employed in transporting heavy luggage; it was used in a hundred different ways. Ah, this dumb ox, the peasant was sick and tired of its slow, deliberate pace. And following his ox, he all the while would cast envious glances at the youthful driver mounted on his steel monster across the line.

The bey and the kulak, knowing that the Soviet State would never permit them to own tractors and realizing that the tractors were the most eloquent propagandists for collectivization, were bitterly opposed to them. They spread lies about them. "Fields worked with tractors yield nothing. It is a sin to touch a tractor for it is lubricated with the fat of impure animals." Is it surprising that one of the Bolshevik slogans in Central Asia was "The enemy of the tractor is our class enemy?"

But even the whispering campaign of the class enemy could not for long be effectual alongside of the loud paeans of praise that rose from the lips of those who had seen the great achievements and understood the still greater potentialities of the modern machine. In the spring of 1930, 4,677 tractors were ripping the arid soil of Central Asia. Of them 2,297 were working on the state farms; and the remaining 2,480, of which 1,310 belonged to the Cotton Coöperative and the 1,170 to the Machine and Tractor Stations of the Tractor Center, were employed on the fields of the collectives and, in some cases, of individual poor and middle peasants. The Central Asian had ample opportunity to see the machines in action, or at least hear the marvelous tales about them.

Fully as impressive as the machines were the spectacular organizations employing them. There was, for instance, Pakhta Aral (Island of Cotton) the magnificent state cotton plantation administered by the Cotton Trust. Stretching along both sides of a newly built canal, over an area fifteen miles long by three miles wide, and embracing six settlements with several thousand inhabitants, this giant plantation was producing cotton seed sufficient to meet the needs of almost one-fourth of the whole of Central Asia. The natives had witnessed the birth of this giant. The thrilling story of how an army of men and tractors and excavators and motor trucks had invaded the Hungry

Steppe and within a short time had miraculously transformed the sterile territory into a flourishing island had been assiduously circulated among the remotest villages in the region. Peasants would go miles out of their way to visit Pakhta Aral, to see the electric plant, the machine shops, the schools, the hospital, the club, the cinema, and the modern workers' homes, and above all to see the columns of giant caterpillars advancing through the fields.

And Pakhta Aral was not the only state plantation in Central Asia. In 1930 there were twelve state farms covering an area of 39,821 hectares of newly irrigated lands —25,013 in Uzbekistan, 8,008 in Tadjikistan, and 6,800 in Turkmenistan.

Of even greater propaganda value were the Machine and Tractor Stations. Up to the end of 1929, the few collective cotton farms that existed in Central Asia had almost exclusively been created on the basis of pooling the land and the few and primitive agricultural implements of individual peasant households. The benefits the peasant derived from such collectives were more generous credits, lower taxes, better and more certain supplies of bread for family maintenance (received from the state), and the general feeling of greater security derived from collective effort and government aid. As regards machines and technicians, the benefits were not so great. The major part of the work on those farms was still done in an antediluvian way, with the crude implements that had characterized agriculture in Central Asia for many centuries.

The few tractor brigades sent out by the government were only supplementary. They helped when help was urgently needed. Though the collectives had the first option, poor and middle peasants not in collectives were also helped by the brigades. As a result, each spring the few tractors at the Government's disposal were scattered through the endless spaces of Central Asia, in groups of two and three, and no one region received technical aid of real consequence. The tractors were merely used as tantalizers. The brigades were primarily missionary in character. The whole thing was to a large extent an ambitious advertising stunt. But it was an expensive stunt. Scattered over a vast area, the tractor brigades were never sure of oil or skilled mechanics.

In anticipation of the collectivization campaign of 1930, the authorities in Central Asia hastened to reorganize the whole system of technical aid to the villages. Machine and Tractor Stations, along the lines successfully operated throughout the extensive grain sections of the Soviet Union, began to be put up with great speed. Toward the spring of 1930, nineteen Machine and Tractor Stations were in operation—six of which were in Uzbekistan, and four in Tadjikistan. In the first sowing campaign the MTS's of Central Asia fulfilled 117.7% of the task imposed by the government.

MTS and Coöperatives

To appreciate more fully the rôle of the MTS in industrializing and collectivizing the cotton plantations of Central Asia, a knowledge of the manner in which an MTS functions is indispensable.

Every MTS is an independent, coöperative, economic unit, created for the purpose of rendering, on a contractual basis, mechanical aid to the peasantry. At the same time, each MTS serves as the center from which the collectivization of the surrounding peasant households and the "socialist reconstruction of the district" is conducted. In districts having an MTS the collective farms do not own any tractors. All tractors designated for kolkhoz service are delivered to the MTS, and it is the duty of the MTS to give the kolkhozi preference in the use of the tractors and other agricultural machines. Next to the full-fledged kolkhozi, peasant associations organized for the purpose of common soil cultivation are entitled to the services of the MTS.

The usual contract between an MTS and a kolkhoz is signed for a period of five years, and is registered at the Land Department of the Region. Under the contract the

MTS is obliged to provide the collective with a specified number of tractors, implements, and various services. In case of necessity the MTS is also obliged to make all the repairs of and provide all the necessary parts for the collective's own machines. Furthermore, the MTS undertakes all this at a price not to exceed the actual cost. All expenses involved in repairing its own machines and implements, in providing the necessary fuel and lubricants, as well as in employing agronomists and technicians, are to be fully paid for by the MTS.

On its side, the kolkhoz assumes a series of obligations. First, all boundaries between separate plots of land must be eliminated; the kolkhoz must represent one continuous stretch of land. Second, in view of the fact that the Machine and Tractor Stations are not yet equipped with adequate transport facilities, the collective's draught animals must, when necessary, be made available for MTS use. The kolkhoz, in consideration of the services rendered by the MTS, is obliged to transport fuel, lubricants, farm implements, and other freight from the nearest railroad station or river port to the MTS. However, heavy freight, such as threshers, combines, etc., is to be handled by the MTS itself. The kolkhoz also promises to transport an adequate supply of water and food to the points where MTS tractors are at work. Accordingly, "the kolkhoz waives the right to sell any of its draught animals or agricultural implements without the consent of the MTS." Also, when roads are to be improved or built, the kolkhoz must provide a specified quota of men and horses, and the MTS the required number of tractors. To insure greater productivity, the kolkhoz, in all matters pertaining to agricultural improvement, planning, organization of labor, irrigation, pest eradication, and hilling, must follow instructions of MTS experts.

The contract also specifies the exact amount of land the kolkhoz is to use for cotton-growing. And to encourage the extension of cotton-sowing, the MTS undertakes to make the first plowing of all new cotton lands free of charge. Tractor drivers are to be supplied by the kolkhoz from among its own members. Prospective "tractorists," men or women elected by the kolkhoz, must be sent for training to the MTS, their living expenses for the required period to be paid by the kolkhoz. For all its services the MTS receives 25% of the crop.

(Incidentally, from the tapering off of the NEP and up to 1932, it was illegal for kolkhozi, as well as individual peasants, to sell their surplus products on the open market. Such selling was branded as "speculation," irrespective of whether or not the kolkhoz or the individual peasant had faithfully delivered to the state the amount of produce provided by the contract.)

A very important feature of the contract is the following point: "In order to establish close contact between the kolkhozi and the MTS and to assure peasant control over the activities of the latter, a special council is formed consisting of delegates elected from all the kolkhozi in the district and of representatives of the administration of the local MTS." Also, the MTS must call periodic production conferences at which the most active kolkhozniks and MTS workers are to discuss immediate problems of work and organization. Finally, failure on either side to live up to the terms of the agreement is sufficient ground for rescinding it, and the injured party has a right to sue for damages.

This cursory account of the organization and functions of the Machine and Tractor Stations ought to be sufficient to convey to the reader the tremendous part they played in the success of the 1930 collectivization campaign in Central Asia.

There was another, perhaps still more powerful factor in preparing the native masses for collectivization—and that was the producer-buyer relationship between the peasant cotton-grower and the Soviet Government. At present, this relationship is based on a bilateral contract under which the Government, in consideration of the peasant's promise to sow a stipulated amount of cotton on a specified plot of land and to sell to the Government such minimal portions of the cotton crop as are indicated by the terms of the contract, agrees through the cotton-growers' coöperative to purchase from the peasant, at a previously fixed price, cotton in quantities equal to, or in excess of, those mentioned in the contract, as well as to supply the peasant with the agricultural implements, selected cotton seed, bread grains, and manufactured products the peasants may require. Up to about 1926, however, such preliminary agreements were not common, and the state cotton-ginning industry used to obtain large quantities of cotton by haphazard purchases from the peasants during the fall and winter months. Such a system was advantageous to the beys, kulaks, and speculators, who, in addition to their own cotton, were selling to the Government cotton they had themselves bought at low prices from the poor peasants—a system highly unsatisfactory whether viewed from the angle of cotton or that of socialist planning. On the other hand, preliminary individual contracts with millions of small cotton growers, though highly desirable as a means of eliminating the parasitical middle-man, would have entailed another evil—a formidably cumbersome and expensive bureaucratic apparatus. Here was a problem that challenged Bolshevik ingenuity. The answer was, a mass agricultural coöperative organization, built up pyramidally from the bottom.

The basic unit of the coöperative is the village producers' association—in Central Asia, the village cotton-growers' association. These village associations which unite all the poor and middle, individual and collective, farmers in the village are joined in regional cotton-growers' coöperative unions, which in turn are united in one central Cotton-Growers' Coöperative.

The chief function of the coöperative is to act as intermediary between the cotton growers and the government cotton-ginning industry. Accordingly, contracts for cotton are concluded by the cotton-ginning industry not directly with the individual peasant households or separate collectives, but indirectly, through the local coöperative association which represents the interests of all its individual and collectivized members.

Planning Made Possible

The way the thing works is rather simple. The planning commission of each cotton-growing Central Asian Republic draws up a tentative plan for each region, designed more or less to fit into the general cotton plan of the Soviet Union. The tentative figures, called "control figures," for they offer a basis for checking up or controlling results, are communicated to the several regional branches of the Cotton-Growers' Coöperative. The latter examine, discuss, and if necessary amend the "control figures" for the various village branches of the coöperative. These village "control figures," too, are drawn up so as to agree approximately with the tentative plans received from above. Each village branch, balancing the control figures received from the regional center with the statements filed by all its members as to how much cotton each of them expects to sow in the coming spring, goes through a parallel procedure with regard to all individual and collective cotton-growers in the village. At village soviet gatherings, at general mass meetings, at kolkhoz conferences, the "control figures" for each household are weighed and discussed and fought over. Peasants who are anxious to get larger advances from the Government tend to over-estimate, while kulaks who are the enemies of cotton tend to under-estimate their respective cotton-growing capacity. Both are challenged by the rest. In a small compact community it is rather difficult to hoodwink one's neighbors. In case of disparity between the control figures for the village and the total proposed by the individual and collective members, a general meeting of peasants decides just where the figures may be adjusted. When cotton assignments are increased, land, implement, and labor possibilities are taken into consideration. If certain households require special help to enable them to fulfill the assignment, such help is generally granted by the meeting.

The treatment of the kulak is less gentle. First, he is not

allowed membership in the association. Second, the Government does not enter into any contract with the "class enemy." The village soviet, guided by resolutions adopted at the general meetings of the poor and middle peasants, gives each kulak an inflexible, a "hard" cotton assignment. The kulak is paid for his cotton like all other peasants, of course, except that he does not get any advances and, as we have already mentioned, he is obliged to deliver to the Government a specified quantity of cotton determined in advance by the local authorities.

After every peasant in the country is thoroughly familiarized with the general cotton plan and the part he personally is expected to play in fulfilling it, contracts are signed. First, agreements are made between the village branch of the Cotton-Growers' Coöperative and each individual member in that branch; second, between the regional and village branches; third, between the central and regional branches. So far all the agreements are among the various branches of the Cotton-Growers' Coöperative. The last step is a contract between the central office of the Producers' Coöperative and the state cotton-ginning industry. The cotton grower's numerous contractual obligations, such as weeding, watering, hilling, picking at proper times, are in the final analysis but part of his main obligation—to produce and deliver to the coöperative warehouses as much (or more) cotton as the coöperative had contracted for. The main obligation of the coöperative is to buy all the cotton produced by each individual or collective farmer at a price not lower than the contract price. The coöperative is also obliged to pay to each individual or collective cotton-grower advances (monetary or in the form of manufactured products, seed, fertilizer, implements, bread, MTS service, etc.) in amounts and at intervals specified in the contract.

In the spring of 1930, there were in Central Asia 2,192 village branches of the Cotton-Growers' Coöperative. There were 1,630 branches in Uzbekistan, and 50 in Tadjikistan. These simple coöperative associations, in drawing many poor and middle peasants out of their economic isolation, in making them feel that they were active parts of a complicated economic whole, in perpetually holding before them the advantages of coöperative effort, in educating them socially and politically, in taking the initiative toward the economic and cultural reconstruction of the village, have been incomparable training schools for kolkhozniks. Together with the state farms and Machine and Tractor Stations, they rendered the peasant's transition to higher forms of collective ownership and collective enterprise not only natural but inevitable.

That this was so can be judged by what took place in Uzbekistan during the next few years. As in all the Central Asian Republics, the 1930 collectivization campaign in Uzbekistan did not seriously affect the cultivation of cotton. Indeed, judging by the growth of the cotton area, 1930 showed more than normal progress. In 1925-26, the cotton area in Uzbekistan was 380,000 hectares; in 1926-27, 444,300 hectares; in 1927-28, 529,900; in 1928-29, 585,700; in 1929-30, 824,000; and in 1930-31, 1,020,200 hectares. In the fall of 1930, over 27 per cent of the cotton lands were collectivized; and in 1931 over 55 per cent. In 1931 the state cotton plantations stretched over areas amounting to 80,000 hectares. Instead of the six MTS's in 1930, Uzbekistan had fourteen large and thirty-four small stations in 1931. Instead of 368 tractors in 1930, there were 2,300 in 1931. The total value of all agricultural production in Uzbekistan, silk, fruit, grain, wool and dairy included, jumped from 523 million rubles in 1928 to 1,216 millions in 1930 and it is significant that the increase in 1929 over 1928 was only 5.2 per cent, while in 1930 it was 29 per cent over 1929.

PART FOUR

BUILDING SOCIALISM IN TADJIKISTAN

"... The revolution would not have triumphed in Russia, and Kolchak and Denikin would not have been crushed, if the Russian proletariat did not have on its side the sympathies and the support of the oppressed peoples in the former Russian empire. But to win the sympathies and the support of these peoples, it had first of all to break the chain forged by Russian imperialism and free these peoples from the yoke of national oppression. Without this it would have been impossible firmly to establish the Soviet power, to implant true internationalism and to create the remarkable organization for the collaboration of nations which is called the Union of Soviet Socialist Republics and which is the living prototype of the future union of nations in a single world economic system."

—JOSEPH STALIN, *The National Question.*

XII

A BOLSHEVIK IN STALINABAD

> *Who has brought to our steppes the gay, ringing streams?*
> *Who has tamed the wild waters of the turbulent Pianj?*
> *Who has brought our poor peasants sweet joy and sweet rest?*
> *The men from the North! The men of great freedom!*
> *The men of Marx and Lenin—the Bolsheviks!*
> —ALI-BE, Turkoman Poet.

Structures and Superstructures

I SHALL never forget the powerful impression made on me by Sluchak, the assistant to the native vice-president of the Tadjik Republic. I lived in his hastily built, sparsely furnished apartment for over two weeks and I had an excellent opportunity to observe this wiry, energetic, blue-eyed and dark-skinned Bolshevik at close range.

The apartment gave one the feeling of military headquarters. Except for the time that my host spent in the office, his home, from early morning till late in the night, was crowded with people—officials with portfolios and batches of papers, engineers with blue-prints and grandiose plans, accountants and economists with endless columns of figures and ingeniously plotted graphs and curves, managers of state farms, chairmen of collective farms, representatives from coöperatives, the transport, labor unions, educational institutions—callers without end.

Not infrequently the callers would begin to pour in even before Sluchak was dressed. And heated business discussions would resound through the half-empty rooms while Vice-Chairman of the People's Council of Commissars brushed his teeth, gargled his throat, and pulled on his breeches. A meal was never a meal in this household; it was "snatching a bite" in the midst of some conference. It was so in the evening, too. Always working, always on the go, always in the thick of a "campaign."

The first time I met him, I did not catch his name. I did not know his official position. The conversation turned to the then unfolding "cultural campaign." Sluchak spoke so enthusiastically about the victories on the Tadjik cultural front that I was certain he was a native. My astonishment was great when I discovered that he was a Jew from Gomel. This was strange enough. But even stranger were his enthusiasm and complete identification with his subject. He actually spoke of "our" culture, when he meant Tadjik culture.

Apparently my companions were surprised too, for one of them remarked: "The way you spoke, I surely thought you were a Tadjik." "Not a Tadjik, but a Bolshevik," corrected Sluchak. In Tadjikistan, he proceeded to explain, the Soviet task of overtaking and surpassing the capitalist countries—a task common to all the republics in the Soviet Union—was particularly difficult because of the great cultural backwardness of the population. The government, therefore, had the additional and immediately urgent task of removing, in the briefest possible time, the cultural and economic inequality between the Tadjik people and the peoples of the other republics in the Union. This meant that the rate of development of Tadjikistan's national economy and, *primarily*, of its social and cultural life, had to be much greater than in the rest of the Union, so that this backward country might catch up with her sister republics and together with them overtake and surpass the capitalist countries. Accordingly, Sluchak assured us that it was not as a Jew or a Russian or a Tadjik that he spoke, but as a Bolshevik—a Bolshevik who realized that "a victory on any of the Soviet Union's cultural fronts was a victory for Bolshevism."

When Sluchak's use of the word "primarily" was challenged by some of my Communist companions, his answer was illuminating.

"The precedence I have given to cultural over material advance must, of course, be understood in the sense of my having placed the end anterior to the means. The end is a nobler and richer life, a happier humanity. The means are a thorough and complete change in the material, the economic base of the social structure. My use of the word 'primarily' was, strictly speaking, wrong. However, there is some psychological explanation. Subconsciously, perhaps, I stressed the aim first because in my own life, and I suspect it holds true of most of our comrades, the constant awareness of the aim has served as incentive and justification during the most crucial periods."

Here Sluchak walked over to the bookshelf and pulled out a well-thumbed paper-covered collection of Communist Party Resolutions. He swiftly turned the pages, glanced through a couple of them, and obviously finding something to support his argument, smiled mischievously:

"You, comrades, are finding fault with my formulation. Now listen to the Resolution of the Twelfth Congress of the Russian Communist Party, passed in 1923. Here it is, on the National Question, Section One. I'll read only part of it:

> "The legal national equality achieved by the October Revolution is a great gain for the peoples, but it alone does not solve the whole national problem. A number of republics and peoples, which have not passed, or have only to a small extent passed, through the stage of capitalism, which have no proletariat or only a very small proletariat, and which, accordingly, are economically and culturally backward, are not in a position to make full use of the rights and opportunities conferred upon them by national equality and are unable to rise to a higher level of development and thus overtake the more advanced nations, without effective and prolonged outside help. The causes of this actual inequality lie not only in the his-

tory of these nations, but also in the policy of the Czarist government and of the Russian bourgeoisie, whose endeavor it was to transform the outlying provinces exclusively into sources of raw material exploited by the industrially developed central regions. It is impossible to abolish this inequality and eradicate this heritage in a short period, in one or two years. The Tenth Congress of our Party noted that 'the abolition of actual national inequality is a long process demanding an obstinate and persistent struggle against all survivals of national oppression and national slavery.' But abolished it must be. And it can be abolished only by the Russian proletariat rendering effective and prolonged assistance to the backward nations of the Union in their economic and cultural advancement. This assistance must consist primarily in the adoption of a number of practical measures for the creation of industrial centers in the republics of the nationalities which were formerly subjected to oppression, and in drawing the greatest possible number of the local population into this work. Finally, as indicated by the resolution of the Tenth Congress, this assistance must proceed side by side with the struggle of the laboring masses for the consolidation of their social positions as against the exploiting elements, both native and from outside. Unless this is done no hopes can be entertained of establishing proper and stable coöperation between the nations within a single federative state. Hence, the second immediate duty of our Party is to struggle for the abolition of the actual inequality of nationalities and for raising the cultural and economic level of the backward nations.

"Here you have it—'cultural and economic.' In the concluding sentence 'cultural' is mentioned first. Not the means but the end," said Sluchak triumphantly. Seeing, however, that his foreign comrades felt a little sheepish, he hastened to console them by pointing out that in their actual practice, even as the Resolution showed, the Bolsheviks placed chief emphasis on the means.

This is Leninist practice. The Bolsheviks hold that the

cultural and psychological aspects of life are "superstructures," that there is no such thing as "immutable human nature," and they are out to change the economic and social foundations of society in the conviction that they will thus bring about corresponding changes in the psychological and cultural superstructures. As regards cultural innovations, they employ strategy, leveling their first, direct and most powerful attacks at the determining, i.e. the economic, factors. But the Bolsheviks are not crude materialists. They are Marxists. They look at life dialectically. Their conception of social "structures" and "superstructures" is monistic: there is no rigid line of demarcation—the sap of life runs up and down; there is an eternal give and take. In the social complex, they realize, psychological and cultural patterns, though determined by economic patterns, in turn affect those patterns. This being the case, it is obvious that the Bolsheviks could not ignore, even from the very outset, psychology and culture. Their efforts on these fronts have been persistent. In a tense revolutionary situation, they have found, clearness and firmness of purpose, tempered by intelligence, caution, elasticity, and above all genuine sympathy are absolute prerequisites for any effective changes, especially on the cultural front. Besides vested interests to combat, there were native prejudices to be taken into account—traditions, customs, habits, faiths, superstitions, and fears.

Naturally, some things required less delicate treatment than others. It all depended on the ease with which the government could demonstrate to the masses the advantages and desirability of a specific change, and that depended on the depth of the prevailing prejudices against such change. On the whole it is safe to say that in their work the Bolsheviks had to be exceedingly subtle and diplomatic. This was particularly true in Central Asia, and especially in Tadjikistan, where equilibrium, when established, was rendered highly unstable by the proximity of vigilant English imperialism and by tireless anti-Communist propaganda.

National in Form, Socialist in Content

In our conversations with Sluchak, we would often revert back to the problem of culture, especially national culture. Once one of my companions expressed amusement over the grotesque forms which Bolshevism has assumed in some of the remoter regions of Central Asia—Communists going to the mosque, members of the Party clinging to all kinds of superstitions which harked back to pre-Moslem days, to magic and Shamanism.

"This does not worry us," Sluchak assured him. "Our first test in these backward regions is this: Is the fellow with us in the matter of taking away the lands from the beys, is he with us in the matter of collectivization and industrialization, is he ready to fight for our program? If he is, he is eligible for Party membership. Don't you see? We must be flexible in approaching the masses. We have the responsibility of reconstructing a whole society, and we cannot permit ourselves the comfort of sectarianism. Here acceptance of Marxist and Leninist materialist ideas is not a prerequisite for Party membership, but it invariably happens that a few months in the Party result in a gradual acceptance of our ideas. When a native is drawn into the Party, he is much more amenable to our influence and teaching. We are in a transition period. Naturally, you encounter some grotesque specimens."

Another time, Sluchak and I had a long discussion as to the wisdom of Bolshevik emphasis on the development of national cultures. My feeling was that such emphasis was bound to lead to greater cultural differentiation, to a lessening of mutual understanding, increased friction and disunity. I confessed that I was quite irritated in the Ukraine when all theaters, moving pictures, signs in the shops, and businesses and offices employed the Ukraianian language. There was a time when one could go to Kiev or to Kharkov or to Odessa and feel that one was in a Russian city. Indeed, the cultured Ukrainians used the Russian language almost exclusively. And writers like

Gogol, Dahl, Korolenko—Ukrainians all—contributed to the enrichment of literature by employing Russian, a language spoken by many more millions than was the Ukrainian language. Now Russian has become a foreign tongue in the Ukraine!

"If you were a Russian, we would call you a Great Russian chauvinist and we would make it rather hot for you," Sluchak laughed.

Following good Bolshevik precedent, however, I tried to defend my position by a reference to Lenin. Long before the Revolution, in his polemics with the Jewish *Bund*, Lenin declared that national culture was a bourgeois concept and that socialism, together with abolishing national oppression, would remove all national barriers and that the interests of all nationalities would combine in a single whole.

"But this is a mechanical interpretation of what Lenin said," exclaimed Sluchak. "You take no cognizance of time or place. Furthermore your arguments have been excellently answered by Stalin." Jumping up impetuously and pulling out the second volume of Stalin's *Leninism*, Sluchak pointed out the passage where the Communist leader, after defining Great-Russian chauvinism as "the desire to ignore national differences in language, culture, mode of life ... the desire to prepare for the liquidation of the national republics and regions ... the desire to undermine the principle of national equality," proceeds to castigate those "deviators" who "take their stand on the argument that, as with the victory of socialism nations will fuse into a single whole, while their national language will be fused into a single common tongue, the time has come to liquidate national differences and renounce the policy of developing the national culture of the peoples which were formerly oppressed."

There it was, black on white. My arguments, stamped as "the most subtle and, therefore, the most dangerous form of Great-Russian nationalism"!

"Read on, read on," urged Sluchak. "Stalin also answers your reference to Lenin very specifically."

I read: "In the first place, Lenin never said that national differences must disappear and national tongues be fused in one common tongue within the boundaries of a *single* state, *before* the *victory* of socialism *all over the world.* Lenin, on the contrary, said quite the opposite, namely, that 'the national and state *distinctions* between peoples and countries... will exist for *a very long time even after* the establishment of the dictatorship of the proletariat on a world *scale.*' How can people refer to Lenin and forget this basic statement of his?"

"Don't you see," Sluchak further pressed his point, "we communists do not discuss 'national culture' in the abstract. For us this is a concrete problem in a concrete situation. And we have to deal with it concretely. In order to have a Soviet Union at all, in order to gain and hold the sympathy of all the peoples that had been oppressed by czarism, in order to make them love and understand the Soviet Union, it was essential that we make the Soviet government not a Russian but an international government. We, of course, are interested in socialism and not in national differences. But we realize that the ultimate fusion of nationalities under socialism is a matter of very many years and that the road to that fusion is through the complete liberation of all peoples. We must reach the native masses, the peasants, the workers, and the only way we can reach them is through their own national language, the only language they know, and their own national cultures, the only cultures for which they have a genuine love. Accordingly, not only the schools, but all our institutions and organs, both Party and Soviet, have had to become naturalized step by step. They have had to employ the language understood by the masses and take into consideration the habits and customs of each given people. Only such a policy has enabled the Soviet government to function not as a Russian but as an international government understood by, and near and dear to, the toiling masses of all the republics, particularly to the nations which have been economically and culturally backward!"

My Norwegian companion, Luyn, now took up the

argument with Sluchak. While admitting that the Bolshevik cultural policy was wise and necessary as an initial step in the creation of the Soviet Union, he still failed to see how the perpetuation of that policy would bring about the ultimate fusion of peoples under socialism.

In reply to Luyn, Sluchak gently chided his foreign comrades for soaring in the realm of the superstructures without occasionally alighting on the economic and social foundations.

Had not feudal economic and social relations in Europe created a specific feudal culture which even then transcended national lines? And had not capitalist economic and social relations created a quite distinct bourgeois culture? Indeed the proverbial visitor from Mars would find infinitely more similarities in the cultures of, say, Italy, Germany, Finland, Japan, and other capitalist countries than he would find differences. This, despite the constant incitements of national and religious suspicions and hatreds. Now what was the situation in the Soviet Union? argued Sluchak. Here the economic foundations of society in all the nationalities were basically changed. Exploitation, the profit motive, private property in the means of production were being rapidly eliminated. The socialist proletariat and the industrialized and collectivized peasantry, which was ideologically coming closer and closer to the proletariat, were in power among all the Soviet peoples. The Soviet Union was already creating a classless society, and it was advancing towards the economic and cultural equality of all the peoples in its fold. Was it unreasonable to believe then that the Union of Socialist Soviet Republics would in the course of time evolve a socialist culture quite distinct from the feudal or bourgeois ones? Look at Stalinabad! Of course, old forms did tend to persist, but already a new content was being poured into them. This was a part of the transition. Hence, so many cultural hybrids in the land. With a socialist economy assured, with all causes for national hatred, jealousies and suspicion removed, with travel made infinitely easier and encouraged, with internationalism constantly implanted in the psychology of every Soviet child, what reason was there to believe that in time a fusion of peoples would not be effected?

But this would take a very long time. It would come about gradually, naturally, not through administrative pressure. All the Bolsheviks could do was to create the conditions which would make this normal development possible.

Meanwhile, suggested Sluchak, the Soviet course during the transition period, the proletarian dictatorship, had been very fully worked out in Stalin's *The Political Tasks of the University of the Peoples of the East:*

> But what is national culture? How are we to make national culture compatible with proletarian culture? ... How are we to reconcile the development of national culture, the development of schools and courses in the native languages, and the training of Communist cadres from among the local people, with the building of proletarian culture? Is this not an impenetrable contradiction? Of course not! We are now building proletarian culture. That is absolutely true. But it is also true that proletarian culture, which is socialist in content, is assuming different forms and different means of expression among the various peoples who have been drawn into the work of socialist construction, according to their languages, their local customs, and so forth. Proletarian in content and national in form—such is the human culture toward which socialism is marching. Proletarian culture does not cancel national culture, but gives it content. On the other hand, national culture does not cancel proletarian culture, but gives it form. The slogan of "national culture" was a bourgeois slogan so long as the bourgeoisie was in power and the consolidation of nations proceeded under the aegis of the bourgeois system. The slogan of "national culture" became a proletarian slogan when the proletariat came into power and the consolidation of nations began to proceed under the aegis of the Soviet power.

In Happy Exile

Once, as we sat over a glass of native wine, Sluchak looked so nervous and worn that some one in our group suggested that it would not be a bad idea if he took a vacation.

His eyes lit up: "A vacation! I haven't had a vacation for years! If I ever get one, the first thing I'll do is fly to Moscow—theaters, music, and all that sort of thing. And next I would go to Minsk to see my mother. I haven't seen her for over eight years now, and I am anxious to see her. Poor woman, after my father was killed in the Gomel pogrom, she did everything to bring us up as good Jews. And how grieved she was to see me, a student of the Talmud, intended for the Rabbinate, become a revolutionist, a *goy*. When I joined the Bolsheviks she cried bitterly, though she said nothing—I had always suspected that her opposition was caused more by her fear for my life than by actual dislike of the Revolution. After all, a Jewess whose husband had been killed in a pogrom was not likely to cherish tender feelings for the czar and his régime. My sister writes me that the old woman is now quite reconciled to the new life. In her relations with God she has remained steadfast. She goes to synagogue regularly, keeps *kosher* house, observes all the fasts and holidays; but politically she has become quite a Bolshevik."

Sluchak laughed with a tenderness one scarcely suspected in him. What a mighty thing is Revolution! How it had hammered and hardened this obviously sensitive being into the sharp, steel-like instrument of the proletarian dictatorship he now was. In the smithy of the Revolution, this child of the ghetto, this student of the Talmud intended for the Rabbinate, had been forged into a Bolshevik, a military hero, into a torch-bearer of Communist Internationalism on the borders of Afghanistan, India, and China.

When Sluchak was asked how he happened to land in that remote periphery of the Soviet territory in Asia, he answered with a long disquisition on the manner in which the Bolsheviks organized the government of Tadjikistan, and on Tadjikistan's early need of cultured non-Russian Bolsheviks to aid in the work. Only toward the end did he mention himself and how he happened to be in Tadjikistan. He was here, because he was a Bol'shevik representing a national minority and as such more able to appreciate the problems and aspirations of other national minorities. He had fought three years in the Civil War; during the famine he worked in the Volga region; then he was shifted from one job into another, in White Russia, the Caucasus, and finally in Moscow. But in Moscow he remained only a short time. Just as he had begun to take things a little easier, to permit himself an occasional evening in the theater or the opera, the Party ordered him to Tadjikistan.

Sluchak had scarcely heard of Tadjikistan before. He knew it only as a wild and primitive country of mountains, deserts, bandits, and nomads, somewhere near India. And how he hated to leave Moscow, the center of everything in the Union, and go to some forsaken place in Central Asia! He felt hurt and resentful. Tadjikistan meant exile to him. But orders were orders. He came here and plunged straight into the work, into the very thick of it. At first he worked furiously, simply to forget his resentment, but the deeper he became involved in the work, the more absorbing, the more fascinating he found it. This was his third year here, and now nothing could tempt him to leave Tadjikistan except on a short vacation. "If one wants to work, to build," said Sluchak, "Tadjikistan is the place. If one wants to fight—Tadjikistan affords ample opportunity for that, too. Even now, in 1931, we have our hands full with Ibrahim Bek and his Basmach bands. What makes this place so alluring is that the struggle here is extraordinarily intense—extraordinary even in the Soviet Union. You have done well to come here. Geography, history, religion, customs—everything seems to have conspired to make this obscure place the ideal spot for any one who wishes to study Bolshevism both as an international force and a domestic generator of highly charged economic, political, and social drama. First, we are at the gates of Hindustan, Afghanistan, China, countries with considerable Tadjik populations. Second, we have to deal with the most fanatical Moslems in the world. Third, it is an inaccessible mountainous country—tucked away in the Hissar and Kuliab valleys and hidden among the Zeravshan, Altai and Pamir mountain ranges—and native counter-revolutionary bands supported and armed from the outside have an excellent opportunity to harass us constantly. Fourth, we have here an involved national question, and particularly and quite naturally a tendency toward Tadjik chauvinism. Fifth, Tadjikistan was an incredibly ignorant and impoverished country. Only one half of one per cent of the population was literate. And you can gauge the effect of the revolution and the Basmach movement on the life of the people by the fact that at the end of the Civil War Eastern Bokhara had lost 72 per cent of the sown area, over 60 per cent of the cattle, and 25 per cent of the population. There was a great exodus of the more prosperous peasant families. Two hundred and six thousand people (43,000 peasant households) with stocks and cattle and implements migrated to Afghanistan. We found here a completely devastated country, and we have been striving to transform it in as brief a time as possible, and despite all the Ibrahim Beks, into a highly mechanized, collectivized, and industrialized center of Egyptian cotton."

Ibrahim Bek Again!

Sluchak's frequent references to Ibrahim Bek provoked a series of questions from the group. Sluchak dismissed the whole affair as rather inconsequential, a brief but unpleasant interlude in the republic's march toward collectivization and cotton. According to him, minor Basmach raids from across the Afghan border had occurred here regularly since the formation of the Tadjik government. Ibrahim

Bek was still the most important Basmach leader. His following among the thousands of kulaks and beys who had emigrated to Afghanistan after the Revolution was so great that he had begun to play quite a rôle in intertribal Afghan struggles, lending his forces and prestige to this or that Afghan chieftain. By the time Amannula Khan, the Afghan king, was overthrown and Nadir Khan seized the reins of the Afghan government, Ibrahim felt sufficiently powerful to oppose the new king. There were rumors that Great Britain was backing Ibrahim Bek, intending to utilize him in the creation of a buffer zone between Soviet Tadjikistan and Afghanistan. The zone was to be settled by Ibrahim's followers, and he himself was to be the ruler of Britain's choice.

However, Ibrahim Bek was defeated by Nadir Khan and was forced to retreat to the north, where for three and a half months he had complete sway over the Karategin and Badakhshan provinces. But he could not withstand the pressure of Nadir Khan's troops. Early in April, 1931, a fierce battle on the banks of the River Pianj left Ibrahim Bek's forces completely smashed. When his warriors and their families and cattle tried to cross the Pianj to the Soviet side, they were attacked by the Afghans in the middle of the river. Hundreds more were massacred. Women and children and cattle were drowned. Those who managed to cross were received by the Soviet authorities with serious misgivings.

The misgivings were wholly justified. Beaten in Afghanistan, Ibrahim Bek had conceived the notion of restoring his fortunes by invading Soviet Tadjikistan which was in the throes of the collectivization campaign. Ibrahim relied on reports of peasant opposition to collectivization, and he had hoped that the invasion of Soviet territory by a large force might provide the impetus for a widespread counter-revolutionary uprising. Like most people in Tadjikistan, Sluchak was inclined to credit Great Britain with the plan. He maintained, and I subsequently heard many other people in Tadjikistan say the same thing, that the ostensibly peaceful reimmigration of 6,000 people on the

25th of March, 1931, had been a maneuver of Ibrahim's to create a strong anti-Soviet base for himself on Soviet territory, especially in his native Lokai Valley.

Soon after the coming of the 6,000, a long proclamation, printed on good paper, and decorated with Ibrahim Bek's seal, began to circulate in the villages of Central Asia.

The proclamation, displayed to us by Sluchak, had been issued "In the name of Almighty God." It opened with a verse from the Koran, "With God's help, victory draws nigh." It read:

> To all the peoples inhabiting the territory of Russia, Turkestan, Tartarstan, Kazakstan, Kirghizstan, Uzbekistan, and Tadjikistan, greetings from Divon Bek and Tachasm Bachi, Mohammed Bek, also from his Majesty Emir Alim Khan!
>
> We herewith recall to your mind that at the time the Russian Czar Nicholas and Emir Alim Khan were reigning, all nations lived happily and peacefully on their respective territories and were allowed freely to practice their religion. But in the year 1295 Czar Nicholas, and in the year 1298 Emir Alim Khan were removed from their thrones, violently, at the instigation of Lenin (his name be cursed)....

Ibrahim accused the "representatives of the government of Lenin, cursed be his name" of breaking their promise to rule "fairly and justly." He presented a long bill of complaints: The Bolsheviks were dishonoring the Moslem women and turning them into harlots; they were taking the lands and the water from the rightful owners, forcing the poor peasants to plant cotton instead of corn, thus spreading hunger and devastation through the land. They were foisting new-fangled iron instruments and machines ("bought in foreign lands"!) on the peasants, for which the peasants had to pay with their last kopeks; taxes were crushing and were being collected by force. The bazaars were ruined, prices were sky-high, and the "poor peasants can obtain goods only by submitting to insults and injuries." The Bolsheviks were deceiving the peasants by forcing them into collective farms and depriving them of their horses and cattle. Besides seizing their property, the Bolsheviks were planning to exile the peasants "to faraway lands." That was not all. The "treacherous and horrible," the "satanic" government would soon begin to destroy mosques and prayer houses and sacred books, to burn the dead, to take the women away from their "masters" and force them into the Communist Party and make harlots of them. Before long any one daring to even so much as breathe the name of God would be mercilessly destroyed.

Ibrahim's proclamation also announced his international connections:

> As these things were developing through the criminal policy of the Bolsheviks, the meeting held February 8, 1928, by the League of Nations in Berlin [sic!], where a representative of the refugees from Russian Turkestan was present, as well as the session of the League of Nations held in December 1929 participated in by representatives from America, France, Japan, Germany, Persia, Turkey, Italy, Afghanistan and Poland [the name of England is discreetly omitted], resolved, in accordance with the statements of the representatives of the emigrants from Russian Turkestan, and with the new political information furnished in the year 1930 by Comrades Trotsky and Zinoviev, to abolish the Party's government in Russia as well as in Bokhara, and to organize instead a monarchy.

"Empowered" by his Highness Emir Alim Khan and by the above-mentioned nations "to raise armies of the required strength on all borders," Ibrahim urged the peasants of Central Asia to advance upon Soviet Bokhara and "invite in writing the whole Red Army, the whole militia, all the workers' fighting detachments, and all of the Emir's subjects" to join in the war against the Reds. After promising "in the name of Allah and his prophet ... to pardon all those who served the Bolsheviks, but who had repented in time," Ibrahim's declaration concluded: "Our aim is clear. Oppressed peasants, we are engaged in this war to liberate you from the Bolshevik yoke!"

BUILDING SOCIALISM IN TADJIKISTAN

"The trouble with Ibrahim Bek," Sluchak commented, "is that he does not know Soviet Tadjikistan, the mood of the Tadjik masses. He is an able leader and no fool. But, like most émigrés even better informed than he, Ibrahim tends to believe what he wishes to believe. Of course, the proclamation was not written by him. It must have been written by one of his mullahs, but it no doubt expressed his ideas. Ibrahim and his gang thought that they could undo what we have done, that they could return the past. They sought to take advantage of our difficulties during the reconstruction period. Backed by the English, they thought that they could upset our spring sowing campaign and that with the support of the dissatisfied elements in the villages—the kulaks and the mullahs—they could start a counter-revolution here. Well, they know better now. We have beaten them to a frazzle. Ibrahim Bek has not been caught yet, but we know where he is and we'll get him, too."

A Bolshevik Legend

To show the utter fatuousness of Ibrahim's adventure, Sluchak began to cite the great achievements of Soviet Tadjikistan. "Study Dushambe and Stalinabad," he urged, "and then make your trip through the country and you will see what the Soviet government has accomplished here. But as you study, always bear in mind that we have started here with less than zero."

What Sluchak said was no idle boast. Before the revolution there had been no industries in Tadjikistan. In 1931, Tadjikistan had nine cotton-ginning mills, one cotton-seed oil factory, one volatile oil factory, numerous flour mills, a huge factory specially employed in preparing fruit for export, etc.

There was in 1931 the beginning of a mining industry —coal, oil, and salt. The production of Shurab oil had been doubled in 1930, and was expected to be trebled in 1931, and oil transportation had been facilitated by the new sixty-five kilometer railroad branch to Shurab. Scientific commissions were studying the Karamazar zinc mines and the Nauket copper mines. The first was expected ultimately to yield ten thousand tons of zinc and the second five thousand tons of copper yearly. The exploitation of Khanakin anthracite had begun. A huge hydro-electrical station was being constructed on the river Varsob near Stalinabad. The most gigantic undertaking was the Vakhshstroy, the analogue of the Ukrainian Dnieprostroy, which was planned to supply most of the country with electrical power and with the basis for a modern system of irrigation. Thirty thousand people had already been drawn into the domestic crafts industries, of which the silk industry was the most important and most promising. In addition to the silk factory employing one thousand people, which was already working in Khodjent, one of the biggest silk factories in the Union, which was to employ three thousand Khodjent women, was approaching completion. Another huge silk factory was being built in Stalinabad. In 1927-28, the government had put 268,000 rubles into its industries; in 1928-29, 1,400,000 rubles; in 1930, over 10,000,000 rubles; in 1931 the figure was 14,000,000 rubles. In 1928-29 the value of Tadjikistan's manufactured products was 10,000,000 rubles; in 1931, 51,000,000 rubles. In 1928-29 the value of Tadjikistan's agricultural products was 94,000,000 rubles; in 1931, 153,000,000. In 1928-29 building operations amounted to 20,000,000; in 1931 the allotted sum was 128,000,000.

Great progress had also been made in agriculture. As had been pointed out by Sluchak, in 1925 the sown area was 72 per cent lower than in pre-war days. This spelled catastrophe. All kinds of wild rumors spread through the countryside. Soviet enemies went around whispering that Tadjikistan would never recover under the Soviet power, that God had inflicted hunger upon the people for accepting the *"Bolshevois,"* that unless they continued to struggle against the Communist régime the whole population would die out. A few years passed and the sown area was greater than in pre-war days. And what was particularly important was the rapid extension of industrial crops. The growing of cotton, which had almost ceased before 1925, developed to tremendous proportions—from thirty-five thousand hectares in 1914, the growing area had fallen to four thousand in 1925. In 1930 the total area had increased to one hundred and thirty-two thousand. The year 1931 showed a further 25 per cent increase in the cotton area of Tadjikistan.

The growth of the cotton area here depended a great deal on irrigation. In 1929 Tadjikistan spent three million rubles in round figures on irrigation; in 1930, twelve million rubles, and the budget for 1931 was sixty-one million; i.e., approximately fifty rubles for every inhabitant in Tadjikistan. And most of that money was obtained not from taxing the local population but from sums granted by the central government of the Soviet Union.

In the matter of collectivization, the intensive educational and propaganda campaign brought altogether unexpected results. By May 1931 sixty thousand out of a total of two hundred and twenty thousand farms were in collectives. And by June over sixty per cent of the cotton lands were collectivized. The percentage of all collectivized lands (cotton and grain) was about thirty per cent. No mean achievement this, when one considers the backwardness of the country, the newness of the Soviet régime there, and the bitter struggle against collectivization carried on by the combined forces of reaction under the leadership of Ibrahim Bek.

"Of course," Sluchak said, "there are plenty of difficulties, but we overcome them—advancing along the general line laid down by our Party, fighting simultaneously the opportunists, the doubters, the creepers, and the chauvinists on the Right, and the infantile, over-enthusiastic babblers on the Left. Whatever aspect of the work you tackle, industrialization, collectivization, education, woman's emancipation, coöperation, transport, the problems of religion, law, administration, the building of Stalinabad, everything is full of thrills and romance.

"Even to me the mere fact that Tadjikistan, an obscure

little country the size of Czecho-Slovakia, is one of the seven sovereign constituent Republics of the Soviet Union, enjoying a political status on a par with the infinitely larger and incomparably more important economically R. S. F. S. R., still seems a legend, a myth! Imagine what it means to the natives!"

XIII

DUSHAMBE VERSUS STALINABAD

> *Both Samarkand and Kandagar I saw,*
> *And the dream of the desert and the bazaar*
>   *I saw,*
> *And one-third of the Mohammedan world I saw,*
> *And the snows of the tall Pamir I saw.*
>
> *Canals I dug, and molded pottery,*
> *And carried burdens up the mountain's back,*
> *Along steep paths I stumbled days and days*
> *And reached the mountain's rocky peak....*
>
> *But never such a wonder have I seen*
> *As the iron road to Dushambe....*
>   —Tadjik Song of Wonderment.

Donkeys—Camels—Mullahs—Merchants

IN the morning sun the Dushambe Bazaar shimmers like a vari-colored Oriental carpet. From the winding streets and alleys, raising clouds of gray dust, streams of bearded natives—peasants, peddlers, craftsmen—riding graceful mountain horses or tiny native asses, pour leisurely into the teeming square. Now and then the fantastic curves of a loaded camel undulate gently above the crowd. The older Tadjiks and Uzbeks are dressed in their brightest cloaks and headgear. Occasionally the snow-white turban of a mullah flutters in the air. Everywhere one sees sallow fakirs shambling behind their donkeys heavily laden with bundles of dry brush or sacks of grain or baskets of fruits and berries.

The merchants, the more solid ones, those who own places in the double row of stands, are spreading their wares—the cheapest sorts of gaudy Bokhara silks and skull caps and calicoes and carpets, beads, hand-made stilettos, pins, needles, threads, combs, moldy pastries and little tin jars with all kinds of miracle-working salves and potions. Most of the merchants, however, have no stands and they spread out their wares on the ground. One has leather and leather-goods, shoes especially adapted to mountain climbing, overshoes, wallets, trinkets. Another crouches near a heap of *nas,* a green tobacco which the natives always keep in their mouths, and tobacco containers made of gourds. Still another has a pile of *uriuk*—small and very sweet apricots—or cherries—it being as yet too early in the season for the pomegranates, melons and grapes for which this part of the world is so famous.

Noise, shouting, laughter. Bargaining.

For the most part under the open skies, but occasionally under a huge umbrella, are spread out the tonsorial establishments. Barbers are hovering over their kneeling victims, scraping dull razors over resignedly lowered pates. Knife grinders are displaying their dexterity. Water carriers, their sweating, long-nozzled copper vessels or dark dripping water skins on their shoulders, are proclaiming the cooling properties of their wares.

In the center of this milling crowd, sits a mountain Tadjik, the proud vendor of two huge chunks of ice which he had hauled down from that glacier that looms in the distance. It was a difficult task to carry the ice from the steep height down the narrow and slippery mountain paths, but it was worth the pains, for ice in this torrid land is rare and precious, and, judging by the number of purchasers, quite irresistible.

A coffee-colored lad is trying to find space for his business. There is a log not yet preëmpted. He makes a dash for it, and, dragging a suspicious-looking cut of mutton from his sack, sticks his knife into it and begins to yell at the top of his voice: "Gusht—Gu-usht!" But a dignified graybeard, holding a heaping basket of apricots in his arms, chases away the lad and usurps the place. How slow and deliberate the old man is, with what concentration he balances his tiny scales, carefully, carefully, as if these were not apricots but gold ingots, and he looks up into the eyes of the customer and seems to say: "Well, well, young fellow, I wonder if your intentions are really serious?" A few paces away a tall, barefooted youngster in a greasy old cloak is selling fritters, still steaming. The densest crowd has beleaguered the stand belonging to the Tadjik State Coöperative. Everybody is hungry for manufactured products sold at the low government prices. All the money of the bazaar ultimately finds its way into the cash box of the Coöperative. As the sun comes nearer to its zenith, the hubbub increases. A heavy, sticky smell, a mixture of the sweat of human bodies, of animals, and of shashlik, penetrates the cloud of fine dust which hangs motionlessly over the bazaar.

I step into a Red Chai-khanah and order a pot of Kokchoi—green tea. It is wonderful how refreshing hot tea is in these arid regions. During my journey through Uzbekistan I used to gulp down from thirty to forty *pialas* a day. An eternal Central Asian cycle—one is hot, then he drinks hot tea, then perspiration breaks out all over his body, then the perspiration quickly evaporates, then he feels cool; before long, however, he feels hot again, then again hot tea, again perspiration, again evaporation, again cooling, and so ad infinitum!

When I reach the third stage of the cycle, I drop into lazy meditation.

Suddenly, I am startled by a burst of martial music from the other side of the bazaar. The fellow in charge of the establishment is amused. "A parade. We are celebrating our victory over the Basmachi," he reassures me.

I rush out of the Chai-Khanah. As the head of the parade approaches, the whole crowd on the square splashes to one side, like water in a tilted vessel. The OGPU band is playing the Budionny march. It is followed by ranks of native and Russian Red Army men, Pioneers with red bow ties, young Communists in semi-military khaki uniforms, by older Communists, workers, peasants, members of unions and coöperatives, all carrying banners and streamers and slogans in the Arabian and Latin alphabets—"Down with the Basmachi!" "Long Live the Cotton Campaign!" "Death to Ibrahim Bek!" "Long Live Socialist Collectivist Tadjikistan!"—all marching in the direction of the new city.

Bargaining is at once terminated, and the whole crowd, on foot, on horseback, on camels, on donkeys, men, women, children, merchants, peasants, mullahs, fakirs, form an amorphous, heaving mass, milling around and trailing behind the paraders.

By a kind of miracle, the churning mass of beasts and men flowing out of the large space of the bazaar is sucked into the narrow winding gullets of ancient Dushambe to issue again, an hour later, and much augmented, onto the wide paved streets and the broad sidewalks of Stalinabad. Two motor buses, fifteen motor trucks and eight passenger cars join in the parade, and by wildly tooting their horns add to the already unbearable noise. The parade halts before the imposing house of the Soviets. They are calling for Gusainov, the Secretary of the Central Committee of the Party, for Maxum, the President of the Republic, for Khodzhibaiev, the Chairman of the Soviet of People's Commissars.

"Death to Ibrahim Bek!" "Long Live the Cotton Campaign!" "Long Live Socialist Tadjikistan!"

No Mosques, No Churches, No Synogogues

Stalinabad is young. It is the youngest city in the youngest country in the world.

Stalinabad is the tempestuous capital of the seventh member of the Union of Socialist Soviet Republics. Its foundations were laid in 1926 adjacent to the ancient village of Dushambe, in a broad valley where the Varzob river bids farewell to the snow-capped Hissar Mountains and plunges headlong into the Kafirnigan. Stalinabad is young. And the turbulent Varzob, youthfully leaping and laughing, supplies the *leit-motif* to the bold chant which

Red Stalinabad sings to the peoples of the East—sirens of factories, rasping of cranes, chattering of pneumatic hammers, panting of engines....

One need not be a primitive Tadjik mountaineer to break out into a "song of wonderment" on seeing Stalinabad. It started with nothing—no population, no materials, no skilled workers, about three hundred kilometers from the nearest railway, Basmachi lurking in the surrounding mountains.

True, there was the village of Dushambe. For centuries the fame of the Dushambe fair, held on a memorable Monday once a year, had resounded through these regions. Caravans heavy-laden with goods from lands as remote as Persia and China wound their way for months through the deserts and across the mountains of Central Asia to be on time at the Dushambe fair. But the Emir's rule and years of revolution, civil war and banditry brought ruin on the old village. And in 1925, when the Autonomous Tadjik Republic was born, there was practically no Dushambe. The village was deserted, the population gone....

In Dushambe one can still see a cluster of tumble-down, insect-ridden mud huts which the natives jestingly call "The Kremlin." That was the first seat of the Tadjik government. Here they met, here they lived, here they worked. When the heat became unbearable, the Executive Committee of the Soviet would retire to the yard, there, under an ancient tree, by the side of the malodorous Hauz, to attend to the affairs of state.

It was a Gargantuan task—the building of Stalinabad. Timber had to be brought from the north, from the Urals, via Termez. And the thousands of kilometers between the Urals and Termez, despite the inefficiency of the single track line, were much easier to negotiate than the three hundred kilometers from Termez to Stalinabad. One camel could pull only two logs. By the time a camel reached Stalinabad, each log was about one meter shorter than at the beginning of the journey—the result of one end being dragged for ten days or so over stones, gravel, and sand!

It was difficult to lure skilled builders from Russia. The four- or five-day journey by railroad from Central Russia to Termez through the arid, sandy steppes was bad enough. But then one had to go by cart from twelve to fifteen days, or on a donkey—a matter of twenty-five days!

It took three years to extend the railroad line from Termez to Stalinabad. The first train arrived at the capital on May 1, 1929. And now, in addition to the railroad, there is a regular air service connecting the Tadjik capital with Termez, Bokhara, Tashkent, and Moscow, and another air line connecting it with the Garm grain region.

Day and night, day and night dozens of motor trucks, hundreds of wagons, *arbas,* carts, and camels haul building materials to the city. Houses spring up by magic—cottages of unburned and burned brick, houses of stone and cement. The site of the city is cluttered with stacks of brick, with piles of lumber, with mountains of stone, gravel, cement. The streets are ripped open—pits, holes, ditches, swamps.

People live in barns, in hastily rigged-up barracks and arbors, in tents, in covered wagons. A more or less stabilized, normal life is out of the question. The population is swelling. Every train disgorges into the city hundreds of new workers. Food is irregular and bad. The water system develops too slowly to meet the growing demands.

Still the outlines of a modern industrial city are visible. Stalinabad is beginning to look its part—the capital of a progressive land. The stately building of the Executive Committee had been erected back in 1926-1927. It was the first European edifice in the heart of Asia, at the foot of the Pamir. It was built literally under the bullets of the Basmachi. Two buildings away is the magnificent home of the People's Commissariat of Justice—a befitting monument to the sixty Communists who had been slain and buried on that spot by the Basmachi. Since 1929, Stalinabad has been growing at a prodigious rate, one official building after another: Post and Telegraph, the Red Army Club, the Commissariat of Education, the Hospital, the Tropical Institute, Tadjikstroy, Khlebstroy, the Municipal

Soviet Building, the State Publishing House, various schools and dormitories, an electric power station, an electric flour mill, a huge electric bakery, a silk factory, a state theater, a cinema laboratory, a railroad station, a railroad depot, a modern restaurant, and, of course, many standard houses accommodating thousands of soviet workers and employees. Stalinabad is illuminated by electricity. It boasts a radio broadcasting system, a beautifully kept park, and a well-equipped airdrome. In 1930 the population was sixty thousand, and the city is still growing, spreading, expanding. Within a few years Stalinabad is projected to become one of the important industrial centers in the Soviet Union.

Incidentally, one distinction of Stalinabad the Tadjik Communists never omit to mention—Stalinabad is the first, and so far, the only capital city in the world free of any religious institutions. No mosques, no churches, no synagogues. This in the dark depths of Asia!

Stalinabad Press—Self-criticism

The two local papers, in addition to the inevitable *cotton* and *collectivization* subjects, bristle with self-criticism, with exposés of inefficiency, laxness, dishonesty on the part of organizations and officials. Inadequate sanitation and food provoke the bitterest comments from the worker correspondents.

The inhabitants of the workers' settlement on the outskirts of Stalinabad complain. For two weeks a dead camel has been spreading such a terrific stench in the neighborhood that one can neither pass the street nor open a window without becoming sick at the stomach. Repeated appeals to the militia (police) have brought no results. The item in the newspaper concludes with two despairing questions: "How long does the militia intend to let the rotting camel poison our lives? How long will the inhabitants of the settlement continue to be treated as the stepchildren of Stalinabad?"

A few months later the residents of the same suburban settlement register another complaint in the press. They write:

> Remoteness from the bazaar, from shops and the coöperative stores, the absence of a restaurant, of a water system, of street illumination, a bath, not to mention our unsatisfied demands for a club, a cinema, a library, etc., make life in the suburb rather unenviable. Last year the Consumers' Coöperative did attempt to do something for us. It had opened three stands in our suburb, selling manufactured products, vegetables, and meats. The remoteness from the center let itself be felt forthwith—near each stand there was a permanent long line. Still, though the service was not commensurate with the needs, the opening of the stands removed the necessity of daily journeys to the bazaar or of buying from private traders. Alas, this did not last long. One fine morning the meat stand vanished, then, shortly after, the vegetable stand. Now we cannot even get bread in our neighborhood. Apparently the Party's order that the coöperative stores be brought closer to the consumers has not yet reached the bureaucrats in our coöperative organizations.

The worker *Dust-Mamat* complains that "the conditions of the workers in the brick factory are exceedingly bad. They are not even supplied with a sufficient number of cots. Many sleep on the floor. The dormitories are filthy. There is no cleaning woman. The dining room doesn't function well. It is about two or three months since the workers have received any manufactured goods—clothes, shoes, etc. No production conference has been called for over two months. The workers work blindly, not knowing either the plans, achievements or failures of the factory. The administrative and technical staffs offer no leadership. The Workers' Committee, too, is asleep, making not the slightest effort to remedy the situation."

Here are a few characteristically bitter headlines: "Restaurant or Pigsty?" "Vegetables Are Perishing, but the Coöperative Sleeps." "Height of Vegetable Season, but

Workers not Supplied." "Who Ate Up the Potatoes?" "No One is Ready to Receive the Vegetables." "Coöperators Sleep, While Private Trade Prospers." "Fit for Pigs." "Drinking Mineral Water Expensive Vice." "Worms a Delicacy." "Restaurant Manager Inefficient."

And the August 31st issue of the *Tadjikistan Communist*, the official Government and Party organ, has the following streamer running across the entire width (8 columns) of the page:

A GOOD AND CHEAP DINNER HELPS OUR
INDUSTRIAL AND FINANCIAL PLAN

This is followed by a quotation from a decree issued by the Central Committee of the Party:

> Every worker, every Party member, every Young Communist, and above all, every person employed in organizations directly connected with Communal Feeding must actively struggle against the defects in our communal feeding, and must endeavor so to improve it as to render it one of the most important links in improving the life of the working class.

There are different ways of interpreting such items in the press. The skeptic is likely to find in them substantiation for his skepticism. To one who knows Soviet conditions, however, they are likely to bring unadulterated delight. Here is a young city in the heart of the impenetrable mountains and deserts of darkest Asia, striving towards forms of social life so advanced as to be inconceivable in our western, capitalistic civilization. Failures? Naturally. Absurdities? Inevitably. Abuses? Galore! But after all, these negative items have been selected from a batch of papers covering a period of five months. I said "negative." But to one who understands the situation they may not appear quite so negative. Do they not reveal an extraordinarily active participation of the masses in the molding of their own life? Do they not reveal an unusual willingness of the authorities to listen to the voice of the people? For, it should be noted, any such complaint sent to the Soviet papers, whether published or not, is immediately followed by an investigation, and by an invariable improvement.

In the very same issue which contains the complaint of the "step-children" of Stalinabad (Nov. 21, 1931), the reader may also find the interesting daily feature: "Our Replies." To quote:

"To Tkachev—The statements contained in your note 'Are Such Facts Permissible?' are now being investigated."

"To Krivoshein—Your material is being investigated."

"To Dokshin—Your revelations are a duplication of an exposé already published in the paper. There is therefore no point in publishing your note."

"To Zatziepin—Your note concerning Protosov's unauthorized appropriation of electrical wire from the storehouse has been substantiated. Protosov was tried by his co-workers and was ordered suspended from the union for a period of six months and removed from his job at the storehouse. The court also decided to issue a public reprimand to the manager of the storehouse, Medvediev, for his failure to keep careful inventory of the materials in his custody."

In the same column featuring "Our Replies," under the conspicuously set caption, "Better Children's Lunches and Coöperatives Needed," the following startling paragraphs appear:

"The hot lunches served to the children in our schools are of poor quality. This must be attended to immediately. Considerable improvement can be achieved at relatively low cost.

"Also, the Commissariat of Education, together with the Coöperative Organization, must forthwith begin to organize children's coöperatives in the schools. After a sufficient number of children have been persuaded to join these coöperatives, low price stands and buffets must be opened in all the schools. This measure is important both from the standpoint of health as well as education."

Hundreds of thousands of black and white children of unemployed American workers might well envy the enlightened solicitude which the "uncivilized" Asiatics of Stalinabad bestow upon their young!

For Sanitation! For Education!

It is by such measures, by such exposés, that conditions are gradually being improved, not only in Stalinabad but in the whole country. Consider sanitation and education. Up until very recently, and partly even now, the *tabibs,* the local healers, played the chief rôle in the care of the sick. The health of the country was in their hands. Swallowing little pieces of paper with quotations from the Koran was considered the most efficacious remedy against any disease. Wearing amulets was the sole prophylactic the natives ever knew. As regards preventive health and sanitation measures, the densest ignorance prevailed. Malaria was the most frightful scourge in Tadjikistan; there are still regions where fifty per cent of the population are affected by malaria. There is leprosy here, and dysentery, and a hundred other local diseases that take an incredibly large toll of the ignorant population.

It is only recently that Soviet medicine has made its appearance in Tadjikistan. Up to 1929, there was only one dispensary. In 1931, there were sixty-one hospitals—ten in the cities and fifty-one small hospitals in the villages. There are now 2,125 beds to accommodate the sick, where before there was none. There are thirty-seven dental clinics, where before there was none. There are special concentration villages for the victims of leprosy, where before lepers were allowed to mingle with the rest of the population, the only restriction being that they were required to walk in the middle of the street. There are two hundred medical doctors in Tadjikistan who are gradually effecting a revolution in the health habits of the natives. One of the best naturopathic hospitals in the Soviet Union is now located in Hodjent. Moreover, the young Tadjik Republic can already boast of four medical research institutes. And while in 1929 the Tadjik Government spent only 725,000 rubles for health purposes, the expenditures for 1931 leaped to 6,898,000 rubles. However, even this sum was trifling considering the needs. Stalinabad has a long way still to go before it can be considered a healthful sanitary city. And it is all up to the Stalinabad Press.

The greatest strides made by the Tadjik Republic have been in the field of education. Nowhere in the Soviet Union have I observed such an overpowering thirst for knowledge as that evinced by the young Tadjiks. The few old Moslem schools, where for years children were made to study the Koran by heart, and where no secular subjects of any kind were tolerated, have passed into oblivion. Gone, too, is the old type of teacher—the mullah or the student of the Moslem religious academies. The schools are modern schools; the subjects are modern subjects; and the teachers are modern teachers. A people that was almost entirely illiterate (only $\frac{1}{2}\%$ could read and write) suddenly woke up to the need of education! Schools are being built everywhere. And it is noteworthy that for the most part the initiative comes from the peasants themselves.

One of the thrills during my trip through the country was to see a group of peasants in a remote mountain village waylay the President, Maxum, and denounce him and the government for being dilatory in providing building materials. "No nails, no window panes, no lumber—and the summer is passing, the school season about to start. It's a disgrace!" argued the peasants. And not until the President took down all the details and promised to attend to the complaint personally did the peasants evince a willingness to discuss other matters.

The papers are full of discussions of the school problem, and persistent demands for schools. A mere glance at the headlines of the *Tadjikistan Communist* is sufficient to give one some idea of the situation. The paper is impatient. It clamors for schools. One headline screams: "Building Organization Disrupts School Construction." The subhead reads: "Immediate Acceleration of Tempo. The Plan Must Be Carried Out. We Shall Brook No Delay."

I quote a few characteristic paragraphs from the article that follows these headlines:

> One hundred and two new elementary schools, eight kindergartens, several pedagogical technicums, a number of schools for the workers' children at Santo and Shurab, five libraries and reading rooms, five red tea rooms—this has been our plan for the coming school season, this, we have hoped, would serve as a basis for the unfolding of our vast cultural and pedagogical work, in conformity with the general plan for a cultural revolution in the various districts of our Republic.
>
> The turbulent economic and industrial growth of Tadjikistan, the unheard-of rate of development of our socialized sector, have stimulated the toilers' legitimate craving for education.
>
> What was sufficient yesterday, is utterly inadequate to-day. Everywhere there is a shortage of schools. We cannot accommodate all those who wish to study. The existing schools are crowded, and therefore not very efficient. The slogan "Liquidate Illiteracy Within the Next Couple of Years" has been taken up by the masses and is being carried into life.
>
> Naturally, school construction does not keep up with the rapidly growing demand. During the coming season, the lack of school building will greatly hamper any attempt to liquidate the illiteracy of tens of thousands of toilers.
>
> This is the reason our building organization must give special attention and care to the construction of the schools and the other cultural mass institutions projected and financed by the People's Commissariat for Education.
>
> This is the reason, with a deep feeling of protest and indignation, we are forced to call attention to the threatening failure on the most important front of school construction.

The four other school items are all written in the same vein. Protest, indignation, irony, but no despair. The schools projected for the years 1931-32 would be constructed, despite some natural delay. For delay is natural—bringing lumber and nails and glass from the north and distributing them among the villages is no simple matter, in view of the inadequacy of the transport. Another cause for delay is the time required for the training of teachers.

Still, a great deal has been accomplished. In 1925 there were only six modern schools in Tadjikistan. Toward the end of 1926 there were 113 schools with 2,300 students; in 1929—500; in 1931, over 2,000 educational institutions with over 120,000 students! The budget for 1929-30 was 8 million rubles. The budget for 1930-31 was 28 million rubles.

"These tempi, as you see, are colossal," said Khodzhibaiev to me, "but the results are insufferably small. There is a disproportion between the economic and cultural growths in Tadjikistan. What I mean to say by that is that in the realm of economics our achievements are much greater than in the realm of culture."

To me it seems, however, that Khodzhibaiev was wrong. He was too impatient. Furthermore, his criteria were not the correct criteria. Altogether a cultural revolution is not a ponderable matter. Certainly, the number of schools (this is what Khodzhibaiev judged by) is in some way an index of what has been accomplished, but to me this is not quite as significant an index as the overwhelming number of people who are clamoring for schools, for modern education, for science! This is the real achievement. Schools will come, once the demand has been created.

It is very characteristic that during the Basmach troubles, the village teacher was usually the first to be killed by the invading bands. The teacher stands for modernity, for science, for the emancipation of the enslaved Moslem woman, for collectivization, for cotton, for everything abhorrent to the supporters of the old. The village teacher in Central Asia is the worst enemy of reaction and bigotry; the best and most enthusiastic carrier of the Communist ideals. The village teacher is a symbol of an awakened Tadjikistan forging ahead to heights no Tadjik could even dream of six or seven years ago.

XIV

A SHEAF OF TRAVEL NOTES

Neither mullah, bey, nor merchant would I like to be,
Nor a dervish, blind and funny, would I like to be,
Nor a son of a rich man, dressed in gold and silk,
With a rouged and powdered face would I like to be.

Nor a boss of ferry boats would I like to be,
Nor a fat emir's official would I like to be,
Nor a healer of old women would I like to be,
Nor a vendor on the market would I like to be.

An agronomist, a doctor, I would like to be.
A librarian, a teacher, I would like to be—
One who sows the words of Lenin in the minds of men
Like a peasant in the meadow, I would like to be.

And a People's Commissar I would like to be....

*S*LUCHAK was right.
 Evidences of the dramatic conflict between the Old and New, between Europe and Asia, between Socialism and Feudalism, between Mohammedanism and Marxism-Leninism are more numerous in Tadjikistan than anywhere else in Central Asia. The steady encroachment of modern Stalinabad upon ancient Dushambe is only one of the more obvious symbols of this conflict. Every road, village, home, indeed the very soul of every Tadjik, even of the Communist, has its Dushambe and Stalinabad aspects. The clash between the two is all-pervading.

Except for the few highways built during the last five or six years, there are practically no roads in Tadjikistan, only narrow bridle paths winding over dizzy mountains and trailing along black precipices. We are told that there are sections in the mountains where the principle of the wheel is still unknown and where the inhabitants have been introduced to airplanes before they had ever seen a wagon. When the mountain Basmachi first saw a car advancing along a recently built road, they thought it was a devil and scurried off into the hills. On the Afghan border, some Basmachi, upon capturing an automobile, smashed the headlights, thinking that they were disabling the beast by destroying its eyes. According to the chauffeur, the consternation of the bandits when they saw him get back into the car and escape was so great that they did not make the slightest effort to catch him.

The average Tadjik seems cheerful, hospitable, and peace-loving. One can scarcely imagine him as a Basmach. He loves to work on his field or in his garden, but his ideal is the bank of a road, an orchard, and a breeze. In some mountain regions, however, the Tadjiks are distinguished by their austere, direct, and warlike nature. I am told that the Yaftal Tadjiks in Afghanistan are extraordinarily daring, and that the Tadjiks of the Kabul region supply the best soldiers of the Afghan army.

We are in Sarai Komar, discussing the terrible ravages wrought by malaria in that section. The local representative of the OGPU is boasting of the efforts of the Soviet Government to introduce modern methods of sanitation and hygiene. Uzbai, a middle-aged Tadjik, a member of the local Soviet and a candidate for membership in the Communist Party, does not seem wholly convinced of the efficacy of modern medical science. To the utter embarrassment of the other Communists in the room, particularly of the representative of the OGPU, Uzbai even goes so far as to put in a good word for the old healers, the *tabibs*. He says: "I was once sick with malaria. One healer gave me an egg and a spool of thread, and told me to first wind the thread around the egg, then, after unwinding the thread, to throw out the egg and twist the thread around my neck. He told me to wear it around my neck for three days, then to remove it and throw it into the stream. Then, he said, I would be cured. And would you believe it, I was cured." "But you still have attacks of malaria," exclaims the representative of the OGPU. "Yes," answers Uzbai imperturbably, "but that was eighteen years ago!" "And you a candidate for Party membership!" says the smiling Russian Communist, shaking his head reproachfully.

Through most of the country, camels, horses and donkeys are the sole means of transportation. Donkeys are invaluable. I once heard Maxum, the peasant president of the Tadjik Republic, refer to them as "our dear little Fords." You see these poor creatures everywhere, carrying inconceivably heavy burdens. Before the coming of the tractors which everywhere in the Soviet Union work day and night, the most characteristic night noises in this part of the world were (and in some sections still are) the heart-rending braying of the donkeys and the weird monotone of the bells of passing caravans. One commiserates even with the awkward camels, though, according to the native authorities, they are mean, vindictive and cowardly. The camels always have a martyred look. Everywhere along the roads one sees the bleached bones of their brothers who fell in the line of duty while helping build socialism.

One often hears of the Basmachi. We travel armed, and throughout the journey in the mountains we have two Red Army men, with rifles and hand grenades, accompanying us. Ibrahim Bek is on every tongue. England, said to be in back of Ibrahim, is most cordially hated by every Tadjik peasant. Everywhere the peasants are organized in Red Stick detachments. There are, we are told, sixty thousand Red Sticks in Tadjikistan. Most of them have no firearms, but they carry heavy cudgels, knives and other weapons when they go out into the hills in search of the Basmachi.

Occasionally one meets a Tadjik Communist who still frequents the mosque.

Nabidjon, a Communist, is accused of having three wives. His defense: "I had them before I joined the Party. It would be cruel to drop them now."

Even the new highways in the valleys are not very good. They are so thick with dust that motors are bound to be ruined within a short time. During the winter, our chauffeur tells me, traffic is almost impossible because of the mud. What is worse, many of the roads in the valleys are crossed by numberless ditches (parts of the irrigation system), very few of which have as yet any bridges. Getting stuck in a ditch, therefore, is a very common misfortune.

On the Aral road something rather significant happened. The front wheels of our truck landed in a ditch, and the car refused to budge. The usual bustle ensued. The natives from a neighboring village came with spades and dirks, and had a good time at our expense: shouting, scratching of heads, laughter, all kinds of good or bad advice. When it seemed that everything was ready for us to pull out, our truck began to hiss and sputter and shiver and with one grand effort leaped with the front wheels out of the ditch only to have the hind wheels sink in the mud. Just at that moment there appeared a brightly attired native mounted on a donkey, holding a sheep in his lap and with a little boy clinging to his back. He halted for a moment, glanced at our painfully breathing truck, smiled in his black beard, and without uttering a word, very proudly crossed the ditch. Then he turned around, smiled once more, and proceeded on his way. That smile was so devastatingly contemptuous that our chauffeur, a young Tadjik Communist, fairly writhed under it. He couldn't stand it. Jumping into his seat, he violently threw in the clutch and, lo and behold, the truck, with a tremendous jerk, struggled out of the ditch. The chauffeur screamed with delight. The natives burst out into loud guffaws. The discomfiture of the contemptuous Tadjik was complete. Modern technique won the day. And as our car dashed forward leaving a trail of smoke and dust behind it, we could hear the hilarious laughter and shouting of the natives.

In Khodjent: One Tadjik, twenty-four years old, given a month's vacation and railroad ticket. Goes to the station. Waits till the train pulls in. Becomes frightened. Goes back and gives up his trip.

Still found among some sections of the Tadjik population is the worship of living *saints,* the so-called *ishans.* These are the spiritual leaders and exponents of the mystical teaching of *sufism.* Their followers are known as *miurids.* When an ishan arrives in an out-of-the-way village, his followers go out in crowds to meet him and do him honor, and a religious Tadjik considers himself fortunate when he manages to touch the clothes or even the stirrup of the saint. The miurids whip themselves into a frenzy of mystical exaltation and ecstasy, and into a feeling of close proximity to Allah, by reiterating, without let up, for hours at a stretch, the various names of the deity. They also hold to the belief that some of the most saintly of them belong to the forty mysterious beings who keep watch over the universe. Sufism and Bolshevism!

In almost every village the story begins: "We had expected the Basmachi here in the spring" or "the Basmachi came here in the spring" or "We had a battle here with the Basmachi in the spring"; and in almost every village the story ends: "But we carried out the cotton plan just the same" or "The sowing campaign was a success just the same" or "Collectivization went on just the same."

Some of the stories are quite dramatic. In the mountains, much more than in the plains, there is no choice between battle and retreat. And the battles are fought without mercy, to the death. Even in this land of strange doings, they speak with bated breath about the Garm battle in 1929, a battle which, as described by Ludkevich, was indeed a combination of tragedy, movie-thriller, and revolutionary opera all in one. Garm is a village of gardens and orchards. It rises from the banks of the tumultuous Pianj and is surrounded by a ring of snow-capped mountains. Now there is an automobile road being built which will connect it with Stalinabad, but in 1929 there were only narrow mountain paths, and it took three days to cover the distance between the two points. On the other side of the Pianj, behind those mountains, lies Afghanistan. In 1929, Faizulla Maxum, a notorious Basmach leader, scaled the Darvaz glaciers, crossed the treacherous Pianj, and suddenly appeared in Garm. The village was quite defenseless; no garrison, no armed forces and no one to come to its aid. A dozen teachers, three Soviet employees and three members of the border OGPU shouldered their guns and went out to meet the enemy. They were slaughtered. But just as Faizulla was celebrating his victory and augmenting his troops by recruiting the "best people" of Garm, a huge and ominous bird came soaring over Garm. The natives ran for their lives. What then was their astonishment to see their old friend Maxum, the President of the Republic, accompanied by a military man, emerging from the steel bowels of the bird! And then down flew other birds, from which came forty-five warriors armed with machine guns. "Faizulla, his troops shot to pieces, fled back to Afghanistan like a mountain goat. He is now an inn-keeper in Kabul."

Garm again. This spring, in April, Ibrahim's bands raided this neighborhood under the leadership of Mullah Sherif. The population rose against them—half of them were drowned, including a brother of Faizulla Maxum, and perhaps even Mullah Sherif himself. And only three weeks before we came, another Ibrahim detachment passed through this region. This time the Basmachi were fleeing back to Afghanistan. The Garm Red Sticks intercepted them in the mountain. Many were killed. The rest vanished.

On our way to Khovaling we stop in the village Degris to rest under a huge plane tree on the bank of the Yakhsi.

BUILDING SOCIALISM IN TADJIKISTAN

Lozowick falls asleep. His Swiss watch attracts the admiring attention of some of the Tadjiks, also my field glasses. ... As I write this note my writing stirs the curiosity of a few young people. I tell them that I am writing English. This creates a tremendous sensation. By signs, sounds, and grimaces they make me understand that one of them is a Pioneer, the others are Young Communists. They inquire as to my nationality, as well as to that of the others in the group. The variety of nationalities represented creates another sensation. "A real International!" exclaims one. The Pioneer asks Vaillant-Couturier: "Communist?" "Yes." Great jubilation.

An illustration of the sudden leap Tadjikistan is making from primitive to ultra-modern forms of life is the almost daily task of transporting our splendidly modern two-and-a-half-ton truck on one of the antediluvian, ramshackle native ferries across the many mountain rivers.

The level of the water in these mountain streams is most uncertain—now very high, now very low—changing erratically, depending on the weather. The little ferry wharves are invariably rickety wooden structures, with plenty of loose boards and protruding nails. Neither the wharves nor the ferries, of course, are meant to support trucks or cars. And usually the floor of the ferry is either considerably below or considerably above the wharf.

The problem of getting a truck across such a wharf and on such a ferry is most complicated and involves skill and teamwork of the highest order. When, for instance, on getting on, the floor of the ferry is below the wharf, everybody clusters on the farther side of the ferry in the hope that the combined weight of all the passengers may raise the boat on the opposite side to the required level. The first violent sensation one gets is when the front wheels of the truck jump the perilous gap between the wharf and the ferry. (Provided, of course, that they land there; for as often as not the boat tips too much and the truck plunges into the water.) Not before the front wheels are safe in the middle of the floor does any one dare to make the least move. But getting the truck on the ferry is only one-third of the job. The weight of the truck naturally loads the ferry deeper in the water, and in nine cases out of ten it scrapes bottom. Then the real trouble begins. Everybody strips naked, jumps into the river and pushes, not always with much success. The last operation is getting the truck off the ferry—a job obviously as delicate as getting it on. I once complimented our driver on his skill, and his answer was: "If your American manufacturer ever saw what we were doing to his machine he would weep."

In Chubek. Kolroshchikov speaking: "We have been even more exposed than the comrades in Garm. Here the Pianj breaks up into eight branches. In the fall the river at this point is so shallow that the Basmachi find it easier to cross here than anywhere else on our Afghan border. Furthermore, our reed jungles provide an ideal place for hiding; while Khadzha Mumin, our white salt mountain, is an excellent help in finding one's bearing on a dark night. . . .

"Ibrahim Bek crossed nearby with three hundred horsemen. There were only two Red soldiers on guard— Neviazny and Solovey. They waited for the Basmachi to get very close to them before they began shooting. The two guards were soon joined by two more—Tynok and Lomechuk. The Basmachi, crying 'Allah,' fell upon them, but the guards held their ground. The Basmachi then broke into two parts. One part got across while the others continued the fight. The shots were heard at the garrison. Twelve more soldiers joined. Commander Golodovnikov and one army man lured the Basmachi to the ambuscade. Fighting continued all night. All in all fifty-eight dead Basmachi were found in the morning. More had been killed, but some of the bodies had been picked up by the Basmachi. Leaving forty-five horses behind, the beaten remnants ran toward the Kyzyl Mazar region where they were taken care of by the regular army. There were no losses on the Soviet side."

BUILDING SOCIALISM IN TADJIKISTAN   259

We are told of two more Basmach raids—small ones, in Chubek, and several more in other sections of this district.

In the mountain village of Mumanibad the students in the local school for adults ask us the following questions:

1. What is the American workers' attitude toward the Soviet government?
2. What is the cause of strikes?
3. How large is the membership of the Young Communist organization in Germany?
4. What is your attitude toward the Soviets?
5. What is the percentage of literacy in France, Germany and America?
6. Do you have co-educational schools in your countries?
7. What is the position of woman and what are her rights in America? The same about France and Germany.
8. Is there freedom for workers? Can they go to school? Can they get any kind of work?
9. Have you kulaks? How do you treat them?
10. Which countries are nearest to socialism?
11. What are the subjects taught in your schools? Are the students taught *politgramota* (political education) and from which point of view?
12. What is the social composition of your universities?
13. How does the revolutionary movement develop in your countries?
14. Which country is the most developed technically?
15. Which country has the biggest armaments?
16. Is the Communist Party legal in America?
17. Is education in America "all-sided"?

At the end, a young fellow, addressing himself directly to me: "Tell them in your country they should stop oppressing our Negro brothers!"

Numerous sacred spots, springs, rocks, trees with miraculous and healing properties—so-called *mazars* are to be found all over the country. These are associated ostensibly with the names of Moslem saints. In point of fact, however, most of these mazars, it seems, are of ancient, pre-Moslem origin.

In Mumanibad, the local Communist Nazarov tells me of such a mazar in the Shurab district. As he describes it, it is a long, narrow, dark cave. In the center of the cave, which is always very damp and in which there is an eternal vapor, there is a huge stone grave. On top of the grave there are three stone objects: a turban, a tea pot, and a pair of overshoes. By the side of the grave there is the stone image of a camel. Water constantly drips from the roof of the cave. This water has magic properties. When you say, "how cold," the water becomes hot. When you say, "how hot," the water turns cold. When the water falls on your hand, it looks like a wet crystal, and it can heal all kinds of ailments. This cave is named after the saint Imam Iskari.

I confess I am more amazed by the hushed voice of the credulous Tadjik Communist than by the magic properties of the water and the mysterious petrified objects in the cave. When I ask Nazarov whether he had ever visited that cave, he tells me that he never had. Yet there he is, a Communist, a member of the Soviet, ready to believe the most preposterous legend about some very dubious saint.

More skeptical than Nazarov is Ibrahimov, the secretary of the local executive committee of the Party. "It must have been built by a gifted fellow, a sculptor, who then decided that it would be a good way to play on the superstition of the ignorant masses, and to collect money." To prove his point, Ibrahimov cites another mazar, in the village Pushan in the district of Kuliab. In Pushan, Ibrahimov informs me, there is a beautiful stone which has the imprint of a horse's hoof and near which there is a stone *manger* which attracts many sick people. According to ancient tradition Ali, the warrior, the son-in-law of Mohammed, the *Shah-Mardan* (King of Man), the *Khazret-i-Shah* (Holy King), had been on that spot and had rested his horses there.

Ali is the most popular hero in Tadjik folklore. He is credited with the conquest of Central Asia and the conversion of that region to the Moslem faith. Near the ancient city of Balkh a large settlement had sprung up by a grave in which, presumably, the body of the holy Chalif Ali rests. Since, however, according to Ibrahimov, it is known definitely that Ali was never in Central Asia, it follows that in this case, as in so many others, popular imagination transferred to Ali the legends and stories and beliefs which had been built around some earlier, more ancient, popular hero.

Meeting at Kolkhoz Gulston (Land of Flames), with the participation of the neighboring Kolkhoz *Stalin* and the Commune *Poor Peasant*. Meeting place at mosque. Red flags all over. The order of the day is: 1, Report on the political situation in the district and on recent events; 2, Introduction of brigade of foreign writers; 3, Election of extraordinary political commission for struggle with Basmachi; 4, Enlistment into Red Sticks. One peasant argues: "Why enlist when we will all fight?" The oldest member, Duse-Mahomet-Dovlet Zada, sixty-six years old, wants to join and is put out when told that it would be better if the younger folk did the fighting. "I'll lick any two of you younger folks," grumbles the old man. Also the fourteen-year-old Hait Sherif Zada! Also a woman! One hundred and ten enlist altogether.

Most of the villages we pass are in valleys. Not infrequently, however, the traveler's eye is met by a village clinging to the side of a mountain, arranged picturesquely like an amphitheater, and bathed in a heavy sea of verdure: gardens, vineyards, fruit trees, mulberry trees, nut trees, apricot and pistachio trees, plane trees, poplars. All of these trees grow luxuriantly in the mountains, at times to incredible thickness and height.

The mountain villages are not very large, only a few households. But each household is large, the married sons and their families living with the parents. The buildings are squat, thick-walled, with apertures in the ceilings for the smoke to pass out. Often the buildings are simply piled-up rocks which are whitewashed and which give the dwelling a rather cozy appearance. Almost every village has a Red *Chai-Khanah*. In many villages we find mosques turned into modern schools.

The furnishings and utensils in a mountain Tadjik's household are poor and crude: an iron kettle for cooking the simple fare, a *kumgan*—a brass or copper pitcher for tea, a few crude, home-made clay dishes, a couple of wooden spoons (most of the food is eaten with the fingers—spoons are used only for soup; forks are never used), and finally a leather sack in which provisions are kept. The last is the invariable companion of the mountaineer when he is on the road. At times one may find in a Tadjik household a very primitive weaving loom and tall wooden overshoes. Occasionally, one also finds the pictures of Lenin or Stalin or the local leaders.

Alongside of books on Leninism and talk about the Five-Year Plan, one finds vestiges of the ancient Iranian reverence for the sun and for fire all over the country. An orthodox mountain Tadjik will never extinguish a fire by blowing, for the human breath is impure, but by the waving of his hand. He will never pour or throw anything impure into burning embers. During the wedding ceremony, he will follow custom in making a bonfire in order to drive away all evil from the newlyweds. And the first remedy he will resort to in treating sickness will be the lighting of candles.

Belief in all sorts of evil spirits that bring sickness is still extant. There is, for instance, the "Div" or "Dev." (Forms of this word are found in various modern European and Asian languages.) Div, according to the Tadjik, is a spirit haunting mountains and deserted places, an evil creature, harmful to man, the cause of sickness and madness.

In Tadjik fairy-tales frequent reference is made to the land of the *Divs*—an enchanted region utterly unlike arid Central Asia—a land of dense forests and perennial rains, located somewhere at the farthest extremity of the Iran, by the southern shores of the Caspian Sea.

There are numerous other Iranian superstitious remnants: the rite of leaping over bonfires and leading the sick members of the community thrice around the fires, and then making them jump across them; the fixing of marriage engagements by the breaking of bread; the distribution of little pieces of bread to those present when a baby is being put in its crib; the belief that after death man's soul crosses a bridge, as narrow as the sharp edge of a knife, suspended over the precipices of hell; the spring festivities of the Red Flower, similar to the May festivities among some European peoples; the custom of coloring eggs, precisely the same as is practiced at Easter time in the Russian villages. All these superstitions, our guide assures us, are rapidly disappearing "in the light of Marxism-Leninism."

"Give us roads and bridges and we'll give you a Soviet Switzerland in return," once said Khodzhibaiev. He was right. One sees very few bridges here which can support more than a single horseman at a time. Not infrequently even a single horseman appears too heavy for the logs and cross boards connecting the two beautifully constructed timber supports that stretch toward each other across the river and form something in the nature of an arch. From a distance one cannot but admire these marvelously graceful and ethereal structures. But to be on them, and to look down into the rushing milky waters below, is another matter. Everything shakes. The head goes round and round. One is ready to faint. Shortly before our visit, a letter-carrier who was taking mail to the Pamir had fallen off such a bridge together with his horse and had been dashed to death.

There was a fine newly built wooden bridge across the Kafirnigan River, a bridge wide enough and apparently solid enough for any vehicle. But it is not for nothing that the river is named Kafirnigan—the faithless one, the treacherous one. After a few weeks the bridge was washed away, though I am not quite certain whether it was the river or the engineer who in that case was guilty of treachery.

When I had to cross the Kafirnigan a second time, I had to do it on what the natives called a "crib." This odd device consists of a few boards roughly nailed together and attached by four flimsy ropes to a pulley which rolls on a steel cable across the river. The "crib" accommodates only one person at a time. I climbed into it, stretched flat on my stomach, and was pulled across. I do not know whether this crossing was as perilous as it appeared to me then. The sensation was certainly unique, with the stream roaring angrily far below as it hurled its glacier waters against the million bowlders glistening in the hot sun.

The most usual way of crossing a river is on a *burdiuk*, a blown-up sheep skin. A few such *burdiuks* tied together make an adequate raft. The natives steer the raft with their legs. It is borne obliquely down the stream, drifting sometimes miles out of the way before it reaches the other side. This, too, is not the safest nor the most comfortable way of crossing a river. One wonders how many Five-Year Plans will be needed to make travel safe and comfortable in Tadjikistan.

Higher in the mountains. Less verdure. The buildings are much poorer, gloomy little huts made of stone. Alongside many of the huts there are places for the cattle. More often, however, the cattle are housed together with the human beings. Every dwelling has a hole in the center of the floor, at the bottom of which in cold weather a dish with burning coal is placed. Over the hole there is a special wooden grate in the shape of a little bench. The whole thing is covered with a huge quilt. The only way to keep warm is to shove your legs under the quilt. During the winter the entire family gathers around this "hearth," with the legs beneath the quilt, and sits this way for hours trying to keep warm. In view of the dearth of fuel, this is probably the most expedient and economical way to obtain and preserve heat. And yet it was in just such a primitive hut that a Tadjik village teacher was talking of "overtaking and surpassing the capitalist countries!"

The Tadjiks are very hospitable. They run out to meet you; they hold the bridle of your horse while you alight. They spread rugs and quilts under some shady tree and immediately bring out the best they can offer. What often repels the Westerner in the old-fashioned Tadjik home is the greasy cloth which is placed in the center of the rug and on which the food is served. The greasier the cloth, the more reason for the host's pride, for it is evidence of his frequent entertainment and his rich cuisine. In such homes hygiene is still observed in the ancient Central Asian delightful manner. Thus, since practically all of the eating is done with the hands, it is desirable that the hands should be washed before each meal. The old host recognizes that, and he always brings out a pitcher of water and pours a few drops on the hands of each guest. If you look for something to dry your hands with, the host, if he is not yet touched by modernity, very solemnly lifts the corner of his old cloak, which he has probably worn for years and under all kinds of conditions, and offers it to you. When he wants to show special consideration, he very carefully fishes out a handful of mutton and rice (*pilaf*) and solicitously raises it to the mouth of his guest. And the latter is expected to be pleased with the honor of eating the first mouthful from the host's greasy hands. Almost invariably the younger members of the family make some apologetic remark about the old man's not knowing any better.

Many divorces take place because of the husbands becoming too cultured. Such men like to marry European women.

As we pass through the villages we hear repeatedly that the peasants have applied to the government to form a kolkhoz. But the government has not yet approved. Bazarov explains: "It's no use encouraging the organization of a kolkhoz when you're in no position to assure its successful operation. Organization without help is worse than no organization. We must give service when we organize a kolkhoz."

In the inaccessible mountain regions in the Pamir, we are informed, remnants of the Shiite sect are to be found. According to that sect, the family line of Ali has not been broken. Ali's offspring is Aga-Khan, who is revered by the Ismailites as the living God. "Aga-Khan," explains our Tadjik guide, a student, "resides in Bombay, under the solicitous protection of the English. He owns huge factories. The English are trying to win over the ignorant mountaineers of Soviet and Afghan Badakhshan by being kind to Aga-Khan. They shower all kinds of benefits and titles upon him. They have even granted him the title of 'Highness,' and of 'Prince of the British Empire.' The present Aga-Khan has received a European education. Dressed like an English dandy, he makes frequent trips to England, where he mingles in highest society. The living God of the Ismailites is passionately fond of races; he gambles away fortunes playing horses. And while Aga-Khan fox-trots in London or Paris, while he is busy yachting and gambling, the poor, half-starved Tadjiks on the Pamir gather their last pennies to be sent as the yearly tribute to Aga-Khan, the incarnation of God on earth. According to Lapin, every year in the month of July, the Ismailites elect representatives, *vakils,* whose duties it is to pay their respects and to deliver the collected moneys to their god. These messengers are sometimes bitterly disappointed, for it happens quite often that his Worshipful Highness is not disposed to meet his faithful followers. When he does invite these rude mountaineers to appear before his presence, this Europeanized gentleman is not above resorting to trickery to impress them. These ignorant Tadjiks, on their return to their villages, spread all kinds of legends about Aga-Khan: 'He is a God! He walks over to the wall, turns a handle, and a stream of crystal water gushes forth into his glass. And his house is tall, tall.... You enter a box below, and suddenly you find yourself on top. The food appears before you mysteriously....'" On hearing that, Bazarov, a valley Tadjik, exclaims: "We can show them greater wonders than that in Stalinabad!"

The village of Kazak in the Sarai Komar region organized a collective farm composed exclusively of former Basmachi. It is reputed to be the best kolkhoz in the whole region.

Kuliab. Demchenko of the OGPU speaking: "On March 22nd one of Ibrahim Bek's bands attempted to seize Kuliab. Our Red Sticks, thirty people in all, could not take care of them. The army provided an additional thirty men. In the battle that followed, our losses were only two wounded Red Army men. The Basmachi lost thirty-five people in killed. The number of wounded I do not know. Among the killed Basmachi we found three Russians. One of them was Marshevsky, our own technician on the water works. On him we found a pair of field glasses and a map showing a plan of attack on Kuliab. Marshevsky had absconded on the nineteenth of February with two thousand rubles of Government money and our best horse. His purpose was to get away to England, but in Afghanistan he joined Ibrahim's band. Marshevsky was a son of a Kiev kulak. Two of his brothers, White Guards, had left with the Wrangel army. Marshevsky remained in Russia. Hiding his identity, he managed to enter the Moscow University, but when he was in his third year, he was discovered and expelled. He worked in Kuliab about six months. It is interesting that when he disappeared, the other specialists on the water works insisted that he must have been killed by the Basmachi. But recently they had a meeting at which they denounced him as a traitor. Who knows how many Marshevskys we have around here!"

Guliam Kadir was a Basmach. He has come over to the Soviet side. "When I was on my way to Faizabad from

Afghanistan," he says, "I saw forty women working on one field. This was something new. I stopped my horse and asked the women about it. It was a kolkhoz. And I thought it was forced labor. I could not imagine women working voluntarily. That was the first sign of the new life."

In the village of Sarmatai the peasants took violent exception to the local Soviet program on the ground that it made no provisions for a school for women.

The head of the Communist Party in Sarmatai: "We were gathering Red Stick volunteers. We issued a call to the nearest three villages. The peasants of another village, quite as near, felt offended. 'Can't we be trusted to defend the Soviet government?' they asked. 'We'll complain to the highest authorities.' We had to apologize and take some of them in."

"And here is Varsobstroy!" exclaims Khodzhaiev, as he leaps out of the still moving truck.

We are nonplussed. Words ending with *stroy* are very common in the Soviet Union. Who hasn't heard of Dnieprostroy, Volkhovstroy, Vakhshstroy, and a hundred other *stroys* all over this vast country of Soviets? But *stroy* means construction, building; it implies bustle, hubbub, panting trucks, rasping cranes, the hissing of steam engines—in short, it implies visible, audible, tangible evidence of work, and, in the Soviet Union, of feverish work. While here there is nothing; only a steel cable drawn across the foaming Dushambe, only a wooden box (the natives call it a "crib") suspended from the cable; and at a distance, near the village of Shafte Mishgoi, a few rough hewn barracks and some workmen. Instead of activity, there is desolation, quiet, bare mountains frowning on all sides....

"Varsobstroy—that sounds big!" jests the German comrade.

"It doesn't only sound big; it is big," smiles Gindin, the hydro-electric engineer in charge of the construction, as he shakes our hands. "In Tadjikistan a hydro-electrical station giving 10,000 h. p. is no small matter."

"It certainly isn't," corroborates Khodzhaiev. "Not with the difficulties we are having here."

Slapping Gindin vigorously on the back, Khodzhaiev declares proudly, "Aaron Markovich Gindin is a real engineer, a Soviet engineer, one of the heroes of the *piatiletka*. Tell them how you got here, Gindin; the reception we gave you in Stalinabad, the encouragement."

Both laugh gayly.

Gindin, however, is reticent. Sunburnt, his skin as black as a native's, stocky, vigorous-looking, this Russian-Jewish fellow is almost girlishly bashful. He is glad to tell you all about the Varsobstroy project, about the difficulties, and the prospects, but he becomes as silent as a clam when the conversation turns to his personal achievements. "It doesn't really matter," he protests feebly, as Khodzhaiev proceeds to expatiate on Gindin's self-sacrificing work. At the first opportunity, he slips away to the barracks, "to see the men."

Gindin gone, Khodzhaiev becomes eulogistic. "He has the real stuff in him, he is genuine pioneer material. Nothing scares him, nothing stops him. He is not a Party man; but his loyalty, his devotion are unflinching. When he came here, he had nothing but a portfolio under his arm, and determination. For two months we had no living quarters for him, so he slept on a desk in one of the offices of the VSNKH. The bureaucrats here refused to take him seriously, he was too young, they said, to be intrusted with a big job. It was only after Gindin produced proof of having been graduated from the Temiriazev Academy in 1926, of having been in charge of the construction of a huge dam in the Transcaucasus, of having then been appointed chief engineer of the hydro-electric irrigation works in Tashkent, that he was given a hearing. Then he was confronted with the lack of funds. Then the question of building materials came up, then of transportation, then of workers, then of food and shelter for them. Furthermore, in the spring there arose the additional danger of the Basmachi. Varsobstroy is seventeen kilometers from Stalinabad, it is an almost completely deserted gorge, exposed to bandit attacks at almost any time. But Gindin never wavered. The project was practicable, and he had made up his mind to see it through. His dream is to have the entire Varsob region electrified. To construct an electric railway from Stalinabad to Samarkand, to turn this valley into the hunting ground of European tourists, to eclipse Switzerland in a hundred different ways, to make a Soviet Switzerland. He has all kinds of dreams for Tadjikistan; and he neither a Communist nor a Tadjik!"

When Gindin comes back, he tells a little about the work here. I am no engineer; and many things aren't clear to me. However, the skeleton of the plan is this: a dam 180 meters long, from there a canal 1,126 meters long and from 3 to 4 meters deep. The excavation work will amount to about 28,000 cubic meters. The total cost will be nine million rubles. The cost of current won't exceed 3 kopecks per kilowatt hour, whereas the present cost in Stalinabad is 70 kopecks. By September first, there will be here a settlement of 1,800 people, with stores, bakeries, clubs, etc.

"Now tell of the difficulties," suggests Khodzhaiev. "Let the comrades know what it means to build socialism in this wild country."

"It's too much to tell," laughs Gindin. "Briefly, we need ten automobile trucks, 150 horses, 140 wagons, 400 tons of iron. We have—not one truck, only 34 horses, only 25 wagons, only one ton of iron."

There is a considerable slump in our enthusiasm: it is one thing to plan, and another to carry out the plan.

"How in hell do you expect to carry on the work?" asks the French comrade in a choking voice.

"We have pulled through worse fixes," rumbles the irrepressible Khodzhaiev reassuringly. "We know that the materials are on the way; when they arrive, we'll have to do some real hustling, that's all."

"If everything were on hand," rejoins Gindin, "if there were no bureaucrats, and saboteurs, and self-seekers, there would be no trick in building. Sure, it's hard. But we'll do it, won't we, Khodzhaiev?"

"We certainly will!" shouts Khodzhaiev, laying his heavy hand on Gindin's shoulders. "And three years from now we'll invite our comrades to come here and take a trip through the mountains on our luxurious mountain railway...."

"The Bolsheviks certainly know how to dream," remarks our Norwegian companion.

"Fortunately, they are also learning how to work," retorts Gindin.

The workers are gathering around the long flat shed which serves as the temporary dining room at Varsobstroy. It is twilight. The hot sun has sunk behind the mountains. The village, the gorge, the river, the barracks—everything seems to be enjoying the cool evening shadows.

In the long shed two oil lamps cast a dim light on the heads of the workers. In its flicker, faces look rather queer, figures tenuous, shadows grotesque. There is something strangely similar between this country and this rough-looking crowd and what my imagination has always pictured our American Wild West to have been. The workers who have come to this remote and forsaken place are not just ordinary workers one meets anywhere in the world. They are adventurers, pioneers, seekers after the unusual. Cutting tunnels through mountains, erecting electrical stations in the desert, laying roads in the heart of Asia, building bridges across black chasms, this is the work that attracts them. Are they Bolsheviks because they have the pioneering spirit in them, or are they pioneers because they have been stirred by the spirit of Bolshevism? It is hard to tell. The two things are so inextricably interwoven. One thing is unquestionable: these men have set out to build a new order, a new proletarian society. A gigantic task? Certainly. But such men are made for such tasks.

The meal over, a short meeting to honor the foreign guests is proposed. The whole thing is spontaneous, informal. One of the guests delivers a few words of greeting and invites the workers to ask questions about the foreign lands and suggests that there be an exchange of opinions.

The workers hesitate to speak. These people are no orators, no after-dinner speakers. Words do not come readily to them.

Finally, one worker rises and asks in a halting Russian whether he may speak in German. He is met with encouraging exclamations: "Go on, Karl! Let it be German, the comrades know German! Shoot!"

Karl tells an unpretentious story. He had been a farm hand before the Revolution, working for the rich German kulaks on the Volga. It was veritable slavery then. The Revolution has done a great deal for him and for the other poor peasants in that region. He glories in the national equality granted to all peoples in the vast Union of the Soviets. In short, "long live the Soviet Union, long live the Communist Party!"

Karl has broken the ice. Many workers get up to speak in their native languages: a Persian, a Tadjik, a couple of Russians, a Jew, an Uzbek, a Tartar, a Turkoman, an Armenian.

The least articulate and the most effective speaker is the Armenian. He and a group of other Armenians have come here from Baku, they have organized their own shock brigade, and they have signed up to remain in Tadjikistan up to the successful completion of the Piatiletka. "We want to help the Soviet Union build a better society," he concludes.

The person who seems to be most affected by the meeting is Khodzhaiev. "A real international gathering here, in the wilds, on the shore of the Dushambe.... Isn't it wonderful!"

When the meeting is over, we file out of the shed, followed by the crowd of jostling workers. There is warm shaking of hands, and countless requests for proletarian greetings to be transmitted to the workers in the capitalist countries. "Tell them to start something real, and we'll come to help them," shouts Karl. And as our truck plunges into the deep Southern night, the Internationale sung in a dozen different tongues to the accompaniment of the roaring Dushambe, crashes through the crisp mountain air and, reverberating in a million echoes through the Varsob valley, rolls along the mountain tops, hits against the snowy peak of Lenintau, and vanishes in the starry spaccs.

XV

NEW WOMEN IN OLD ASIA

> If you throw a stone into a deep well,
> It will go to the bottom, O mother dear.
> If you sell your young daughter to strangers,
> She will cry her eyes out, she will perish,
>   O mother dear....
>
> Along the road that takes me from my home,
> Sow thorny weeds and thistles, O mother dear.
> And when you see the thistles droop their heads,
> You'll know that I have faded out of life,
>   O mother dear.
>   Pre-Revolutionary Turkoman Girl's Song.

Gray or Dark-blue Coffins

TO a Westerner traveling in the Orient, one of the most haunting experiences is, no doubt, his first encounter with those strangely amorphous, ghost-like creatures that glide, silent and mysterious, through the narrow-winding, deserted alleys of any Central-Asian town or village. The experience is even more ghastly if one chances upon such a figure while it is at rest—a gray or dark-blue coffin standing stiffly on end, covered with a black, bulging, heavy lid.

These are the women of Central Asia, vestiges of a remote past, living corpses eternally imprisoned in their coffins. It is difficult to imagine anything quite so monstrous and degrading as this traditional costume (*paranja*), this formless cloak with its long, wide, empty sleeves tied on the back, and its thick, black, horse-hair net suspended in front of the face, from the top of the head to a little below the waist. This is how the local

Moslem, still untouched by Communist teaching, protects his woman from the impure glances of the stranger. The woman can see the world, but the world cannot see her. Even little girls of nine or ten are thus protected from immodest appraisals of their pulchritude. This custom is rigid, absolute. The emotional ramparts built around it by vested economic interest and religion are well-nigh insurmountable. Despite Bolshevik onslaughts, they have held out in the more inaccessible regions and even in such cities as Tashkent and Samarkand.

It is almost impossible to snap a photograph of a native woman. The slightest suspicious move in her direction and she flees as if pursued by a thousand devils. More than once our cavalcade, on espying women working in the fields, would begin to focus cameras, only to have the women drop precipitously to the ground and cover themselves with whatever they could lay hands on. Not before they heard the clatter of our horses' hoofs die away in the distance would they venture to peep out from under their covers.

Besides being offensive to the eye, the *paranja* is irritating to the nose. It always emanates a faint odor of perspiration mingled with that of mutton. Generally, it is filthy and insect-ridden, and is the cause of multifarious eye and skin diseases. It shuts from the woman and her suckling babe the benefits of sunshine and fresh air, and is accountable, in large measure, for the prevalence of lung-trouble among the women and for the frequent stunted growth of children.

What makes the *paranja* especially significant is that it serves as a symbol of the utter degradation and humiliation of the Moslem woman in Central Asia. "Obedience and silence are a woman's greatest virtues," says the Prophet. "If a Moslem is in need of good counsel," the Uzbeks say, "let him turn to his sire; if there is no sire, let him ask his older brother, or uncle, or neighbor; if there is no one of these about, let him consult his wife—and do exactly the opposite of what she says." Contempt for the woman seems to be one of the most sacred articles of a Central Asian's faith.

Boys are a blessing in a home; girls a curse. When too many girls are born into a family, it is the mother who is held responsible. (Childlessness and infant mortality are also blamed on the mother.) To congratulate a father on the birth of a daughter is a mortal insult and may entail a bitter family feud. I knew a woman in Tashkent, Mozol Kolontarov, who had given birth to six girls in succession. Mozol felt terribly guilty before her husband. After an interval of seven years, she had another opportunity to redeem herself. Frantic with fear and misgiving, she kept on reiterating that she would much rather die than have another girl. Fate was unkind to her; she bore a girl once more. When she beheld the newly born infant, Mozol died of grief.

According to both the common law code (*adat*) and the religious code (*sheriat*), a woman may be bought and sold and transferred from one man to another without herself being in any way consulted. According to the *sheriat*, the husband has a right to punish his wife's disobedience by keeping her incarcerated in the house and by discreet use of corporal punishment. Cruelty, torture, and even maiming are not sufficient grounds for divorce. According to the old law, the testimony of one man is equivalent to that of two women. The woman is rarely permitted to leave her home without a male escort. While at home, she is confined to the *ichkari*—woman's section of the house—where she remains whenever her husband entertains visitors in the man's section. In the street, a woman dare not stop, or cough, or linger, or look back; she must just keep on walking. Polygamy, child marriage, and purchase of brides (*kalym*) are all essential features of woman's status in Central Asia. She is a chattel, a slave.

Yet there is evidence—often cited by the emancipated Tadjiks and Uzbeks—that the woman had not always occupied such an abject place in the social scheme of these peoples. Numerous legends and myths preserved by some Tadjik mountain tribes make mention of heroic women and of brave and wise female rulers. There is the story of Queen Tamiris, of how she and her nomadic subjects had won a mighty victory over the great Persian ruler Cyrus. There is the memory of Queen Khatun, the wise ruler of Bokhara, who reigned during the troublous years of the early Arab invasions of Central Asia.

It was, indeed, with the coming of the Arabs and the gradual triumph of Islam that the position of the woman among the Iranian aborigines of what is now known as Tadjikistan began to decline, less rapidly among the nomads in the steppes and the peasants in the mountains, where the woman was an important economic factor in the family organization; more rapidly among the settled urban population—merchants, mullahs, officials, etc.— where the woman was economically unimportant and where the influence of the Mohammedan religion had taken firmer root.

This process continued during and after the Tiurko-Mongolian invasion. However, originally, that is before they surrendered to Moslem influences, the Tiurko-Mongolian nomads, too, had known of no special disabilities for women. Like the Aryan folklore, Tiurkish folklore has references to heroic women. There is the legend, for example, of a detachment of female warriors who had fought a valiant battle on the walls of Geok-Teppe. Also there is the beautiful Tiurkish legend about the woman musician Khelai-Bakhshi who had triumphed over all her male rivals, especially the celebrated musician Ker-Jepali who had challenged her to a contest. Khelai-Bakhshi was with child then. Her labor pains were about to begin. But she accepted the challenge of Ker-Jepali. The unusual contest lasted a long time. When midnight came, Khelai-Bakhshi turned to her husband, asking him what he preferred, a child or victory. "Victory," said the husband unhesitatingly. Then Khelai-Bakhshi excused herself for a little while. She gave birth to her child, handed it over to her relatives, and came back to proceed with the contest. She beat the old and famous Ker-Jepali, and he rode away with lowered head.

Green Frogs and Free Women

It was toward evening, after our customary visits to the schools, coöperative, the orphanage, the primitive silk works, and the other interesting places in the village, that our group, while lounging on the huge woolen rug and pile of blankets spread out under the magnificent plane tree on the side of a pool and sipping interminably the inevitable tea from capacious *pialas,* induced our hostess, the organizer of the local Woman's Department, to tell us a little of her life. Prompted and guided by our questions, occasionally interrupted and put back on the right track, Khoziat Markulanova told us her story.

She was born in Fergana. Her father was a weaver, a devout Moslem. Her mother was of peasant stock. From her earliest childhood, Khoziat, her two sisters and her mother were working at embroidering skull caps. Her two brothers were bakers. Hers was an industrious, hard-working family.

When Khoziat was eight years old, her mother made her a little *paranja.* Khoziat cried and refused to put it on. But her mother said that she was too pretty and that if she didn't go covered the Bek's procurers would grab her. Khoziat did not know what that meant, but she had heard so many stories of how little girls died in the Bek's palace that she was glad to put on the *paranja.*

When Khoziat reached the age of fourteen, her mother began to be worried. Most of her daughter's former friends were already married. Marriage now began to be discussed in Khoziat's presence. Once, her father, looking very pleased, marched into the *ichkari* and whispered something to her mother. Khoziat did not know what he said, but she had a feeling that it was about marriage. Her heart sank, as she was terribly afraid of being given to an old man. Pretending to be busy with the dishes, she strained to make out what was being said. She heard her mother ask: "Have they anything?" and her father answer: "Not rich, but they have something." Her mother nodded assent.

What happened was this: The village *imaum* and Ali Nazarov had come to feel out the old Markulanov as to what his attitude might be with regard to a match between his daughter and Nazarov's nephew. Upon receiving a tentatively favorable reply, the suitor's older sister, together with a woman neighbor, came to interview Khoziat's mother. They brought the traditional bread and a couple of kerchiefs as presents.

On the third day, the *imaum* and Ali Nazarov paid Markulanov another visit. Now the kalym—the price—had to be discussed. After arduous haggling on both sides, it was finally agreed that her father was to receive two rams, 160 pounds of rice, one cow—to compensate for the milk Khoziat had been fed—two donkey-loads of fuel, and three quilts. The cow was never delivered.

After that Khoziat's mother sent some more gifts to the suitor whom neither she nor her daughter had ever seen. Three weeks passed between the engagement and the wedding. On the day of the wedding, people began to crowd the bride's house from early morning. Everything was in a turmoil. Elaborate preparations were being made. A ram was slain. Pilaf was being cooked in the yard. All kinds of vegetables and fruits were being piled up—radishes, cucumbers, scallions, egg-plants, apricots, pistachio nuts, and melons and grapes. During all that time Khoziat sat in the *ichkari,* nervous, worried, but also a little glad that she was the cause of all this hubbub.

Soon Khoziat's mother came in and said that the mullah had arrived. She then assisted Khoziat with the *paranja,* and led her close to the door. On the other side of the shut door the mullah began to chant his prayers. Then he cried out in a loud voice, so Khoziat might hear on her side of the door: "Khoziat, do you consent to take this man as your husband?" He repeated the question three times. Khoziat did not know what to say, until prompted by her mother: "Hai" (yes).

After the ceremony, Khoziat's mother and some other women spread many rugs and quilts on the floor of the *ichkari.* The great moment was approaching. Khoziat was to meet her husband for the first time. While she and her friends, all in *paranjas,* were huddled in a corner of the room, two young fellows, in bright turbans, brought in the bridegroom. A robe was thrown over his head. His escorts helped him sit down on the quilt and retired in silence. Khoziat's mother, aunts, and neighbors then surrounded her and, leading her over to the bridegroom, seated her next to him. Then everybody began to withdraw from the room. Khoziat's girl friends were sobbing: "You are leaving us. Don't forget us!"

They sat near each other, their faces covered, scarcely daring to move, petrified with fear and embarrassment. Khoziat could hear the gurgling of the stream outside and the rustling of the poplars. Her husband moved a little closer to her. She heard his heart beat. Finally he removed her *paranja,* and uncovered his own face. Khoziat did not dare raise her eyes. After a while, she glanced at him furtively. He was pleasing to look at. She felt a great gladness in her heart. Then their eyes met. He smiled at her and to reassure her he put a cushion under his head and shut his eyes. Khoziat was fortunate—he was kind and delicate. She too shut her eyes. They slept like brother and sister. The oil lamp burned all night.

Khoziat and Khadza lived together for about six months. Then Khadza left for Tashkent to work on a cotton plantation. He died soon after. Khadza's death was a terrible blow to Khoziat, for she had come to love Khadza and appreciate his gentleness. She then returned to her parents.

Echoes of the revolution finally reached Khoziat's village. There were rumors of fights and battles in the surrounding hills. Then a band of counter-revolutionary guerillas appeared. The village was terrorized. Markulanov and many other workers were killed. It was whispered that the bandits had sent out agents to look for pretty women. Khoziat's uncle heard it in the *chai-khana* (tea room) and he hurried to Khoziat's house that night and he brought his daughter with him and insisted that the girls must be hidden. Khoziat and her cousin dressed up like old women, padded their backs with heaps of cotton, and, accompanied by Khoziat's mother, they fled that night to Kokand.

The refugees walked two days and two nights before they reached their destination. In Kokand they had neither relatives nor acquaintances, but it was a big city and they felt safer there. Khoziat's mother then decided to hide the girls in the household of the famous local *ishan* Rokharatub, who consented to take them in as servants. Striking his long, carefully combed beard and rolling his clever little eyes to heaven, the *ishan* said: "The flesh is ours, the bone is yours." By which he meant to say: "While they live, they work for me; if they die, they belong to you."

The *ishan's* household was a busy place. Many *miurids* (followers of an *ishan*) came to visit the holy man, bringing all kinds of gifts in meats, fruits, vegetables, and so on. Every night the ishan, surrounded by his *miurids,* sat on a mountain of quilts, ate fat *pilaf,* and recited the *Koran.* For him and his fanatical *miurids* every night was a feast night. But for the women in the household it was endless drudgery—cooking, and baking, and cleaning, and washing dishes from early morning till late at night. The girls received no pay; they weren't even given any clothes. They ate only the left-overs, and were chased and hounded by the *ishan's* two senior wives. Every night Khoziat and her cousin would shed furtive tears on their pillows.

After a few months, the *ishan* gave Khoziat's pretty cousin to one of his old *miurids,* Hokim Saidov, who had only one wife. The girl was afraid to refuse, though she hated the sight of Saidov. A few months later, Khoziat's uncle came and brought her regards from her mother. His daughter whom he also visited implored him to take her away from Saidov. But the uncle said it was bad this way and it was bad the other way. But he thought that Saidov was the lesser of the two evils, and he said that he couldn't take his daughter back before it was all over with the Basmach bandits.

Vague rumors would sometimes penetrate the walls of the *ichkari;* Khoziat heard the old women curse the infidels, the Russians, the "Bolshevois." One day there was a great commotion in the *ichkari;* some one brought the news that he had seen a whole group of young Moslem women strutting brazenly through the street with their faces uncovered, like shameless harlots. The only one who did not appear to be outraged was the *ishan's* youngest wife, a pale little creature not much older than Khoziat. She, poor thing, had had a sad life, with the older women always jealous of her, and always picking on her, and gossiping about her. She was wasting away very fast, coughing up blood all the time. Maybe she was dreaming of a happier life of freedom, when she heard all those rumors that came from the outside world. That day she became so excited that she coughed more than ever, and had to be put to bed. The *ishan* had a consultation with a *tabib* (healer), and they decided that the best cure in such cases was a broth made of green frogs, which was to be given to the patient secretly for seven days in succession.

One of the old woman servants and Khoziat were then sent out to catch frogs. Taking a bag and iron pincers, they went to a distant pond in which green frogs were said to be plentiful. They had caught only a couple of them; so on the following day Khoziat went out by herself to hunt for frogs. As she approached Soviet Street, she saw something extraordinary happen. The street teemed with people. Red banners, and streamers, and placards gleamed and fluttered in the hot sun. A throng of women, mostly young, though there were a few middle-aged and even old ones, many with faces uncovered, were parading along the street. There was a brass band playing unfamiliar music. The young people were singing strange songs. Occasionally, one would hear the voices of youngsters: "Down with the *paranja!* Long live the free women of Central Asia! Down with the beys and mullahs! Long live the Soviet Government!"

This was new and fascinating. Poor Khoziat forgot all about the *ishan's* pallid wife and the green frogs, and, in a trance, followed the crowd. She watched the parading girls. They looked so free and gay and proud, and she longed to be with them, to be like them, to sing their songs, to hold their banners.

Then the women marched into a spacious courtyard, with many trees and rugs and teapots. The paraders arranged themselves in a huge circle. They sat under the shady trees, and drank *kok-choi* (green tea), and ate apples, and listened to speeches. The girls called out to the women standing in the throngs of onlookers to remove their *paranjas* and to join in the feast. Khoziat did not dare to remove her *paranja*. "I live with an *ishan*," she thought. "If he ever learns about it, he'll kill me." But she did sidle up to the girls, and timidly sat down on the edge of the rug. The girl next to her handed her an apple, and called her *rafik* (comrade). Khoziat was happy.

She listened to the speeches. Most of what was said she did not understand. What she did finally grasp was that this was Woman's Day, a day to celebrate woman's freedom. And she believed the speakers, for their eyes looked honest.

Then a middle-aged woman, with ample bosom and mild eyes, got up to speak. "Ibrahimova," whispered the crowd, "the director of the Woman's Department." She spoke as a mother would speak to her children, quietly, gently, simply—so that every one could understand. She wasn't a smooth speaker. She often stopped, and smiled a little guiltily, fumbling for the proper word. She spoke of the sorrows of the woman's life. Of ignorance, and darkness. Of how children died by the thousands because the mothers didn't know how to take care of them. She spoke of the humiliation of wearing a *paranja*.

When Ibrahimova finished, Khoziat felt drawn to her, like a mother. To her she could tell everything, of the terrible life at the *ishan's* and of her fear to go home. She sought out Ibrahimova in the crowd and anxiously touched her arm. She said only a few words and the older woman understood everything. "You have no one in Kokand? You are a widow? You live at the *ishan's*? Don't worry, my little woman, don't tremble so. We'll take you to our girls' dormitory. We'll take care of you. We'll teach you; we'll train you; we'll make something of you."

Khoziat cried with happiness when she entered the girls' home on Karl Marx Street. She was taken into a nice, clean bathroom and shown how to use it. She was given clean underwear, European clothes, bed, quilt—everything.

On the very next day, Khoziat's teacher gave her the first lesson. Things came easy to her. In a couple of weeks, she knew how to read and write. She soon started arithmetic and elementary politgramota (civics). The girls used to have long talks with their teacher. She was a very intelligent woman, and one of the first woman Communists in Central Asia. Her name was Makhi Djamal Seifutdinova. She had seen a great deal in her life. She had been a woman's delegate in Samarkand and in Tashkent. And she had been a member of the first delegation to the First Congress of Eastern Women in Moscow. She often spoke of the life in the various big cities she had visited, and she very often spoke of Lenin. It was through Seifutdinova's conversations that the girls came to know and love Lenin. She described how well they had been received in Moscow, how Lenin and his wife, Krupskaya, came to visit them. On the sight of Lenin, one of the Uzbek women fell on his shoulder and began to cry, and she couldn't stop until they gave her some drops. Then Lenin conversed with the women, and told them what the Soviet Government was trying to do for them. Then Alexandra Kollontai spoke to them. Then they were taken to museums, and theaters, and factories. They stayed in Moscow twelve days.

Khoziat lived in the dormitory for nine months, and was very successful in her studies. She got encouragement on all sides. Among her teachers there was a young man by the name of Feizula. He was also the superintendent of the dormitory. He took a special interest in Khoziat and helped her a great deal. Once she had to fill out a questionnaire; and in helping her fill in the answers, Feizula learned much about her former life.

"Does your mother know about you, where you are?" he asked Khoziat. "Don't you think you are a little unkind to your mother? From what you tell me, she is a very good and kind woman. Don't you think we better notify her as to your whereabouts?"

Khoziat felt ashamed before Feizula for being so callous, but she said that she was afraid her mother and her uncle might take her away from the school, back to the village.

Still, Feizula, without consulting Khoziat, did write a letter to her mother. One afternoon—she was monitor that day—Khoziat was busy cleaning up one of the rooms. Suddenly she saw a veiled woman, followed by a little boy, crossing the threshold. "Are there no men around?" the woman asked in a low voice. "Not a soul, my good woman," replied Khoziat gayly. The woman uncovered her face. It was Khoziat's mother! And the little boy was her youngest brother. For the first few moments, both her mother and little brother were so stunned by Khoziat's European outfit and bobbed hair that they couldn't utter a sound. It wasn't Khoziat. At any rate, it was not their Khoziat. She was a stranger. She looked like an infidel. And they both burst into tears. It was only after Khoziat rushed to them, and embraced them, and kissed them, and made them feel at home and welcome, that they became a little composed. Gradually, they got used to her alien appearance. It was their Khoziat, after all, whom every one in the village thought dead!

What happened was this: After Khoziat had vanished from the *ishan's* house, she had been searched for by her master's servants all over Kokand. When no traces could be found of her, the *ishan* called in a fortune-teller who, after mumbling all kinds of strange words and pronouncing many queer prayers and invocations while casting little balls of cotton into a bowl of water, finally solved the mystery. "The light has gone out of Khoziat," she finally muttered. "A big man, a *kaffir*, a Bolshevoi abducted her while she was returning from the pond carrying the green frogs. He abducted her, then killed her, then threw her into the water."

Khoziat laughed at her mother and her fears, and called the *mullah* an old fool, and told her mother very definitely that she had not the least intention of going back to the village. Her mother was hurt, and Khoziat had to explain. She talked to her, and tried to convert her to a more modern point of view. She told her of Ibrahimova and Seifutdinova. She tried to explain to her the disgrace of wearing a *paranja*. She presented to her all the arguments that she had learned in favor of woman's emancipation. But the mother shook her head sadly, and told Khoziat that she wasn't convinced, that the Tadjiks had lived that way for centuries, and that she saw no good in breaking up everything, in destroying everything. "I can't go back to the village without you," she kept on saying. "Ah, Khoziat, Khoziat, what have you done to me and our family? You have disgraced us in the eyes of every good Moslem. Everybody will be pointing at me. I won't be able to look anybody straight in the eyes. If, Allah beware, I am in trouble, no one will help me. Ah, Khoziat, Khoziat...." Still, her resistance was a little broken. There was even a glimmer of pride in her eyes when Khoziat displayed her ability to read and write and make long additions and subtractions.

Later, the girls came in, and Feizula, and Seifutdinova, and were all very courteous and gentle with the mother. As to her, while she never said a thing to Khoziat, seeing all those nice people with whom her daughter was associated made her feel a little reassured.

When she was bidding farewell to Khoziat, she said, "Ah, my little daughter, if you only knew how I'm afraid to face our relatives and neighbors. I have learned much while I have stayed with you here, and I have thought that perhaps you young people are right after all. I don't know. But I am an old woman, Khoziat, and I am sorry I wasn't dead before all these new things have come to destroy the old life."

That was the last Khoziat saw of her mother. The old woman died soon afterward—a good, devoted, silent and obedient Moslem woman. Soon afterward Khoziat married. Her husband, who was a member of the Young Communist League, was transferred from Kokand to Tashkent, to study in the University. Khoziat went with him, to study in the Workers' Faculty. Here an altogether new life began for her. From now on her life became bound up with the Revolution.

Tact and Revolution

Long before Khoziat came to Tashkent, the Communist Party there had done a huge amount of work with the native women. The nature of this work is best given in the following statement of F. Marchenko, one of the leaders of the Woman's Department in Tashkent:

Our Department was organized on November 12, 1919, when the Regional Committee of the Communist Party adopted a resolution calling for the formation of special women's departments in all the Party committees in Central Asia. The purpose of these departments was preliminary education, agitation, and organization among the native women. However, the work at first moved along rather slowly.

The European, the Russian, women, the working women and the wives of working men in Tashkent did begin to stir, to show signs of life—now a meeting, now a lecture, here and there a political circle. But the native Uzbek and Tadjik women were neither seen nor heard.

Many a time Dvorkina and myself, seeing how well the work was progressing in the new, the European, section of the city, among the Russians, would say to ourselves: "This is not the main thing, the old city is still untouched."

The trouble was, we did not know the language. Another trouble, there were no Moslem women in the ranks of our Party. And it was only later that Dvorkina fortunately happened to come across Usupova, a Tartar woman. The latter had had a lot of trouble in her married life, and spoke bitterly of the lot of the Eastern women. She seemed to us very promising, but we did not know at the beginning where to use her. She explained to us the local customs, the traditions; she also served as our tongue. We then decided to try first to draw in the Moslem women of the intelligentsia. We called two meetings. Quite a number came, but they all seemed to be half asleep. We made efforts to have elections for a special Moslem Women's Bureau, also to elect some for forming contacts with other Moslem women. But as soon as the meeting was adjourned, there was no bureau, and no one who was willing to do the necessary work. This was quite natural, since the crowd was rather well-to-do, without a touch of social consciousness, and certainly without any disposition to take part in great events.

All other pother came to nothing. We succeeded only in getting hold of a few Moslem, chiefly Tartar, women—Khusanbaieva, Fatikha, Redkina, Karimova, etc.

We failed badly with the intelligentsia. We therefore decided to begin from the other end, to begin with the poorest class.

Even before we arrived at Tashkent, there had been in the old city artels of women weavers. Usually, these women weavers were given the cheapest sort of cotton to work on. The wages were not paid regularly. And the prices they received were very low. Of course it might be better to sell their products at the bazaar; but, first, this was even less certain; and, second, one needed funds for the initial investment in cotton, spindles, etc. And so, these Moslem women, meek, ragged, would come, hand in their week's work, receive their miserable few kopecks, and uncomplainingly go home to starve some more. Many of these women had whole families to support. Either the husband was sick, or there was no husband at all. Such women, heads of families, are more independent, and tend to become more emancipated than the helpless women of the intelligentsia.

It was with this material that we began our work. We entered into an agreement with the Department of Home Crafts. We sent our representative to watch that our women got better cotton to work with; we won a higher price for the piece workers, etc.

We then called a meeting of the women working in the artels. There was no trouble to get them to come. The place was like a bee-hive. Noise. Complaints. In the new city, milk is handed out for babies free of charge. No such thing in the old city. In the new city, a new-born babe gets some clothes. No such thing in the old city. In the new city, they occasionally get a ration. No such thing in the old city. And so it was from the material side that we approached the native woman, and she, of course, gladly responded.

But what to do with the traditions that pressed like a yoke on the Moslem woman? We had to grope along. On the one hand we were advised not to wake the native woman, for it might complicate the political situation; on the other, we were being urged by some bold souls to proclaim the slogan, "Down with the *paranja!*" Such "Down-with" radicals were unhesitatingly sat upon; age-old traditions cannot be knocked out by a straight-from-the-shoulder blow. Let, in the meanwhile, the Moslem woman wear her *paranja*—that is nothing. What we have to do is to help her economically, to put her on her feet, to give her a chance to earn a livelihood. And perhaps she will herself begin to do things. To raise the economic and cultural level of the native woman, to help the Soviet government to find a way of doing it—these were the first steps. And here Dvorkina did everything possible. Not even one of the native women with whom we worked removed her *paranja;* though many of them were at congresses and in Soviets, both as members and delegates.

It was in this careful manner that, together with our work in the artels, we began to do a little cultural work— little plays and concerts preceded by meetings. We began to take our Moslem women to the new city—to the Lunacharsky House. These affairs attracted not only the poor women we had drawn into our ranks. Funny things would happen occasionally. Imagine a concert-meeting in the Lunacharsky House. The speakers and the performers are in the back of the stage awaiting their turn. At the door stands our guard. Men are not admitted. While all around the house there are the Moslem husbands, watching whether it is really true that only women are allowed to the concert. And the women in the hall feel perfectly at home. Some are listening in a reclined position; some help the performer with her song. The kids, too, are here. Altogether, the thing is quite informal and gay. To these affairs we succeeded in attracting wives of most jealous and conservative husbands.

I recall only once that an unpleasant incident took place. A few Hindu comrades who were on their way to Moscow, to the Comintern, expressed a desire to bring their greetings from revolutionary India to the new comrades—the Moslem women of Central Asia. We should have warned the women to pull down their *paranjas* before we brought in the guests. But our guard failed us. The tall, graceful, handsome Hindus, about thirteen of them, solemnly, slowly, one after another marched into the hall just as the women were at the height of informality. A cry of horror pierced the hall. The women dashed for safety. Many literally fell to the floor in an attempt to hide their faces. The thoroughly embarrassed and nonplussed guests were made to occupy the first rows and were instructed not to turn their heads. They must have felt terribly foolish to sit motionless for such a long time. They begged to be excused. Of course, their greeting to the audience of "coffins with black lids" had lost a great deal of its fervor.

Stories about our parties, our appeals, and explanations spread throughout the city, and penetrated far into rural districts. More and more women began to come to our Department—now it was a woman beaten by her husband, now it was a youngster forced into marriage. Weeping, at times bleeding, came old women, middle-aged mothers, little girls; often on their knees, grasping at our skirts, seizing our hands, imploring for help. Willy-nilly we had to meddle in the intimate lives of these people. We tried to be cautious, tactful, not to arouse any resentment. Not infrequently, we had couples come. The husband, serious, morose, in one corner of the office, the wife, sobbing, in another; both demanding justice. We began to appear before the native judges, the *casii,* trying to combat their casuistry and their antiquated laws. And, I repeat, we never got into serious trouble with the native men.

The work of our Department was growing, its influence spreading. Between the years 1919 and 1922 scores of conferences and congresses were held. In 1920, the first trip of Central Asian women to Moscow took place.

This news caused a considerable sensation among the natives. Our message of woman's emancipation was penetrating to the villages. Women's clubs and schools were beginning to be opened in various sections of the country. The Central Executive Committee of Turkestan now felt the time ripe for making polygamy, forced marriages, and marriages of minors criminal offenses. Our labor was bearing fruit.

Husbands and Schools

To return to Khoziat and Feizula. Tashkent, where the newlyweds went to live, was the center of European culture in Central Asia. It had a big European population (in the new city) with several modern educational institutions. It had a large and strongly organized working class, mainly Russian railway workers. As the capital of Turkestan, it was the first city in this part of the world to establish the Soviet régime, and was now the general headquarters of the Communist Party in Central Asia. From Tashkent as a center, the Bolsheviki had sent the Soviet Armies to wage their victorious battles against the counter-revolutionary government of Kokand and against the tyrannical government of the Bokhara Emir. When Khoziat came there in 1922, Tashkent was already in possession of a rich revolutionary tradition: the proper atmosphere for an eager convert. What was most important as far as Khoziat's personal development was concerned was the fact that Tashkent was at the heart of the woman's movement in Central Asia. However, just when she came to Tashkent and was drawn into the work, the Woman's

Department was in a rather bad way. The main reason was, of course, the institution of the New Economic Policy. As a result of the Nep, the Woman's Department had to make fundamental readjustments in its method of work. Previously, students were being paid during their part-time apprenticeship in the schools, offices, and factories. The Nep, by abolishing this privilege, made the task of attracting Uzbek and Tadjik women students much more difficult. Then, again, with the establishment of the Nep, the state ceased to subsidize the artels. And without this support, the rather weak and inefficient women's artels, where the efforts of the Woman's Department were mainly concentrated, began to disintegrate.

On the other hand, as the Party was gaining in members and power, its attack on the old grew bolder and more determined. And one must bear in mind that not everywhere were the representatives of the Woman's Department as diplomatic and tactful as were Marchenko and Dvorkina. In many places the enthusiasts were forcing the issue, removing the *paranjas,* and losing their heads in the process. This naturally brought a sharp reaction. Resistance, at first passive and peaceful, began to assume more ominous forms. In Auliae-Ata, where Khoziat had been commandeered in 1924 to organize a woman's department, the mullahs lodged the following complaint against her before the Revolutionary Committee: "A certain woman in a red dress and a little cap seduces and corrupts our wives. We know that this is not a woman, but a man in disguise. We request that he be arrested in conformity with the laws of the sheriat. If this is not done, we'll take the law into our own hands." To forestall violence, the Committee had to make a pretense at arresting Khoziat. She was then urged by the authorities to stop all propaganda which might result in serious trouble.

Hers was not by any means a unique case. Tadjik and Uzbek Communists were seized, beaten and forced to swear that they would make their wives wear the *paranja;* they were summoned to the mosque and were made to renounce their struggles against religion and custom. They and their kin were threatened with arson, ruin, ostracism. The fighters for the new life were being driven out of their homes and out of settlements. Parents of married women were taking them away from their Bolshevik husbands. Violence and terror spread throughout the land. Women who wished to study, who removed their *paranjas*, were beaten, raped, murdered. Whole villages rose in brutal frenzy against them. Even as late as the years 1927 and 1928, on the eve of Woman's Day, on the seventh of March, several score of unveiled women were slain. From March to November, 1928, 250 unveiled women were slain in Uzbekistan alone.

Such cases can be recounted by the hundreds. The point is that the embattled forces of reaction were putting up a stiff fight. To carry on its work at all, the Woman's Department had to compromise a great deal. It is no exaggeration to say that the Soviet decrees of 1921 pertaining to marital relations were in many places simply not being enforced. It would have been suicidal to try to enforce them. In domestic relations cases the administration of justice was still largely in the hands of the beys and *casii*. The Communists had to be extremely cautious. They had to neutralize the provocative propaganda of the beys and the mullahs.

This does not mean that the Department had suspended its work. By the end of the fifth year, 35 per cent of the best workers of the Department were Uzbek and Tadjik women. The Department was winning the sympathies and often the coöperation of the poorest sections of the population. There were many amusing and curious cases. One afternoon a middle-aged Kirghiz peasant shambled into Khoziat's office and submitted a carefully written request. The request read something like this:

"I, being a poor peasant, have not the means to pay *kalym* and get a wife. I, therefore, apply for your coöperation in that if you have some unmarried Kirghiz woman or one that has run away from her husband, I should be glad to marry her."

Khoziat had much trouble trying to get into his head

that the Woman's Department was not engaged in supplying wives, arranging marriages, and that it did not keep in reserve a stock of old maids and runaway wives. He left the office terribly disappointed.

Invariably, male support of the work of Khoziat's department came from the poorest workers and peasants who could not afford to pay *kalym,* and who were therefore in favor of abolishing it. These people, too, were naturally in favor of doing away with polygamy. First, being poor, they had no hope of ever having more than one wife, however desirable that might be. Second, they realized that with the disappearance of polygamy, many more women would be available for the poor bachelors.

The usefulness of the legal division of the Woman's Department has been attested to by countless men and women of the poorer classes who came in contact with it. It had pushed through the Commission of Justice a statute granting a variety of privileges to women who had had occasion to resort to the courts. For instance, on the Department's recommendation, domestic relations cases involving property were given first place on the court calendars. The state provided the women with legal counsel free of charge.

But legal aid and promulgating and popularizing laws that tended to emancipate the native women constituted only one phase of Khoziat's work. Of no small moment was her work in placing the Uzbek, Tadjik, Turcoman, and Kirghiz women into the Soviet apparatus, in working for their election into local or district Soviets and executive committees, in getting them jobs in the various industrial, commercial, and educational organs of the State, in drawing them into the Party, the Young Communist League, the Pioneer organization, in stimulating their active interest in the coöperative movement, in luring them into the Department's various voluntary social welfare and national defense groups. With the other officers in the Department, Khoziat supervised the conditions under which the women worked, tried to take care of the unemployed women, and coöperated with the unemployment bureaus in placing them in jobs. Mainly, however, Khoziat's attention was focused on the cultural and educational fronts—schools, clubs, nurseries, hygiene, etc.

That was what the Woman's Department did for Khoziat. Precisely the same thing was being done for thousands of women throughout Central Asia. From the very outset, the Department began to agitate for women's schools, an idea unheard of in the old days! Why should a girl be taught to read and write, when even the male population was 95 per cent illiterate, the remaining 5 per cent comprising chiefly the clericals and their children!

A fair idea of the type of girl student the Department attracted, may be obtained from some of the cases told by Khoziat. First, the case of Zeinof Kariheva. When she was seven years old, Zeinof had been sold by her brother to a rich old bey. The transaction had taken place during the famine in Fergana, and the price the brother received was 18 poods of *moto* and a cow. Zeinof's life with the old bey was perpetual misery. Abused by her husband, persecuted by the two senior wives and their grown-up children, the little girl behaved like a wildcat. Once, when particularly infuriated, she jumped at the husband's youngest son, Akhmed, and buried her nails in his face. The spoiled youngster let out one piercing, savage yell. The old bey then decided to teach Zeinof a lesson. He beat her so long and so methodically, that the child-wife lay unconscious for days. When she came to, Zeinof ran away from the house. She hid in the orchard for three days, until, driven by hunger, she made her way into the village. By sheer luck she ran into a group of Young Communists who listened to her story, collected some money among themselves, and sent her on to Khoziat's department. Khoziat had never seen anything quite so pitiful as this child when she was brought into the office. Bloodstained, bruised, shabby, trembling with anxiety and fear, she kept on crying: "I won't go back to my husband; his children beat me; my husband beats me when I don't look happy.... I won't go away from here." This was in

1924. Zeinof is now in her third year at the Tashkent University.

There was Abdunabaiva, who placed her children in nurseries and came to study. There was Kirghizbaiva, who had been given into marriage at the age of 14, but who had left her husband and came to the school. Kirghizbaiva had been sold in 1923 to an old husband. The first time she escaped, she was caught, beaten by her husband and his kin and severely wounded with a knife. After she recovered, she escaped a second time and came to Khoziat begging to be allowed to study. Mukhamed Alieva Khoirakhan had escaped from her husband who attempted to kill her, inflicting on her twelve heavy wounds with his pocket knife. She was still bleeding when she stumbled into Khoziat's office and collapsed. Alieva is now a member of the Party, and is being trained in the Party school for the job of Communist organizer.

Another important phase of the cultural work of Khoziat's Department was the opening of women's clubs; the main purpose being to draw the woman out of her seclusion. When Khoziat came to Tashkent, the first woman's club in Central Asia had already been organized there. It started with only fifteen Uzbek women. Within a couple of years the club boasted a membership of 426. It grew by leaps and bounds. Branches were opened throughout the cities and the villages. There are scores of such clubs now. Men are not allowed to enter the club rooms. This makes it easier to get the women in. At the beginning the women shunned the clubs, for fear that they might be forced to remove their *paranjas*. In its club propaganda, therefore, Khoziat's Department always stressed the point that membership was not contingent on unveiling. To make sure that the women would be tempted to come to the clubs, practical inducements were offered. For instance, the Tashkent club organized under its auspices a sewing artel which gave employment to a considerable number of women members. It established a medical service. Women members as well as non-members are encouraged to come and consult the Department's physicians. The women are taught how to take care of their infants. By means of talks, exhibits, posters, etc., they are introduced to the elementary principles of hygiene. They are given medicine free of charge. Now it is interesting to note that, while going to the club does not require unveiling, unveiling is the inevitable consequence of frequent visits to the club.

Owing to the agitation and pressure of the Woman's Department, Tashkent had in 1924 sixteen specialized medical schools: a school for trained midwives, another school for trained nurses, a school for doctor's assistants, a school for teaching hygiene, for dental hygienists, a pharmacy school, etc. While at the beginning the majority of students in these schools were Russians, the number of native women has grown enormously. The services these schools are rendering are of incalculable value.

A Transition Generation

It was midnight, but Khoziat was not even half-through with her story. By that time, most of us were too tired to ask questions, and one of the group even began to snore— true, quite unobtrusively and delicately, with sudden little starts, and brief pauses, but sufficiently pointedly to make Khoziat a bit self-conscious.

"I had intended to tell you of my work in Tashkent; it turned out, however, that I have told little about myself and a whole lot about the Woman's Department," she said apologetically. "This can be explained by two equally important reasons. The first is—I am a Communist; and this means that like all Communists, I mean real Communists, I am so absorbed in my work and so completely identified with it that when I speak of my work I actually speak of myself. My individual life, my personal emotions, and struggles, and sufferings are relatively of little importance and probably of less interest. So this is one reason. The other is that my recent personal life has been a rather painful one, and I naturally am reluctant to dwell on it. Still, since it throws some light on the psychological difficulties we emancipated women are meeting on our path, I will tell you a bit about it. You will recall I was a young, pretty, innocent, and eager creature when I came with Feizula to Tashkent. I had married Feizula, not because I was attracted to him, but because he was kind to me and my mother, and also because marrying him meant remaining in Kokand, meant continuing my studies, meant freedom. When we came to Tashkent, Feizula entered the University, while I divided my time between the Workers' Faculty and the Woman's Department. I jumped into the hurly-burly of Tashkent life, meeting all kinds of men, working together or under the leadership of some of the most devoted and brilliant comrades in our Party.

"How did the comrades behave toward me?

"Before I answer this, let me give you the psychological setting, which, incidentally, I failed to understand at the beginning, a failure which has cost me no end of needless pain and suffering. Take first our men. The ancient Moslem attitude toward woman, the feeling instilled in every one since childhood that a woman who uncovers her face in the presence of strange men is a harlot, has so conditioned man's psychology in Central Asia as to make it impossible for him to react to an unveiled native woman in a manner that you Europeans would consider normal. This is true of all our men. Even our best, most sincere, intellectually most emancipated, and principled Communists reveal occasionally this psychological aberration. Even they betray at times the inability to suppress a reaction which in its immediacy is tantamount to a conditioned reflex; even they, although unconsciously, tend to assume that peculiar freedom of manner which men allow themselves in the presence of women of 'questionable character.' As a result we have a vicious psychological circle. It is generally the adventurous, daring, and naturally enough, rather good-looking woman who flings aside her *paranja*. As a reaction to her previous enforced meekness, she now tends to become more self-assertive and

BUILDING SOCIALISM IN TADJIKISTAN 299

unrestrained than is good for her. In her relations with the opposite sex she is helpless. Not having been trained since childhood to meet men, she has not built up the particular defenses which a woman needs if she is to meet men freely, on an equal basis. In her work she mingles among men without being emotionally prepared to ward off their equivocal remarks and persistent advances. Whenever she is in a mixed group, the atmosphere becomes charged—passion, jealousy, fear—much more so than you probably find among European men and women. The woman here needs a good deal of discipline and balance, particularly when her habitual defenses have been surrendered and no new ones have as yet been erected.

"In my own case this resulted in tragedy. Meeting men was to me a novel and thrilling experience. A compliment or an embrace was a grand experience. I lost my head. Being a good Communist, Feizula tried to overlook it. But after all, he *was* a Central Asian. For him to let his wife go out unveiled was a tremendous step forward. It was absurd to expect of him the tolerance which I now know is rare even among European men. He suffered terribly. He made jealous scenes. He even struck me on several occasions. He would then cry, and beg me not to bring it up before the Party nucleus. We argued, and discussed, and quarreled. Both young and inexperienced, this new freedom was too much for us. Later, when I began to understand the true nature of most of the compliments and the advances, I suffered doubly. I used to be hurt and insulted. Are these comrades? Are these Communists? I began to lose respect, I began to detest some of the best and most heroic fighters in our ranks. 'They are no better than the Basmachi,' I often thought in my disgust. 'They are worse, because they have pretensions.' In the meanwhile, Feizula and I were becoming more and more estranged. You see, we were the victims of a transition period. In the tortures of our souls, in the fires of our passions a new morality was beginning to be molded. The process is not over yet. Very many are still doomed to burn their wings in their heedless dash for freedom. However, these new ones have people like me and Feizula, people who have gone through the fire, to turn to for guidance and consolation.

"Often the first woman in a village to unveil determines the whole course of woman's emancipation in that locality. If she is too weak, she compromises the whole idea of unveiling. For in the eyes of the village, she is a loose woman, a slut. She compromises, not only the idea of woman's emancipation, but also every other social or economic or educational reform sponsored by the Communists. She plays into the hands of the counter-revolutionary elements who generalize her individual failing into an inevitable consequence of yielding to Bolshevik influence. 'The Bolsheviki are turning our women into harlots,' the enemies whisper. Thus hasty unveilings work at times irreparable harm to our cause. Small wonder we have learned to watch our step. Unless we are absolutely sure that the woman has enough character and intelligence to assume the responsibilities of a pioneer, we actually go to the length of discouraging her. We try to put a brake on impetuous decisions. This is particularly so in localities where the number of unveiled women is still small. For we Bolsheviks, while intransigeant in our aims, are yet, when necessary, patient in pursuing them. We gamble only when we are fairly certain of our chances. And, as I have already emphasized, in dealing with cultural and psychological 'superstructures,' we often resort to Fabian tactics.

"By opening silk and textile factories, by opening cotton-ginneries, by paying more than a woman can possibly earn in her primitive home crafts, by organizing relatively good kitchens and nurseries and dispensaries and clubs in the factories, we lure the woman out of her seclusion, gradually but irretrievably. This may not be as romantic as you first imagined, but it is more certain. Four or five weeks in a factory do marvels for the woman. And the man's objections and jealous fears subside, too, when he discovers that his wife's earnings add considerably to his family income. Also, by encouraging collectivization of agriculture, we enhance the process of woman's emancipation. In a collective farm each individual who works gets paid according to a specified norm. Equal work brings equal pay. The wife of a farmer in a collective knows exactly the extent of her contribution to the family purse; she can leave her husband and still be economically as secure as when she lived with him.

"It is on this base of changed economic and social relations that a new cultural life can be built, and with it a new psychology. We are a transition generation. Knee-deep in our feudal past, we are attempting to build our children's Socialist future. It is hard. Some lose strength and courage. But there are always others to take up the work. Despite the beys, the mullahs, the Basmachi, the plotters from abroad, Ibrahim Bek, the Revolution forges ahead, freeing all of us, men and women of Central Asia, from the memory of a past that seems too horrible to have ever been real."

XVI

THE END OF THE BASMACHI

>Should you want to return to our land again—
>Every stone in the road will arise to restrain you,
>Every tree on the way stick its twigs in your eyes,
>Every vine will become an entangling knot,
>The mountains will shrug their shoulders and throw
>Mighty avalanches down, the rivers will rise,
>And the women will show their rage....
>Do not come back to Badakhshan,
>Know hatred here awaits your bloody band.
>—Tadjik Folk Song.

A Touch of the Exotic

IN Koktash (Green Rock), the center of the Lokai District, we chanced upon a grand celebration. From all over the valley Red Stick detachments, Tadjiks and Uzbeks and Kirghiz, men and women and children, on horseback and on foot, came here in throngs for the festivities.

For years Lokai had been the stronghold of the Basmach movement in Tadjikistan. The local population, mainly nomad Uzbek tribes, had long been renowned for its bold and warlike character. Lokai was the home of the most formidable bands, and the birthplace of Ibrahim Bek himself, the most prominent Basmach leader in Central Asia.

When in the spring Ibrahim Bek came back from Afghanistan, the first thing he did, say the Lokai peasants, was to make his way to Koktash, to his own people, his own tribe. There he had hoped to find his staunchest followers. At a secret meeting of all his tribal kin, he delivered himself of an impassioned plea for support. He boasted of his strength and international backing, of huge armies, with plenty of cannon and machine guns and ammunition, of a huge air fleet across the border. He made little of the Red Army and the Soviet government. "Five years ago," he is reported to have exclaimed, "I abandoned Eastern Bokhara to let you feel for yourselves what Bolshevism meant. Now you have learnt your lesson. Now you have had a taste of Bolshevism. Now you know which flag to follow. I have come back certain of your choice. Join me in a holy war against the infidels, the Reds, for our lands, our property, our women, our faith!"

Then the elder of the tribe arose. He was an old man, the revered upholder of tribal tradition. Everybody grew silent. The old man was under the strain of conflicting loyalties. Say what you would, Ibrahim was a member of his tribe, his clan. He had legitimate claims on his Lokai kinsmen. Yet there were other claims and other loyalties too. The old man was fumbling for words to express the tangle of his feelings. After carefully examining the handful of green tobacco powder he had shaken out of the little gourd, he deliberately stuffed it in his cheek and, staring with his austere eyes above the heads of his assembled kinsfolk, began to tell of the great things that were taking place in the land. It was a pæan of praise to the new life. Then he stopped, spat out his tobacco, and slowly shaking his head, half in sorrow, half in reproach, concluded:

"Ibrahim, Ibrahim, you say you have come to defend us against the Reds, that you have a great army and powerful friends. But why, Ibrahim, do you come to us in the black hours of the night, stealthily, like a thief? Why, Ibrahim, do you keep to the hills like a goat? Our tribe has fought long enough, Ibrahim. Now we have begun to work. Soon the cotton fields will be blooming in Lokai. We do not want you, Ibrahim. Leave us in peace, Ibrahim."

A tumult started. Virtually all of the tribesmen took the side of the elder. Only a few kulaks clung to the Basmach leader. Seeing that his mission in Lokai was a failure, Ibrahim leaped on his black horse and sped away into the mountains like the wind.

This was not the end of Ibrahim. Furious at having been spurned, he vented his anger on the population. Like hawks his Basmachi would swoop down from the Babatagu Mountain upon the peaceful Lokai settlements, seizing food, clothes, horses, setting fire to dwellings, slaying those who resisted. Spontaneously, the Lokai population rallied around the Red forces, formed Red Stick brigades, ferreting out the Basmachi, giving no quarter to the enemy. Within a few weeks the valley was rid of the invaders. And now they were celebrating the victory.

In retrospect, the entire celebration—the setting, the costumes, the games, the speeches, and especially the things that took place the night following the festivities—seems like a memory from the Arabian Nights.

A vast, brilliantly green field encircled by chains of snow-hooded mountains spreads out in an amphitheater to the jagged edge of the horizon. In the middle of the field, six large concentric circles. Shades of red and yellow and orange and blue and white mutinous in the breeze. Turbans, embroidered skull-caps, cloaks of silks and calicoes, and rifles, and sticks, and flags, and sabers. The outermost circle is formed by the equestrian detachment. Laughter, clapping of hands, neighing and champing of horses. A little to the side, a row of huge copper kettles enveloped in smoke and flame—pilaf and tea for the celebration. Overhead the ceaseless screeching of the puzzled eagles.

Our approach creates a flurry of commotion. Young fellows with moving-picture cameras snoop about us. (The Tadjik-kino on the job!) Kodzhibaiev, Chairman of the People's Commissars of the Tadjik Republic, dressed in semi-military uniform, his white linen tunic luminously starched, rises to greet us, placing his hand on his breast as is the custom, and bowing with a great show of ceremonious cordiality. The warriors, on discovering who we are, greet us with loud acclaim.

After the hubbub created by our arrival subsides, the peasants resume their games. In the inner circle a number of wrestling matches is soon in progress. The group of peasants by my side, all of them Uzbeks from the same village, apparently, keep on goading one bearded fellow in their midst to step forth and display his prowess. They are obviously proud of him and his huge frame and they want the whole world to know it. But he pretends to be reluctant. The peasants naturally behave as their hero expects them to. They urge him and pull him and finally succeed in pushing him into the ring. At first he strolls languidly along the inner edge of the circle staring challengingly at the squatting audience. Each village seems to have its own champion. But the bearded chap looks formidable and it takes time to find any one who cares to match strength with him. Finally, a patriarchal Tadjik emerges. An elaborate ceremony follows: genuflexions, bows, etc. Then both rise and begin to walk around each other in circles. First quietly, nonchalantly, almost lazily. Cries of encouragement and derision issue from the crowd. The temperature rises. The contestants begin to whirl around each other faster and faster, each aiming to seize hold of the colored belt or the shirt collar of his opponent. Finally the real struggle is on. The Tadjik patriarch throws out his leg with inconceivable swiftness, trips his opponent (this is allowed by the rules of the game), and within a fraction of a second has him pinned to the ground on his back. A storm of approval from the audience. The victor rises and grinning in his gray beard begins to leap on one leg along the edge of the ring, until he reaches the spot where the prizes are being handed out, where he stops, bows and softly strokes his beard. The sight of a patriarch wrestling and then prancing on one leg seems a little incongruous at first, but when one enters into the spirit of the game the thing seems quite natural. The prize is a strip of calico sufficient for a cloak. The wrestling keeps up for a couple of hours. All the contestants perform all the movements demanded by tradition, kneeling and bowing and leaping on one leg and stroking of real or imaginary beards while receiving the prizes. When all the prizes are distributed, the circles of spectators are broken up. Large wooden bowls of pilaf are distributed through the crowd. Each bowl becomes the center of a small group of peasants squatting around it and diligently fishing out handfuls of rice, as they discuss excitedly the outcome of the various matches.

I eat from the same bowl with Issay Buri, a poor Lokai peasant who had been persuaded by his mullah to join the Basmach movement. However, the behavior of the Basmachi soon disgusted him and he went over to the Reds. To prove his good faith, he slew his chieftain, cut off his head, salted it, and brought it in a bag as a trophy to the Koktash Soviet. The story is told with an air of matter-of-factness quite startling to one who has been used to spilling only ink and waging battles only with his pen.

After the repast, an amusing and rather characteristic incident occurs. A few of the Red Sticks approach Khodzhibaiev with a suggestion that they have a game of goat-tearing. Khodzhibaiev is categorical: "No." The Red Sticks persist, pressing all kinds of arguments: After all, this is an extraordinary occasion; nothing would please the warriors more; furthermore, it would be great entertainment for the foreign guests. Khodzhibaiev looks very sternly at them. "What's the use of asking the impossible? We have a law forbidding goat-tearing. It is an uncivilized game—brutal, savage. We are trying to be better than we have been in the past. We are trying to be cultured."

As a compromise with the demands of "culture," the Red Sticks offer to kill the goat before starting the game. (In the past only a live goat was used.) Again Khodzhibaiev delivers an eloquent exhortation about culture. Though he speaks very persuasively, I detect in his voice a tremulous longing to see the game himself. The Red Sticks are no fools. They detect it too. So they keep on pressing: "Just this once!" Khodzhibaiev becomes angry: "I say no; you understand? And now you can do what you please." We all know that Khodzhibaiev really means "Yes."

It does not take more than a minute before a goat mysteriously appears on the scene. In three minutes the slain goat is flung into the midst of the hundreds of horsemen who are milling on one spot. Immediately there is pandemonium. With wild shouts and whistles the riders begin to beat their horses, pushing simultaneously to the spot where the goat has fallen. The peasant who first manages to bend down from his saddle far enough to get hold of the goat's leg is pressed by the horsemen from all sides, everybody striving to snatch the goat away from him while he tries to break through the besiegers. Suddenly a young horseman, issuing a piercing yell, yanks his horse's bridle so ferociously that the enraged animal rears way up in the air and hurls itself in the direction of the possessor of the goat. While the horse is still in the air, the young fellow slips out of his saddle, though one of his feet remains in the stirrup, and like a vulture, with claws outstretched, falls swiftly on his prey. For a moment the group gives way. He snatches the goat, and with a face contorted with exertion and triumph, swings back into the saddle and makes a dash for the mountain. But immediately he is surrounded by the horsemen again and another fierce struggle begins. This lasts for about a half-hour. Finally, one fellow who seems to have been conserving his strength by always being just at the outskirts of the real fight, makes one plunge for the goat and before any one realizes what has happened flies like a bullet toward the mountain. The pursuit is hot, but of no avail. He reaches the goal. The goat is his. To-morrow his village will feast on goat meat.

Two Documents

The games over, the whole crowd in hilarious procession marches to the village. We pass through a wooden triumphal arch, painted red, and halt in front of a huge rostrum on which the speakers are already assembled. This is the formal part of the celebration, not much different from other formal celebrations in the Soviet Union—speeches, slogans, proud reciting of achievements, etc. The most colorful part of the program is the handing out of rewards—watches, sabers and rifles—to the best Red Stick fighters.

The rewards most cherished are the rifles, and those who receive them are the happiest and proudest people in the Lokai! Among the best Red Stick fighters is Bibitshan Manuir, a plump middle-aged woman. She approaches the rostrum unveiled, with a baby at her breast. Though she has the important post of Chairman of the District Soviet, she is still quite shy. Being the object of so much attention and admiration upsets her. She pulls at her kerchief nervously and giggles. She is handed a watch on which the gratitude of the workers' government is engraved in bold indelible letters. Taking the watch and glancing at it furtively, she tries to hide in the crowd. Her confusion creates much merriment. The crowd insists on her remaining in the front.

A young Tadjik Communist, a student from Stalinabad, recites a poem entitled "From an Undistinguished and Modest Tadjik of the Soviet Mountains to Thee, O English Empire." Roughly translated, the "Modest Tadjik's" address to the English Empire is this:

I know you, Great Britain,
The suffering of our blood brothers—
    is the work of your hands,
The trace of your fat fingers—
    is still on your victims' throats.
Murder, rapine, hunger—
    are the work of your hands,
        O British Empire.
You made the fools amongst us
    fight among themselves.
You dashed their heads together—
You made them fight your wars.
Chains, shackles, graveyards
    are the work of your hands,
And the yellow flame of treason
    is the work of your hands....
Everywhere from Gasn to Kushka
    From Shore to Chushka-Guzar,

BUILDING SOCIALISM IN TADJIKISTAN

*Through the rocky mountains
           you have aimed your blow at us,
                   O British Empire.
But soon the London docker and the farm hand from
   Jalalabad
Will smash your crown, O Britain;
Your victims will walk out of your prisons,
Their fire will sweep through your night;
They will charge their guns with fresh bullets,
And direct their bayonets into thee,
                   O British Empire!*

Among the speeches, that of Rahim Khodzhibaiev is the best and the most warmly received. It is a typical expression of the Central-Asian's revolutionary credo:

"Red Sticks, Comrades, warriors, in celebrating our triumph over the Basmachi, it is well briefly to survey our past. Our country is the youngest brother in the socialist family of nations forming the Soviet Union: it is only eight years since our laboring Tadjik masses have thrown off the heavy yoke of capitalism and feudalism.

"In the grip of a long and torturous agony, the old order squeezed, mangled and crushed this land of enormous possibilities, this land of an heroic people which had for centuries been suffering and battling for the right of free labor, for self-determination.

"The Soviet Union celebrated seven Octobers while our Tadjik peasants, together with the glorious Red Army, were fighting along the narrow mountain paths, winning back step by step the blood-soaked ravines and valleys from the ancient Emirate supported by the crutch of English imperialism.

"That is past. The years of slavery, poverty, hunger have scrawled a bloody picture over the pages of history. Our villages, devastated during the years of struggle, are only now putting out the flames of that terrible conflagration. The Civil War has left deep scars on the economic body of our young, mountainous Soviet Republic.

"The October Revolution liberated the Tadjik people from colonial oppression. It cleared the way for national emancipation, created the conditions for our political and economic development, and said, 'Now build!'

"Our liberated land of green spaces and snow-covered peaks has been engaged in monumental construction for eight years. Ibrahim Bek has tried to disrupt our work, but the toiling masses of our land, our Red Stick heroes, have given him the answer. His bands are destroyed. Our cotton campaign goes on. And to-morrow or the day after we will have him safely behind bars.

"Yes, comrades, the worst is over. Yet it would be a grave error to think that we have already overcome all difficulties. The road before our masses of workers and peasants still calls for tremendous exertion of will. The will toward socialist construction, toward a final attack on the old life of cultural backwardness and ignorance, toward the elimination of the last vestiges of feudalism and landlordism, toward unflagging labor in raising our political and economic power—this is the glorious road our young Socialist Republic must follow. . . .

"With revolutionary enthusiasm the toilers of Tadjikistan will lay stone upon stone, erecting the new edifice of the Tadjik Soviet Republic, and the proletariat of the whole Union will cement these stones with their fraternally attentive help and guidance.

"We are building a model Soviet Socialist Republic at the gates of Hindustan.

"The guarantee of our success is the Communist Party, the party of the vanguard of the proletariat, the party which has led the workers and peasants of the Soviet Union to their great victory.

"Our successes offer the best possible example for revolutionizing the enslaved East—India, Persia, Afghanistan, and others.

"Our existence and the experience of the Soviet toilers will plant in the consciousness of the oppressed masses of the East faith in their liberation and triumph and will unite them in the common task of overthrowing the rule of the imperialists, the landlords, the rajahs, and instituting their own rule—the rule of the working masses."

A Memorable Night

The glaciers are aglow in the flame of the rapidly sinking sun. The last reward is given. The last speech made. Slowly the crowd melts away in all directions to be soon swallowed by the thick southern night and be lost in the near and far settlements in the Lokai valley.

After a brief visit to the ruined home of Ibrahim Bek on the banks of the Kafirnigan, we gather in front of the coöperative store, by the side of the dusty road. Rugs are spread, *kok-choi* served, and the inevitable *pilaf* and *uriuk*.

It grows darker.

A detachment of armed Red Sticks gallops by, raising a thick cloud of dust, and vanishes in the direction of the mountains.

Above, a lonely plane rumbles a while and then, becoming fainter and fainter, is finally dissolved in the night's stillness.

"It'll soon be in Stalinabad," says Khodzhibaiev meditatively as he scrapes the soot off the wick of a small kerosene lamp.

Everything is quiet again. Then a match is struck and Khodzhibaiev's face swims out of the darkness as he lights the lamp and gingerly adjusts the glass chimney. Other native faces, some of them quite familiar to me by now, begin to emerge from the night. The spell of silence is broken.

"He's somewhere not far from here," Khodzhibaiev speaks up again, without giving any indication whom he has in mind. But we all know, for we have all been thinking of him too. "His bands have completely frittered away," Khodzhibaiev continues. "The peasants from Khodzhi-Bul-Bulan and Ishkhabad who were at the celebration told me that they were hot on his tracks; they promised to deliver him to us in Stalinabad within a couple of days. They had left enough Red Sticks behind to keep close watch over his movements. The volunteers of Mukum Sultanov reported the same thing."

Poor Ibrahim! He certainly had not expected such treatment in his Lokai valley.

One of the natives tells an amusing episode: Ibrahim raided a small mountain village near Kuliab. Out of the fifteen peasant households in the village, eleven sent out secret messengers to notify the authorities in Kuliab. Since there was only one narrow path to the town, the messengers naturally collided with one another. And each told the next one some fantastic tale to account for his inordinate haste. They had a good laugh when they all met, out of breath, in the Regional Committee headquarters!

Peasants, singly and in groups, come over to chat with Khodzhibaiev. And he, squatting on a rug, his huge Kirghiz hood of white and black felt in his lap, listens to their stories, complaints and requests. He has been on the go most of the day, and his feet ache, so he pulls off his gray canvas boots and while conversing with the peasants picks on his toes. Neither he nor his interlocutors are conscious of any incongruity. An outsider would find it difficult indeed to tell who in this group is one of the most distinguished officials in the Republic and who an obscure peasant. Several of the peasants submit written petitions, which Khodzhibaiev, after quickly perusing in the feeble light of the lamp, carefully deposits in his capacious hood. Some cases he decides forthwith, others he promises to consider when back in Stalinabad.

Collectivization is still very new in these regions. No end of problems and abuses. Here, as everywhere in the Union, there are signs of what Stalin called "dizziness from success." Here, too, cattle has been wantonly destroyed. And the enthusiasm for cotton has resulted in a certain neglect of the peasants who have been occupied in raising grain or alfalfa or in tending their orchards. The peasants and their village leaders have plenty to learn and plenty to complain about. Now it is a matter of not receiving enough advance credit, now of not being able to determine the relative quantity and quality of work put in by each peasant into the collective enterprise, now of keeping women away from collective work. Experienced organizers, bookkeepers, agronomists, mechanics, tractor drivers, directors are needed.

One peasant hands in a long scroll of paper—a document written in the Persian alphabet and decorated with numerous smudges of black ink. The village is petitioning for artificial fertilizer. And the smudges are the impressions of peasants' thumbs dipped in black ink—the signatures of the illiterates.

It is growing late. We are worn out with the excitement of the day. Thick felt mats are spread out on the floor of the coöperative and all of us stretch out, using our clothes and boots for cushions. But the only one who goes off into beatific slumber immediately is Khodzhibaiev, his head resting on the threshold of the open door. On the other side of the door, under the stars, sleep our two guards. We soft Westerners, however, are tortured by insomnia. The fleas in the place are maddening. Some of us groan pitifully, others curse and scratch and curse again, others, realizing that groans and imprecations won't improve matters, lie quietly, and only when things become absolutely unbearable indulge in sporadic, cautious little scratches. In the struggle between sleep and the insects over the tired travelers, sleep finally wins.

Suddenly we are startled by the scraping of heavy boots and the sound of raucous voices outside. No one moves. I hear the thumping of my neighbor's heart, as I try to peer through the darkness. Then a light appears at the door. In the flicker of a smoking lantern held by a giant hand I recognize our two guards. They are followed by a heavily armed stranger, obviously an Uzbek Red Stick. One of my companions jumps up clutching at his revolver. The last to be stirred by the sudden commotion is Khodzhibaiev.

"What's up? What's the trouble?"

"Good news," replies the Red Stick, handing a slip of paper to Khodzhibaiev.

The guard brings the lantern closer to the chief. One glance at the missive and Khodzhibaiev is wide awake.

"They have got him! They have caught Ibrahim! Hurrah!"

Happy ejaculations resound through the room. The Red Stick smiles importantly in his imposing black mustaches. Khodzhibaiev now reads the message aloud:

TO THE GPU OF TADJIKISTAN—OFFICIAL COMMUNICATION
(Copy to be sent to the Regional Committee of the Party)

June 23. Midnight. We have taken Ibrahim Bek, Sahib Commander, and one Basmach from the ranks. Place—between the villages of Ishkhabad, Khodzhi-Bul-Bulan, and Ak-Turpak. Ibrahim Bek and his companions were on foot. Weapons—2 rifles, 1 Mauser, 1 Browning. We were assisted by the GPU. Also the Basmach Issanbey Babajan has surrendered. I took his Mauser. For the present the Basmach leaders are in Comrade Valeshev's charge. Ibrahim Bek's pistol is still in my possession.

Mukum Sultanov,
Commander of Volunteer Detachment.

"Well, that's that," says Khodzhibaiev, dismissing the messenger. "Now we can sleep some more, and peacefully. There are no more Basmachi in Tadjikistan!"

And he never gave a thought to the fleas....

For days after, the press of Tadjikistan was full of stories about Ibrahim Bek and his capture. His portrait appeared everywhere under the caption, "Bitterest Enemy of the Soviet Power." Messages of congratulation from all over the country, especially from the Central-Asian Bureau at Tashkent and from Moscow, were published.

On July 5, the Central Committee of the Communist Party of Tadjikistan, the Central Executive Committee of the Soviets, and the Soviet of People's Commissars of Tadjikistan issued the following Proclamation "To All Workers, Collective Farmers, Poor and Middle Peasants, Red Army Men, Commanding Staff, Communist Volunteer Detachments, and Red Sticks":

BUILDING SOCIALISM IN TADJIKISTAN

COMRADES!

Owing to the united struggle of the workers, collective farmers, and poor and middle peasants organized in Volunteer Peasant Detachments and Red Stick Detachments against the Basmachi, owing also to the crushing blows showered upon the enemy by our glorious Red Army and its Uzbek and Tadjik sections, as well as by the forces of the OGPU, the Basmach movement has been finally and completely eradicated.

On June 23, 1931, the Basmach chieftains Ishan-Isakhon, Ali-Mardan-Datkho, Tashmat Bek, Gaib Bek, and others were taken captive. Above all, Ibrahim Bek, the leader of the Basmachi, and the pitiful remnants of his bands have been captured by the collective farmers of the Khodzhi-Bul-Bulan and Ishkhabad villages in collaboration with the Volunteer Detachment commanded by Mukum Sultanov.

This concludes the struggle against the Basmachi, the struggle against the enemy who has invaded our lands from across the border in an effort to disrupt our socialist construction, overthrow the Soviet Power, and restore the rule of the Bokharan Emir, his officials, his beys and his ishans.

Our overwhelming victory proves once and for all that the toiling masses of Tadjikistan are ready to fight to the bitter end for the gains of the October Revolution, for the Bolshevik Party, and for the Soviet Government.

The Communist Party and the Soviet Government of Tadjikistan call upon you to draw your ranks even closer around the general Bolshevik line of the Party and to proceed at an even greater rate of speed with our socialist construction, building collective and state farms, striving for the cotton independence of the Soviet Union, for the liquidation of illiteracy, intensifying the ruthless struggle of the poor and middle peasantry against the enemies of the working class—against the beys and ishans and other anti-Soviet elements, against all domestic and foreign enemies of Socialist construction.

Long live the workers, collective farmers, and the poor and middle peasants of Tadjikistan, organized under the leadership of the Bolshevik Party into Volunteer and Red Stick Detachments!

Long live our heroic Red Army and its Tadjik and Uzbek sections!

Long live the trusted guard of our Revolution—the OGPU!

Long live the Leninist Communist Party of the Bolsheviks and its leader Comrade Stalin!

PART FIVE

SOVIET ASIA—1934

"The aim of socialism is not only to abolish the present fragmentation of mankind into small states, and all national isolation, not only to bring the nations closer to each other, but also to merge them.... Just as mankind can achieve the abolition of classes only through the transition period of the dictatorship of the oppressed class, so mankind can achieve the inevitable merging of nations only through the transition period of complete liberation of all the oppressed nations, *i.e.,* their freedom to secede...."

—V. I. LENIN, *"The Social Revolution and the Right of Nations to Self-Determination."*

XVII

A FANTASY BASED ON FACT

> *Never again will you hear the cries of our slain children,*
> *The snorting of Basmach horses, the hisses of murderous lashes....*
> —From a Tadjik Folksong.

Poignant Thoughts.... Bitter Thoughts....

THEY say that when Ibrahim Bek, slightly wounded, was taken by plane to Stalinabad, he looked upon the vast collective and state cotton fields in the fertile valley below, on the new constructions, roads, canals, Machine and Tractor Stations, and his proud head drooped. And as the plane, before landing, circled several times over the humming Tadjik capital, Ibrahim, who since his return from Afghanistan had kept "like a goat" to the hills, gasped with irrepressible surprise. Later, when he was questioned by the representatives of the Tadjik Government, the once terrible Basmach leader crestfallenly declared that if he had known the real extent of Tadjikistan's progress, if he had believed the wonderful tales he had heard among the Afghan peasants along the borders, he would have never undertaken the task of starting a counter-revolution in Central Asia and of restoring the Emir.

That was in the middle of 1931. At that time Ibrahim Bek saw only the vague outlines of the Central-Asian's socialist dream and only the first tangible signs of fulfillment. Four years have passed since then, four unparalleled though difficult years of gigantic socialist construction. The face of Central Asia has changed. The splendid future is already clearly discernible in the achievements of the present. One recalls Bakhrom Amri-Khudoiev of Cold Springs, who in 1924 wrote to his Communist kinsman Sobyr-Djon:

> "Mullah, do not come back. Do you hear the far cry of our hills? They say: "For thousands of years have we lived here guided by the laws of Allah and His Prophet, and there can be no change, there cannot! See, our summits quake, our mighty glaciers crumble away, ready to crush you. We do not want to know you! We shall defend our unreasonable human herd from your teachings...."

And one wonders about him and about all the other pious Moslems whose passionate aversion for the new he so eloquently expressed. One wonders about Ibrahim Bek: If still alive, what does he feel now about the miraculous transformation of his land? One also wonders about Ibrahim Bek's master, Emir Alim Khan.

He, reports say, is still alive. He is a great fur merchant in Kabul. It is almost fifteen years since he had offered to the gentle mercies of English imperialism a land that was no longer his and a population that had violently repudiated him. A very attractive morsel that was, too, but just then, alas, a little too difficult for England to swallow. Fifteen years have passed, years of vast effort and vast achievement for Soviet Central Asia. Each year a decade, each year a half century! It took Europe almost three hundred years to complete the bourgeois revolution, but Central Asia, in fifteen years, has leaped from the stage of feudalism over the whole capitalist era straight into the rule of the proletariat and the beginning of Socialism.

One imagines a quiet evening in the Emir's mansion in Kabul. It is December, 1934. Alim Khan is alone. He is reclining on a richly embroidered soft divan, trying to relax after a long day of worry and irritation. But he cannot rest. How can one rest when all the time nostalgic thoughts of the past, the irretrievable past haunt one's memory?

Noble Bokhara... high, holy, divinely descended Bokhara... sweet, crowned city of Emir Alim Khan's dreams! How happy and hopeful Alim Khan was when in 1931 Ibrahim Bek went forth to reconquer for him his ancient and rightful domain. Surely, it was not his, Alim Khan's, fault that the affair turned out a fiasco. Had he not done all he could, indeed more than he could, to support Ibrahim? Allah only knows how much money he had sunk into that adventure, and all for nothing! A miserable fizzle!

To drive away his bitter thoughts, the Emir glances at the newspaper. But he finds no surcease from his sorrows, no escape. Everywhere are reminders of his great loss. The paper, too, right on the front page, announces in glaring headlines: "Soviet Central Asia Celebrates Tenth Anniversary of the Creation of the Uzbek, Tadjik, and Turkoman Socialist Soviet Republics from the National Elements in the Turkestan of the Czars and the Bokhara of the Emirs." Sadly Alim Khan puts away the paper and turns to the radio. Again the U.S.S.R. Again the by now familiar and hateful voice of Khodzhibaiev, Chairman of the Central Executive Committee of the Soviet Union and of the Uzbek Republic:

... On the basis of the correct prosecution of the Leninist-Stalinist national policy of our Party....

The Emir wants to shut off the radio, but he cannot. A strange paralysis creeps over him. He does not want to listen, but some perverse force compels him to:

... on the basis of the unflagging and systematic concern shown by our Government for the backward peoples of the Union, our national republics have attained tremendous successes in the building of socialism. Uzbekistan and Tadjikistan may serve as clear examples of this. These former colonies of tsarist Russia, where the Emirs and their feudal henchmen once held sway, have, since the October Revolution, made an enormous advance. Once economically and culturally backward, these countries are rapidly reaching a position of foremost importance among the republics of the Soviet Union.

Let us first take agriculture. The sown area in the Central-Asian Republics has increased from 2.4 million hectares in 1920 to 4.4 million hectares in 1934—an increase of 83 per cent. Great progress has been made in the raising of cotton, our basic agricultural product. The cotton area has grown from 325,000 hectares in 1924 to 1,244,000 in 1934—a 400 per cent increase, while the total production of cotton has increased 500 per cent. Furthermore, our agriculture is being rapidly mechanized. In 1924 there were only 358 tractors in the whole of Central Asia; in 1934 the number has jumped to 14,000 and is still growing. In Uzbekistan, 85 per cent of the holdings of the poor and middle peasants are joined in collective farms which are improving all the time and in every respect—organizationally, economically, and culturally. Already the state and collective farms of Uzbekistan provide more than 96 per cent of that Republic's total production of cotton, more than 80 per cent of the grain and 70 per cent of the live stock.

In Tadjikistan, too, despite the ravages of the Basmachi as late as the spring of 1931, agriculture, especially cotton-growing, has made tremendous strides. There the cotton area has expanded from 35,000 hectares before the war to 91,000 hectares in 1934. What is particularly significant is the development of the highly valuable, long-fibered Egyptian cotton. In 1930, only 3,900 hectares in Tadjikistan were devoted to Egyptian cotton; in 1934 we already have 25,400 hectares. Eighty-five per cent of the cotton area in Tadjikistan is socialized. . . .

A Soviet Rhapsody

Numbers! Numbers! Numbers! A rhapsody of numbers! A Soviet rhapsody! Every number is like a dagger. It cuts Alim Khan to the quick. But he listens, drawing a strange masochistic pleasure from the very sharpness of the pain:

... During the First Five-Year Plan, the irrigated cotton area in the Union was increased by 45 per cent, and in 1933 over three million acres were served by the various irrigation systems—the Karabekaul, Savai, and Guyi Canals. A major achievement in this respect has been the new system of irrigation introduced in the Vakhsh valley in Tadjikistan, designed to convert another 247,000 acres of desert into fertile cotton land. The work on the Vakhsh was started a few years ago. The first water was turned into the irrigation canals in the spring of 1933 when an area of 18,500 acres was brought under cultivation. A total of 4,000 kilometers of irrigation canals was constructed before the end of 1933, including the main canal and its floodgate. The latter is forty meters in length and twelve meters in height and can turn 150 cubic meters of water per second into the irrigation system.

The construction of the canal is an important engineering achievement on which twenty-six powerful excavators were employed. Some nine hundred meters of the canal had to be cut through solid rock, the depth of the excavation reaching sixteen meters. The auxiliary constructions completed in 1934 include new workers' settlements, a narrow-gauge railway, a motor road connecting the Vakhsh valley with Stalinabad, the capital of the Tadjik Republic, a telephone line, machine shops, and so on. So far the sum of 120 million rubles has been expended on the Vakhsh system. Several thousand peasant households from the mountain and northern regions have been settled there. This year we expect to settle there twelve thousand more. Another important project is the Fergana Valley irrigation system in Uzbekistan, which will add about one million acres to the total cotton area.

In 1929, the share of the Soviet Union in the world cotton output was still only 3.2 per cent, but in 1932 it already reached 7.2 per cent. From the fifth place, which the Soviet Union occupied before the war in the world cotton production, the country has risen to the third place, and is well on the way of assuming second place at the end of the Second Five-Year Plan.

"Boasting, empty Soviet boasting," Alim Khan consoles himself. "The fact is that this year Uzbekistan and Tadjikistan have failed to fulfill their cotton plan. Uzbekistan, according to their own figures, has given the Soviet Union 90,000 tons of raw cotton less than was expected, while Tadjikistan has carried out only 86 per cent of the plan. Now they can scarcely blame the beys. So it is 'climatic conditions' and—they admit it themselves—'bad work!' It must have been pretty rotten work, if they had to throw out thousands of members from the Communist Party. It must have been bad indeed if Moscow had to send 'Comrade' Kuibyshev to Central Asia to discover the cause of the trouble."

... The yield of our cotton fields this year was low —continues the voice imperturbably—and at the Uzbekistan and Tadjikistan Congresses of Soviets the collective farmers declared that they regarded it as a disgrace that the 1934 plan of cotton-harvesting was not fulfilled and they solemnly assumed the obligation to make 1935 a decisive year in the struggle for freeing the Soviet Union from the need of importing cotton and to give the textile industry extra cotton to make up for the shortage of 1934....

"Just so," smiles Alim Khan, mirthlessly. "Solemn promises...."

... Let us now turn to Central-Asian industry, booms the voice from the ether. Here our progress has been no less impressive. In nine years the output of our heavy industries alone increased 600 per cent, from 140 million rubles in 1925 to 850 million rubles in 1934. The number of industrial and transport workers has risen from 35,000 in 1925 to 213,000 in 1934. Electrical power has grown 500 per cent in the last five years, amounting in 1933 to 93 million kilowats. Oil, coal, zinc, lead, copper—all discovered since the Revolution—form the basis for a rapidly expanding fuel and metallurgical industry.

Thus in the matter of oil, it has been established, as a result of the exploration work carried out in Central Asia in 1933, that the Fergana Valley (Uzbekistan) is capable, not only of satisfying local requirement in fuel oil, but may become the oil center for the whole of Central Asia. Of the new oil-bearing districts discovered, those of Chust, Pakh and Kassansay are of particular interest. New oil fields were also discovered over a large stretch of land from the foot of the Alai range to the town of Fergana. Oil has also been found in Northern Tadjikistan, twenty kilometers from the town of Khodjent, at a depth of 400 to 500 meters. Finally, new oil deposits have been located in Changyrtosh, in the Kirghiz Republic, and experimental exploitation has begun this year.

Or take lead. On January 21, 1934, the first section of the lead combine in Chikivent was started. The annual output capacity of the first section is twenty thousand tons. When completed, it will increase to sixty thousand. The combine, which will be the largest in the world, has its own electric station, where the first turbine of 2,000 kilowatts has been started. The Chikivent lead combine will obtain its ore from the Ashisay and the Kansek lead deposits. A branch railway line eighty-five kilometers long has been built to the Ashisay deposits. The total cost of building the combine has been estimated at 115 million rubles, the cost of the first section being 75 million rubles.

In Uzbekistan, the gross industrial production has grown from 300 million rubles in 1930 to 750 million rubles in 1934. On Uzbek territory we are now engaged in building an extremely large electro-chemical *combinat,* Chirchikstroy, at the cost of from 700 to 800 million rubles. The first unit of a gigantic textile *combinat,* named after Comrade Stalin, is nearing completion in Tashkent. A huge nitrate plant now under construction will provide fertilizer for a million hectares of land per year. A number of other industrial enterprises—factories for the production of clothing, building materials, etc.—are being erected. The

First Five-Year Plan having been fulfilled in Uzbekistan, the Second Five-Year Plan is now being realized. Our budget in Uzbekistan has increased from 37 million rubles in 1924-1925 to 521 million rubles in 1935. The commodity turnover in Uzbekistan for the year 1934 amounted to one billion rubles; the socialist sector—our state and coöperative trade—has won out. The private dealer has been driven out of trade. On a smaller scale, parallel progress has been made in Tadjikistan. There the gross industrial production has increased from 12,378 thousand in 1928 to 84,185 thousand rubles in 1934, i.e. it has grown 700 per cent in six years. From 1930 to 1934 included we have invested 142 million rubles in the development of Tadjik industry. We have built in Tadjikistan a number of large industrial enterprises: a canning *combinat* in Khodjent, two large silk factories (one in Khodjent, one in Stalinabad), etc., etc. The Varsob hydroelectric station is approaching completion...."

"Soviet figures... Soviet statistics..." taunts Alim Khan. "Everybody knows their agricultural and industrial statistics are a fraud, their astronomical numbers a hoax...." Yet Alim Khan finds no consolation in his taunts. Even in Kabul, he has had occasion to observe the considerable growth of Soviet exports of manufactured products in the East. Soviet trade with Afghanistan, he knows, is rising. It reached the pre-war level in 1927-1928 and has been continuing to rise ever since. The same holds true of Soviet trade with the other Eastern countries. In Persia, since 1929, the Soviet Union, he knows, has occupied an important and even a monopoly position as purveyor of a number of goods classifications, and Soviet exports of sugar, oil products, rubber shoes, china and glass, cement, metals, cotton goods, paper, machinery and equipment began to play a considerable part in Persia's purchases abroad. Trade between Chinese Turkestan (Sinkiang) and the Soviet Union, despite competitive efforts of the English and the Japanese, exceeded the pre-war level several years ago. In Mongolia and Toana-Tuva the Soviet Union is not only the leading trading country, but has become the chief guide and helper in their economic upbuilding. In the face of these well-known facts, deep in his heart the Emir feels his sneers to be rather empty and ineffectual.

We Have Been Victorious

The deluge of numbers in the air is overwhelming:

... The lack of roads has been the bane of Central-Asian existence. Roads have been built here at a feverish pace, and in 1934 Uzbekistan fulfilled its road-building plan for the year ten days ahead of schedule: some 1,232 kilometers of roads were constructed, and 16 kilometers of bridges were repaired. In Tadjikistan, during the last five years, 138 million rubles have been put into transport. We now have there over 2,000 miles of newly built automobile roads. The highest road in the world, and one of the longest in the Soviet Union—800 kilometers long—connecting Osh and Khorog in the Pamir Mountains, has been completed. Enormous difficulties had to be overcome. The roads lead over high, inaccessible mountain ridges, across deep rivers and over snow-covered areas. Distances which formerly took 35 days to travel by camel-caravan, now take from three to five days. Another road, almost as difficult of construction, is now being built between Stalinabad and Ura-Tuibe.

... Similar successes have been scored in the realm of culture. In Czarist Turkestan, out of 40,000 students in the elementary schools, only 7,000 were children of natives and the annual expenditure for education amounted to 10 kopeks (5 cents) per child. In 1932, in the socialist republics of Uzbekistan, Turkmenistan and Tadjikistan, into which this territory is now divided, the expenditure per child was 35.10 rubles, 55 rubles, and 41 rubles, respectively. Literacy had increased by 1934 from 4.6 per cent to 52 per cent in Uzbekistan; and from a fraction of 1 per cent to 40 per cent in Turkmenistan, to 25 per cent in Tadjikistan, 45 per cent in Kirghizia, and 24 per cent in Karakalpakia.

In 1934, on the territory of former Turkestan, there were 10,900 elementary and middle schools with an attendance of 997,525 children; 1,023,700 grown-ups were attending classes for the liquidation of illiteracy. Before the Revolution, there was not one higher institution of learning; in 1925 there were only two; in 1934, thirty-five with 15,000 students. There are already thousands of Uzbek, Kirghiz, Turkoman and Tadjik doctors, engineers, agronomists, scientists, teachers, and writers.

The growth in newspapers and books published is equally significant. In 1925 there were 20 newspapers with an annual circulation of 30 million. In 1934 the number grew to 307, printed in 17 languages, with an annual circulation of 177 million copies. More than 20 million copies of books were printed in 1933. Similar figures can be cited to show a parallel growth of public health and social services, children's playgrounds, theaters, rest homes, and hospitals....

"You lie!" chokes Alim Khan. "You lie! 'Public health ... rest homes ... hospitals!' When there is nothing to eat or to wear! When the whole world knows you are starving! When in Germany and Austria they are collecting money for your famine victims."

... Extremely instructive, too, are the figures for the growth in the participation by women in the elections in the villages of the Republics of Central Asia: In the Uzbek Republic, from 7.8 per cent in 1926, participation increased to 72 per cent in 1934. In the Tadjik Republic participation rose from 22 per cent in 1929 to 67 per cent in 1934. Our women are drawn more and more into the government. In Turkmenistan 16 per cent of the delegates to the village Soviets are women; in Uzbekistan, 13 per cent; in Tadjikistan, 22 per cent. In our cities, the percentages are much higher: in Turkmenistan, 21 per cent; in Uzbekistan, 26 per cent; in Tadjikistan, 17 per cent.

It is not amiss to contrast with this the fact that women are still completely deprived of their electoral rights in such countries as Italy, France, Japan, Portugal, Belgium, Holland, Yugoslavia, Greece, Brazil, Argentina....

The comparison of the Central-Asian Republics with the most advanced countries in the world knocks the last bit of resistance out of the Emir. Now he is resigned to hearing almost anything. The voice becomes louder; it sounds triumphant:

> ... This brief summary proves the correctness of the Leninist-Stalinist line on the national question. Lenin's famous thesis that backward peoples can advance toward socialism without having to go through the capitalist stage of development is brilliantly established by our Central-Asian Republics, especially Tadjikistan, where only yesterday the most primitive forms of economy prevailed. We have been victorious. We are now victoriously engaged in building socialism. And the reason for our victory is clear.
> Comrade Stalin pointed out long ago that as compared with all the *colonial* and *semi-colonial* countries in the East, the Soviet Republics in Central Asia have the following distinguishing characteristics: first, they are free from the imperialist yoke; second, their national development proceeds not under the guidance of a bourgeois but of a Soviet power; third, insofar as they are as yet industrially backward, they can rely on the industrial proletariat of the most advanced republics in the Union to help them to accelerate their industrial development; fourth, being free from the colonial yoke, being under the protection of the proletarian dictatorship and being members of the Soviet Union, these republics can be drawn into the socialist upbuilding of the country.
> The reason for our victory is clear. Headed by the Bolshevik Party, the toilers of the Soviet East achieved their success in fierce struggle with counter-revolution, the Basmachi, the beys, in perpetual clashes with nationalistic, pan-Islamistic, pan-Tiurkist

elements, with Great Russian chauvinists, and other anti-Soviet and anti-Party elements. The example of Soviet Central Asia should convince the peoples of the world that only a victorious proletarian revolution and the dictatorship of the proletariat can settle the national question, and that all the talk of the social-fascists about the possibility of solving the national problem within the framework of capitalism is nothing but the ideology of the enemies of the working class, the enemies of the oppressed peoples.

This, of course, does not mean that we are ready to rest on our laurels. Our achievements have been great, but we have not yet caught up with the most developed republics in our Union. Further advances will be accompanied by many more difficulties and will call for even greater exertion and more intense struggle. But that cannot deter us. Guided by the Bolshevik Party, under the leadership of the best friend of the toilers of all nations—Comrade Stalin—and with the assistance of the more developed Soviet republics, the workers and peasants of the Soviet Republics of Central Asia will attain still greater successes in building a classless socialist society on the borders of Afghanistan, India, China. . . .

XVIII

SOVIET ASIA SINGS

> We Tadjiks sing of what we see.
> If we see a fine horse, we make a song about it....
> We have songs made by sweet-tongued poets,
> Songs made to travel along the borders of the years.
> Those which had passed at least three ages
> Told of flowers and beautiful girls.
> But today they do not sing of girls and flowers:
> They sing of our new freedom,
> They sing about an airplane,
> They sing of beautiful future days,
> But more than all else they make songs about Lenin.
> For they know that without him no new songs would have been born
> (Save those like howls of dogs: that is, praises of the Emirs,
> Their generals, their colonels, their soldiers).
> Lenin gave our bards the right to sing of what they pleased,
> And all of them at once began to sing about Lenin. —Tadjik Folksong.

Songs of Sorrow and Revolt

IF numbers and statistics afford an objective standard of Soviet achievement, the reaction of the Soviet people to those achievements, the subjective element, is most clearly reflected in their folk-songs, legends, plays, and literature. In a sense, therefore, the nameless Tadjik creator of the verses prefixed to the present chapter tells us more about the effects of the revolution than mountains of official statistics and libraries-full of ponderous tomes of interpretations by foreign observers, travelers, and newspaper correspondents can possibly convey. "We Tadjiks sing of what we see." A simple mountain folk, the Tadjiks respond to the world about them with an immediacy, a spontaneity denied to the literary and artistic exponents of more sophisticated peoples. What is true of the Tadjiks is of course also true of many other Soviet peoples—the Uzbeks, the Kirghiz, the Turkomans, the Kara-Kalpakians, the Chuvashes, the Buriats, the Circassians, etc. The reader will recall the blind seventy-year-old Turkoman bard Kar-Molli, quoted in the introduction to this book, who, in his song of praise to the Bolsheviks for crushing the Khans and setting his country's soil free, assures his auditors:

> *Of all I've heard and seen I sing,*
> *For now my blind eyes see anew.*

It is in the light of these simple poetic statements that we must read the new literature and folklore of Soviet Central Asia. What do these peoples see? How do they react to the spectacular changes in their environment? What do they sing about? What differences in mood, in form, in content has the revolution brought into the songs and poems and legends of the scores of minority peoples in the Soviet Union? With the profound change in the economic and social structure, what changes have taken place in the psychological and the cultural superstructures?

Take the old folk-songs of Central Asia, the shepherd songs, or the women's songs, or the cotton-growers' songs—what hopelessness, what melancholy, what bitterness! One shepherd complains about his hard life, his eternal wanderings, and about "the many bitter tears I have shed from my eyes." Another, herding camels for the Medzhaur tribe, chants plaintively:

> *Month in, month out I drag behind the camels,*
> *My bare feet are torn, cut; they ache.*
> *If you chance to pass my village, tell my master*
>   *Khyrdan-Bey*
> *That I must have some leather to protect my*
>   *wounds.*

Still another tells of his "heart and blood" having "dried and burned in the fire of the steppe." He intones sadly:

> *Khodzham Shukur is our master.*
> *Pig-weed is our food.*
> *If the worms attack the pig-weed,*
> *How shall we live?*

The Soviet poets in Central Asia who have emerged from the masses sing of the past in tones quite similar to the folk poetry of the pre-revolutionary days. Thus the Turkoman poet Aman Kekilov, in a long and beautiful poem entitled "Days From My Past" paints the old life in the Turkoman village in the blackest colors:

> *Until I was seven or eight*
> *I lived with my mother.*
> *When my mother died,*
> *I remained alone, an orphan.*
> *From that time on, like a slave,*
> *I worked for the same bey,*
> *Herding sheep in the steppe,*
> *Visiting the village only once a year.*
>
> *To live in the steppe all the time was hard.*
> *Always chasing after the sheep and the lambs. . . .*
> *But to stay in the village was even worse,*
> *Always under the heavy hand of the bey.*

And Ata Niyazov, another Turkoman, reminisces:

> *I drag myself behind the grazing camels,*
> *My sister carries water for the herd.*
> *The poor little creature understands everything,*
> *And streams of tears are running down her cheeks.*
> *Our master, we both know, is making ready*
> *To sell to strangers this little friend of mine.*

And so ad infinitum. Melancholy, resignation—not a note of rebellion. Life seemed as immutable as the steppe, as the glaciers on the Pamir. "The poor were subdued by their poverty, and the rich enjoyed the power of their wealth.... The rich were strong like oaks, and the poor and weak clung to them like young shoots of ivy." Above all, "like a granite rock" stood "our mighty Moslem faith."

Among the first voices of revolt was that of the oldest and most prominent Tadjik novelist and poet, Sadreddin Aini. As an authentic expression of the insurgent mood prevalent among the advanced sections of the Djadid movement, Aini's work has scarcely been excelled. Himself an active Djadid, Aini had more than once experienced the brutality of the Emir's régime. There exist two photographs of Aini in Central Asia: one showing his lean, emaciated body with deep traces of chains on his shoulders; another showing his back as a mass of torn, bleeding flesh—the result of a flogging in the Emir's dungeon. Small wonder that Aini's works are aquiver with hatred for Bokhara's savage past! Small wonder, too, that since the first day of the Revolution, Aini, an old man, has been in the forefront of those who have been struggling for a new life and a socialist culture in Central Asia.

A middle-class intellectual, with deep roots in the ancient traditions of Persian culture, Aini came to the Revolution with much of the psychological and esthetic baggage of his milieu. But his progress from the ornate love lyrics, courtly rhetoric, and religious mysticism of the upper class to the modern motifs, revolutionary attitudes, and the simple language of the masses has been steady and admirable.

In August, 1918, Aini, then a fugitive from Bokhara living in Tashkent, wrote a now famous poem entitled "On the Death of My Brother Khadzhi Siradzheddin Who Was Executed by the Emir After Kolesov's Retreat From Bokhara." The poem opens with a description of the author's profound dismay at hearing of his brother's death under the headsman's ax:

And like a sword it struck me in the breast,
And pierced my heart, and robbed me of my breath,
And dimmed my thoughts, and crushed all life in me.

The eight-line stanza, like the two subsequent ones, is followed by the haunting refrain:

*O sweetest friend, O brother, O apple of mine eye,
Thou art gone from me ... gone ... gone....*

The poet's sorrow, however, soon gives way to bitter resentment. His soul cries out for vengeance:

*I swear—henceforth I shall pursue no glory,
Nor read glad books, nor give my thought to chess.
My brother's dead. Life's brightest moon is dimmed.
The steed of grace has perished in the stream.
Henceforth, I swear, I shall not sing of roses,
Nor love, nor beauty.... I shall not sing sweet dreams.
Henceforth, my voice shall rage with flaming vengeance,
Shall cry a burning, bitter chant of hate....*

*O sweetest friend, O brother, O apple of mine eye,
Thou art gone from me ... gone ... gone....*

Overcome with anger and grief, the poet hurls accusations at the "Ruler of Heaven." Out of the depth of his despair, he cries: "Thou, Thou alone art guilty of this crime!" But the Heavenly Ruler does not answer—"the empty sky is dumb...." Suddenly the poet comes to understand that his personal loss, his personal grief are an inseparable part of the whole country's suffering and shame. His country is groaning, bleeding. "O land of mine," exclaims Aini, "here only dreams are bloodless." Despair is followed by hope. Such horrors cannot last forever. The oppressed people will rise once more. The emirs, the khans, the rulers "will drown in the black sea of their own crimes."

The conclusion of the poem is an interesting reflection of the dualism in the psychology of the petty-bourgeois Djadids in the early years of the Revolution. In 1918, Aini is still a pious Moslem. His defiance of Allah in the earlier part of the poem is only a momentary aberration. Towards the end, lifted by a new hope, he turns back to Allah:

> *O God! Shatter the roofs of the palaces*
> *Over the crowns of the vile khans.*
> *O God! Lead us out of this horrible dungeon,*
> *And make the trembling princes kneel before their slaves.*

Two years later, Aini's prayers were fulfilled. The oppressed people did rise. The roofs of palaces did fall on the crowns of the vile khans, and trembling princes did kneel before their former slaves. But that Allah had anything to do with it, Aini himself has ceased to believe. Indeed, in his latest works, Aini, the beloved writer of the Tadjik masses, shows very clearly that the great miracle of his people's emancipation has been accomplished not through the kind intervention of Allah and his prophets but by the revolutionary fervor of the laboring Tadjik masses under the leadership of the Communist Party of the Soviet Union.

Songs of Freedom

"Cast an observing eye over the face of the Tadjik world," invites the Tadjik bard Sukhaili;

> *You will see a new city, resplendent like a bridegroom;*
> *You will hear the bridegroom's happy song.*
>
> *Hark! A propeller hums.*
> *An automobile purrs smoothly on the road.*
> *An iron train sweeps by in clouds of smoke and dust....*

Sukhaili exults over electric lights, over tractors "led by Tadjik hands." He urges:

> *...Enter a peasant hut*
> *Before the sun is settling down to rest;*
> *Hear the song he sings, watch the dancing shadow of his tambourine....*

"Hey, man!" the peasant chants:

Look, the sun of freedom burgeons in the sky!
Spring waters, free, roar joyous down our valleys!
And everywhere our Soviet folk sings....

While the enemies of the Bolshevik Revolution all over the capitalist world are shedding crocodile tears over the tyranny, despotism, hunger, drabness, and horrors of the Soviet régime, the "Soviet folk sings," the "sweet-tongued" poets of Soviet Asia, in the words of the anonymous Tadjik bard, sing of their new freedom, sing about an airplane, sing of beautiful future days, make songs about Lenin:

Do you hear the happy shouting, Tadjikistan?
Your glorious day has come, Tadjikistan!

Your day has come! Your day of joy has come,
My wild, rocky, young Tadjikistan.

This is the mood, this is the dominant motif in the poetry of the awakened peoples in the Soviet East. They sing of their new freedom. The unprecedented sense of release brought by the Revolution has found expression in countless poems and folksongs in all the languages in the Soviet Union.

"Friends, my friends, my dear, my lovely friends," chants the Turkoman bard, B. Karbabiev, on the seventeenth anniversary of the Bolshevik Revolution,

To-day I sing of freshly budding flowers.
The old world is dead. The red roses in my hand
Are like the first-born children of our new, our flam-
  ing epoch.

With our own angry blood and the black blood of
  the khans
We once had drenched these wild, endless sands.
From the acrid days, buried in the mists of the past,
These new red roses have blossomed into life.

*A new sun is in the skies—the sun of a new freedom,
And nothing in the whole world is as beautiful as this
  new sun.*

*One ... eleven ... seventeen.... Year follows year,
Each year in struggle sharpens its sharp edge.*

*Turkmenia, my land, my Soviet fatherland,
Like a flower of joy, life has opened up before you.
Take of it.
Breathe of it.
Make each single day a fragrant day of Socialism!*

Almost all of the songs of freedom contain the contrast between the "acrid days" of the past and the "fragrant days" of the present. Thus, the Central Asian poet Munavvar-Sho tells how he was "beaten with rods ... thrown in black pits ... kept without food for twenty-four famishing days." How he "wept with tears of blood," while the Emir's henchmen peered into his eyes,

*... But the storm of my heart could not be stilled.
I sang to them:
You think you have destroyed me?
Fools, I have learned the dictates of fate.
Rob the poor. Eat their bread.
A day will come and you will be threshed out of your
  castles
As oats are threshed out of their ears by dancing
  chains.*

Soldiers came to my village. They were looking for the sower of rebel thoughts. They slew my father by the doors of the mosque.

*Go out on the hills of rebellion, my horse.
Look! All around there is fire, and smoke. . . .
Like a drove of young steeds the hours fly past.
They vanish—and empty is the palm of the steppe.*

Ah, why recall the past? The hungry and bloody time of our rulers? The cruel years of the Emirs, the dogs? My heart sings of the new!

*O Tadjik land, your time at last has come!
The cruel age is gone—your time at last has come!
Machine that plows our fields, your time at last has
   come!
O Soviet man, your time at last has come!*

Songs About Lenin

Closely related to the songs of freedom have been the countless songs and stories and legends about Lenin. This was natural. From the very first day of the Revolution the name of Lenin had become associated in the minds of tens of millions with their national and economic liberation:

*Lenin gave our bards the right to sing about what
   they pleased,
And all of them at once began to sing about Lenin.*

Indeed, in the literature and folklore, not only of Central Asia, but of the whole of the Soviet Union, the figure of Lenin had at one time begun to assume almost legendary proportions. The personality of the great leader, the noble comrade, the sterling Bolshevik, caught the imagination and stirred the love of millions. The oil-driller in Baku and the peasant in the Ukraine, the Archangel fisherman and the Siberian nomad, the Caucasian mountaineer and the Central Asian shepherd were all contributing toward the creation of a great Lenin epos.

We must remember that the overwhelming majority of the men and women and children who participated in the building of this epos was composed not of trained Marxists and dialectical materialists. They were illiterate or semi-literate peasants—accustomed to the traditional forms, the similes and hyperboles, the nature imagery, and the fabulous heroes of all folk poetry. Lenin the Marxist, Lenin the philosopher, Lenin the revolutionary strategist they neither knew nor understood. To them Lenin was a holy savior, an emancipator, a being great and wonderful in his wisdom and power and love for his fellow men. There had been nothing in their poor, uneventful lives and in their peoples' scant annals to provide a figure even remotely resembling that of Lenin, except their legendary heroes and saints. It was inevitable, therefore, especially in view of the ever-present urge of people to find fulfillment in myths and legends, in saints and heroes, that at first some of the qualities and characteristics of the people's legendary great figures be transferred to Lenin. We must also remember the grandeur of the historical setting. Lenin's name, Lenin's personality invaded the consciousness of these primitive peoples during the most crucial and picturesque period of their history. His was the central figure in the monumental drama. He had emerged in the lurid glare of storms and conflagrations, of wars and revolutions raging over one-sixth of the land surface of the globe. He had passed out of the scene before the sober light of the reconstruction period and of widespread Marxist culture had rendered his silhouette more nearly commensurate with his very great, but also very human stature.

The image of Lenin as a mighty *bogatyr*, a giant, an epic hero, a savior, is particularly pronounced in all the stories and songs treating of him as the champion of the subject peoples of the East. Now he brings hope to the oppressed Georgians, now to a little Hindu boy, now to a hungry and beaten Chinese coolie. The coolie faints when he hears of the death of Lenin:

> *Lenin is dead. But what does it mean:*
> *But what about the Chinese coolies?*

In one Oriental chant we read that at the moment when Lenin was born into the world, he saw man's woe and he sighed. The earth heard that sigh, and people knew that he was born.... And Lenin walked from hamlet to hamlet, from door to door; he beheld man's suffering, and his heart began to glow with a great hatred and a great love. ... Lenin gave his heart to the people. And the heart sent forth countless sparks. And each spark was brighter than a bonfire at night. And people saw the way to happiness.*

In another Oriental chant, Lenin is described as a hero born of the moon and a star, using the magic powers he inherited from his parents to overcome the monster-dragon that lay on the road to happiness. In still another, he very ingeniously outwits the White Czar. In one Eastern legend Lenin rises to colossal stature; he "splits" mountains:

> ... And on the sixth year, when the earth was free of lords and slaves, Lenin vanished.... And when people saw that Lenin was no more, they said that he died. But Lenin has not died. He remembers the testament of his teacher, Khatto-Bash; he is seeking happiness in the mountains. Men see the earth shaking, and they say it is an earthquake. No, it is Lenin splitting mountains in his search for the little rod, in his search for happiness and truth.... And when he finds the little rod, then all peoples, yellow and black and white, will live happily. No one will ask why life is so sweet, because no one will know that life can be bitter....

* Lenin's heart consumed by a great flame recurs in numerous Eastern songs and legends. Here is an example from Tadjik folklore:

> Lenin lifting his head above the stars
> Saw the whole world in a glance,
> The world his hands could guide.
> Vast was his mind,
> With room enough for a peasant's complaint
> As well as the waging of war.
>
> He did not reign long, but his reign was like a bonfire
> Giving to some light and warmth,
> To others flame and fire—
> His life which burned up in the fire of his love....
>
> Long we noticed that he was burning away,
> But we could not drown the fire of love in his heart
> And thereby save his life:
> Can any one put out the blaze of a burning steppe?
> The fire in Lenin's heart was a thousand times more strong.

One of the most beautiful and humanly tender tributes to the memory of the Bolshevik leader is contained in the following Kirghiz song:

> In Moscow, in the great stone city,
> Where the country's chosen lie gathered
> A hut stands on the square
> And in it Lenin lies.
>
> You who bear a great sorrow
> Which nothing can console
> Come to this hut: Look at Lenin!
>
> And your sorrow will be carried off like water,
> It will float away like leaves on a stream,
> But a new, quiet sorrow will envelop you
> That he who was the father of his land
> Was stung with the sting of death.
>
> We love him even as we love our steppes
> And more—our huts and steppes we would give away,
> Our camels, wives and children if these could bring
>   him back....
> But he is in the dark, the awful, the unknown.
>
> Where shall we look for him now? we cry,
> And the steppe cries with us,
> The moon and stars cry with us:
> They remember Lenin.... We remember Lenin.
> And neither ourselves nor our grandsons' grandsons
> Ever will forget him.... Our steppes may choke with
>   weeds
> And tens of Kirghiz generations walk from the earth
> But the last of them will be happy that he goes
> Where Lenin is.

Another song, quite as beautiful perhaps, is one picked up by the Russian anthologist, L. Soloviev, in Kalabadam:

> In April Lenin was born, in January he died.
> These two months in red and black
> Are pressed into our memory.

*Now in April we shall wear
Red clothes to show our joy,
And in January we shall wear
Black clothes to mark his death.*

*In April we will sing joyous songs;
In January, sad ones.
In April the sun will sing happily with us,
In January the cold wind will wail with us.*

It is significant that with the general advance of Soviet culture, the image of Lenin in Central Asian poetry and folklore is perceptibly changing. The superhuman qualities and vague delineation of the mythological hero-emancipator are on the wane. As the details of Lenin's life and work are becoming the common property of new millions of literate workers and peasants, the gulf between Lenin as an objective reality and Lenin as an expression of subjective emotion is disappearing. More and more, the clearcut figure of the Bolshevik leader of the proletariat, with all its specific qualities, is penetrating into the consciousness of the Soviet masses. The garland of traditional anthropomorphic imagery, of legendary little rods, and monster-dragons, of stars and moons and flaming hearts is giving place to the concrete, realistic imagery of the new age.

New Content—New Forms

Thus, in his recent "Wreath on Lenin's Grave," for example, the Tadjik poet G. Lakhuti, instead of the old imagery, weaves in the most poetic flowers of contemporary Soviet vocabulary—"factory sirens," "factory smoke," "Stalingrad tractors ... the steel still warm," "forges," "heavy mauls," "sheaves of wheat from every Kolkhoz," etc. The poem reveals a sharp awareness of the rôle of the Communist Party. It speaks of giving our "Party's oath ... to devote our lives to Communist success." It even refers to inter-party struggles:

*We say: The cause of our truth we fight to defend.
In final combat we engage in closely drawn ranks.*

Against the Left foe and the Right alike we fight.
Victoriously . . . thanks to your wise words that light
our course.

Toward the end the poem asserts Lenin's "immortality," but in a purely materialist-Leninist sense: "Immortal is this great man who left to the world the power of the Bolshevik Party. . . ."

Lakhuti's "Wreath on Lenin's Grave" is symptomatic of what is transpiring in the realm of culture all over the Soviet lands. A changing content is rapidly bringing about changing forms. And to the extent that the content of Soviet life is everywhere fundamentally the same, in the same degree do the cultural forms of the different Soviet nationalities begin to assume amazing similarities. But for the language, Lakhuti's poem might on the whole have been written not by a Tadjik but by a Great Russian, a Jew, or a Laplander. Its distinguishing qualities are not especially Tadjik, they are Soviet.

This trend could be illustrated by innumerable recent examples from all the national minority arts in the Soviet Union, reflecting the processes of industrialization, collectivization, of work and study, of psychological readjustment and socialist incentives, of Party life and Party loyalty, etc. There is no need of burdening the chapter with too many examples. The following literal translation of parts of one of Lakhuti's latest poems—written in the form of a report to *Pravda*, the Central Organ of the Communist Party in the Soviet Union—will, I hope, convey to the reader the character of the most recent trend in Central Asia's Soviet culture:

*Pravda, cultural department,
  Moscow.
Copy for the Central Committee
  Press Section.*

*Comrades, attention!
  Your utmost attention!
A poet reports.
Listen. Take note.*

Comrade Pravda,
  Here in Tadjikistan
The steps of Leninism
  Are growing ever vaster.
Men everywhere have changed—
  Building our Socialist structure.
The very same people
  Who once lay slavishly prostrate
Under the feet of the beys
  And in the claws of the mullahs
Are to-day—I marvel
  At their deeds and their brains!—
Garnering the abundant fruits of October

There was Khalima.
  When she'd see a storm
And lightning in the blue and purple heaven,
  She'd run for shelter.
She'd cry, shut her eyes,
  And tremble like a leaf on an autumn birch.
To-day Khalima is not the same!
  Knowledge has been given to her,
Nature has become her obedient slave.
  I see her busying herself with the antennae—
She has rigged up a radio with her own nimble
      hands!

And there was Tursun.
  Ever since the tractor
Came clatteringly
  To take the place of the old wooden hoe,
Tursun's brain began to ring with different,
      new, unheard-of strains.
  In his consciousness,
Where formerly
  Donkeys and camels
Wandered half sleepily
  Along the customary bridle paths,
To-day in a whirlwind of efficiency
  Dash to and fro autos and tractors and loco-
      motives and airplanes.

Where is the interminable talk,
  More barren than the sands of the desert?
Where is the snail pace?
  Where the Oriental dreaminess?
They have stopped wasting words here.
  They have become efficient, firm, precise.

No wonder! In the olden days,
  Tursun, following the slow steps of his ox,
Would sing his endless, plaintive tune.
  And he never used his eyes
When he swept his ancient scythe—
  Sowing or harvesting, always half asleep.

Now, behold, the Tursuns do not sleep:
  The motors shake them,
The wheels make a mighty noise.
  Sullenness and laziness are gone.
Ears are sharper.
  Eyes more vigilant,
Speech more vivacious,
  Songs more alive.

Comrade Pravda,
  This is no fiction.
This is no exercise of a garrulous poet.
  Exact and truthful is the story I tell,
Upon my Communist word.

"My orchard."
"My mill."
"My cotton field."
  Now you don't hear
These words from our peasants.
  "Our orchard!"
"Our mill!"
  "Our cotton field!"
Everything ours, like the air that we breathe.

To-day we have a Moslem holiday—
  Ruza we call it here.
And what a holiday it was in the past!
  Deserted the homes, deserted the fields,

Crowds kneeling all day in the mosques.
But now who has time to think of Ruza?
Who has time for this nonsense of the slavish past?
Ruza? ...
   Our unions call for brigades!
Shock work in our shops and our schools!

Banu who had only once—
 When she was a bride—
Taken a ride on a horse,
 Now every morning mounts an autobus,
And daily
  Rides gayly
   To school.

Ask even a baby,
 Who are our leaders?
The baby,
 Nestling at its mother's breast,
Still unable even to babble,
 Looks into your eyes
And shoves its plump little finger
 Into the portraits beloved by all....

 No, this is no fiction, no exercise of a garrulous poet. Soviet Asia is marching ahead, struggling, building, singing. The Khalimas and the Tursuns and the Banus are a new generation in Central Asia—bold, confident, efficient. Gone are the interminable talk and the Oriental dreaminess. A new life is creating a new consciousness, a new man: ears are sharper, eyes more vigilant, speech more vivacious, songs more alive. And while the clouds of war are gathering over the great Union of Socialist Soviet Republics, while the imperialists in the East and the imperialists in the West are plotting to attack the Soviet workers and peasants, who for the first time in man's history are freely forging their own happiness, I can think of no better conclusion to this book than the song of the Tadjik collective farmer:

  My breath is free and warm
  When I see our dry plain being plowed.

When water flows along the cotton field,
When I see a finished dam,
And when I see those with me who strive for this new life,
I am as pleased as a father is with his own son.

I cannot help but cry: "Hail, all new men,"
When I see my son driving a machine along the field.

When I see a plow that's piercing root and soil,
I cannot help but cry: "Glory to those who labor!"

When I am threatened: "The old world will return,"
I fall to the ground and freeze in fear.

Give me a gun, comrade; give me some bullets—
I'll go to battle; I shall defend my land, my Soviet land.

CASPIAN SEA
ARAL SEA
FRUIT
E
FRUIT
KHIVA
CASPIAN SEA
D
CHARJUI
OIL
ASHKABAD
FRUIT
MERV
PERSIA